Class, Place, and Higher Education

Understanding Student Experiences of Higher Education

Edited by Paul Ashwin and Manja Klemenčič

As the number of students attending higher education has increased globally, there has been an increasing focus on student experiences of higher education. Understanding how students experience higher education in different national, institutional, and disciplinary settings has become increasingly important to researchers, practitioners, and policy makers.

The series publishes theoretically robust and empirically rigorous studies of students' experiences, including a broad range of elements such as student life, engagement in degree courses and extracurricular activities, experiences of feedback and assessment, student representation, and students' wider lives. It offers a richer understanding of the different meanings of being a student in higher education in the twenty-first century.

Also available in the series

Negotiating Learning and Identity in Higher Education, Edited by Bongi Bangeni and Rochelle Kapp

Everyday Mobilities in Higher Education, Kirsty Finn and Mark Holton

Understanding Experiences of First Generation University Students: Culturally Responsive and Sustaining Methodologies, Edited by Amani Bell and Lorri J. Santamaría

Community-Based Transformational Learning, Christian Winterbottom, Jody S. Nicholson, and F. Dan Richard

Class, Place, and Higher Education
Experiences of Homely Mobility

Alexandra Coleman

BLOOMSBURY ACADEMIC
LONDON • NEW YORK • OXFORD • NEW DELHI • SYDNEY

BLOOMSBURY ACADEMIC
Bloomsbury Publishing Plc
50 Bedford Square, London, WC1B 3DP, UK
1385 Broadway, New York, NY 10018, USA
29 Earlsfort Terrace, Dublin 2, Ireland

BLOOMSBURY, BLOOMSBURY ACADEMIC and the Diana logo are trademarks
of Bloomsbury Publishing Plc

First published in Great Britain 2022
This paperback edition published in 2024

Copyright © Alexandra Coleman, 2022

Alexandra Coleman has asserted her right under the Copyright, Designs and Patents Act, 1988,
to be identified as Author of this work.

For legal purposes the Acknowledgments on p. ix constitute an extension of this copyright page.

Cover design: Charlotte James

All rights reserved. No part of this publication may be reproduced or transmitted in any form or by
any means, electronic or mechanical, including photocopying, recording, or any information storage
or retrieval system, without prior permission in writing from the publishers.

Bloomsbury Publishing Plc does not have any control over, or responsibility for, any third-party
websites referred to or in this book. All internet addresses given in this book were correct at the
time of going to press. The author and publisher regret any inconvenience caused if addresses have
changed or sites have ceased to exist, but can accept no responsibility for any such changes.

A catalogue record for this book is available from the British Library.

Library of Congress Cataloging-in-Publication Data
Names: Coleman, Alexandra, author.
Title: Class, place, and higher education : experiences of homely mobility / Alexandra Coleman.
Description: London ; New York : Bloomsbury Academic, 2022. | Series: Understanding student
experiences of higher education | Includes bibliographical references and index.
Identifiers: LCCN 2022004442 (print) | LCCN 2022004443 (ebook) | ISBN 9781350256217 (hardback)
| ISBN 9781350256224 (paperback) | ISBN 9781350256231 (pdf) | ISBN 9781350256248 (epub)
Subjects: LCSH: Education, Higher–Social aspects–Australia–Sydney (N.S.W.) | Working class–
Education (Higher)–Australia–Sydney (N.S.W.) | Nontraditional college students–Australia–
Sydney (N.S.W.) | Social mobility–Australia–Sydney (N.S.W.)
Classification: LCC LC191.98.A82 S964 2022 (print) | LCC LC191.98.A82 (ebook) |
DDC 378.94–dc23/eng/20220302
LC record available at https://lccn.loc.gov/2022004442
LC ebook record available at https://lccn.loc.gov/2022004443

ISBN: HB: 978-1-3502-5621-7
PB: 978-1-3502-5622-4
ePDF: 978-1-3502-5623-1
eBook: 978-1-3502-5624-8

Series: Understanding Student Experiences of Higher Education

Typeset by Deanta Global Publishing Services, Chennai, India

To find out more about our authors and books visit www.bloomsbury.com and sign up
for our newsletters.

For Tom and Penny

Contents

Series Editors' Foreword		viii
Acknowledgments		ix
List of Abbreviations		x
Introduction		1
1	Homely Mobility: Rethinking Bourdieu	21
2	University and the Promise of a Good Life	47
3	Feeling "At Home" at University	73
4	The Graduate Waiting Room	97
5	On the Social Gravity of People and Place	121
Conclusions		143
Notes		161
References		164
Index		175

Series Editors' Foreword

The "Understanding Student Experiences in Higher Education" book series publishes theoretically robust and empirically rigorous studies of students' experiences of contemporary higher education. The books in the series are united by the belief that it is not possible to understand these experiences without understanding the diverse range of people, practices, technologies, and institutions that come together to form them. The series seeks to locate students' experiences in the context of global changes to higher education and thereby to offer a rich understanding of the different global and local meanings of being a student in higher education in the twenty-first century.

Class, Place, and Higher Education is an insightful and highly engaging account of the role of social class in the experiences and outcomes of higher education. The book affirms the significance of the influential scholarly traditions, notably by Pierre Bourdieu, on the logic of symbolic power in the reproduction of inequalities in the context of higher education. The book extends our understanding of the relations between social class and higher education by introducing place—"microcosm"—and mobilities—notably, the concept of homely mobility—to the investigation. Alexandra Coleman offers us vivid and powerful insights into her own social world in Cranebrook. Her beautiful academic writing and sharp analysis does justice and affirms the lives of the research participants who entrusted her their stories. This is a theoretically sophisticated, empirically rigorous, and beautifully written book which is breaking new ground in our understanding of the intersections between social class, place, and student experiences of higher education.

Paul Ashwin and Manja Klemenčič
Series Editors

Acknowledgments

I am deeply indebted to many people who provided all kinds of encouragement. This book is the accumulation of years of intellectual and emotional support. First, I would like to thank the research participants and those who helped recruit participants. Second, I would like to thank Penny Rossiter, George Morgan, Shanthi Robertson, and Greg Noble at Western Sydney University for their invaluable support and guidance at all stages of the research. I would also like to thank Wolfgang Lehmann and Kirsty Finn for their encouragement and feedback, as well as the Bourdieu Reading Group at the Institute for Culture and Society—Alejandra Villanueva, Francesca Sidoti, Greg Noble (again!), Hanafi Mohammad, Kate Naidu, Megan Watkins, Simon Chambers, and Yinghua Yu. I am also grateful to Cali Prince and Oznur Sahin from the Institute for Culture and Society for their friendship and to Anne Hurni from Penrith City Council for her encouragement. I would like to acknowledge the financial support I received from the Whitlam Institute at Western Sydney University which made the publication of this book possible through the E.G. Whitlam Research Fellowship—especially John Della Bosca, Andrea Connor, Leanne Smith, Maree O'Neill, and Paivi Lindsay. Alison Baker, Evangeline Stanford, and Anna Elliss at Bloomsbury have been great to work with, and I am extremely appreciative of their support. I would like to acknowledge the following publications and thank the publishers for permission to reproduce sections in this book: (1) Coleman, Alexandra. 2015. "Embodied, Emotional, and Ethical Entanglements: Place, Class, and Participation in Higher Education." *Social Alternatives*, 34(4): 35–42; (2) Coleman, Alexandra. 2021. "Whitlam, Western Sydney, and the Promise of University." *The Whitlam Institute*, <https://www.whitlam.org/publications/2021/2/23/whitlam-western-sydney-and-the-promise-of-university>; (3) Coleman, Alexandra. 2022 (forthcoming). "Being Working Class in Higher Education: Place and Belonging." *Research Handbook on the Student Experience*, Edited by Ella Kahu and Chi Baik. Edward Elgar Publishing. Finally, I would like to thank my partner, Tom, and my family—the Colemans, Buttigiegs, and Parfitts—for their care and patience.

Abbreviations

ACU	Australian Catholic University
ATAR	Australian Tertiary Admissions Rank
CAE	Colleges of Advanced Education
CBD	Central Business District
HSC	Higher School Certificate
LGA	Local Government Area
MPC	Master Planned Community
QILT	Quality Indicators for Teaching and Learning
UAI	University Admission Index
UNSW	University of New South Wales
USYD	University of Sydney
UWS/WSU	Western Sydney University (formerly, the University of Western Sydney)

Introduction

Proud as Punch

My Dad, a fitter-welder, recently moved into his own workshop, a medium-sized plot in the industrial pocket of St. Marys, a suburb in Western Sydney, Australia's manufacturing heartland. On my first visit, Dad gave me the "Grand Tour." The site was previously occupied by an Egyptian tradesman who planted the Holy Trinity of the Mediterranean—prickly pears, figs, and olives—amongst the tar, iron, and ungodly smell of garbage compactors, the bread and butter of Dad's trade. Dad was as proud as punch, as happy as Larry, in disbelief at his luck. *"How good is this?."* It's his castle. His "Babylon." Dad showed me his office: it was mostly empty except for two pre-loved tables and chairs and two pine bookcases filled with twenty or so empty lever-arch folders, my old folders, variously labeled "Bourdieu," "Higher Education," and "Class," amongst other things—folders I'd forgotten about when I moved out of my family home, folders out of place amongst the grit and grease of the workshop floor. "Bloody hell, Dad." Dad grinned. The folders are a prop for workshop banter. "What's this 'B-bourd . . .'?" "A fine wine." But the folders are more than a stir, more than a conversation starter—they are part memento, part trophy. Like the workshop itself, which my parents have worked long and hard for, the folders pay homage, however ironic, to his and my Mum's other achievement: their three daughters made it to university.

My parents, like most, wanted my sisters and me to have a good life. Education, for them, was the key. Dad, however, was never interested in going to university. It was never in his field of desirable possibilities. He enjoyed working outdoors, with his hands, and on machinery. Mum, the daughter of working-class migrants from Malta, had hoped to go to university after school, to study fine arts and art history, but that possibility was deferred to earn money and a different type of freedom. Completion of Year 12 was the most, at the time, that could be achieved for a newly settled family in 1960s and 1970s Australia. This was in Gough Whitlam's wake and in his heartland: Werriwa in Western Sydney. Whitlam[1] was prime minister of Australia from 1972 to 1975 and, along with his government, transformed the nation's education system, raised educational horizons, and radically altered what, until that point, everyone thought was possible, but the means to those futures weren't available for all—yet. When Whitlam first represented Werriwa, it was home to the largest population of young men and women in Australia, but few finished Year 12, and even fewer still attended university. Western Sydney's schools were overcrowded and under-resourced, particularly systemic Catholic schools (attended by my parents), and there was no university in the region. Mum and Dad wanted things to be different for my sisters and me. The future, though, was never explicitly about class escape or escape from place—it was about a more open existence, more choice, and access to jobs that are kinder on the body.

Education has, indeed, long been associated with conceptions of a good life (Mill 1998 [1859]). Education was, for example, part of the Whitlam government's "quality of life" agenda. Whitlam (1969, 2) argued that all Australians, no matter where they lived, should have access to the same social, cultural, and economic opportunities: "Equality and quality of opportunity, equality of life and more quality in life, go together." And quality of life, Whitlam wrote, "depends less and less on things which individuals obtain for themselves and can purchase for themselves from their personal incomes and depends more and more on the things which the community provides for all its members from the combined resources of the community" (Whitlam 1985, 3). Since Whitlam's time, however, the policy landscape has radically transformed. Whitlam's version of social democracy has been supplanted by neoliberal forms of governance that privilege the individual over collective forms of existence (Yeatman 2016). The individual is now understood to be the primary beneficiary of a university education. No longer can people expect the government to provide them with "equality of life and more quality in life," but they are instead encouraged to be self-sufficient and entrepreneurial *through* their investment in higher education (Rose 1999, 161). This marks a move away from a "politics of expectation," and a valuing of diverse ways of being, toward a model of "aspirational citizenship," where the capitalizing middle-class citizen is the "aspirational target" (Raco 2009, 438–9). The good life, now, is a middle-class life.

Sociologists have examined how working-class students invest in these governmental expectations. University, Christie (2009, 127–128) argues, has become a "standard" and "typical" pathway for nontraditional students in the UK, and is seen to be a "passport to upward social mobility" and "fulfilling employment opportunities". Similarly, Lehmann (2009a) found that public discourses on higher education in Canada push working-class students toward university. Parental hopes and desires also create strong incentives for "change and transformation, rather than social reproduction" (Lehmann 2015, 25). This is, together, what Lehmann (2009b, 643) calls the "social mobility project." The "social mobility project," he argues, is about a "wish to escape" working-class life (Lehmann 2009b, 643). But, as Lehmann (2013) points out, a focus on class escape can unwittingly pathologize working-class lives. It also doesn't leave much space for the possibilities of attachment to working-class lives and places. And as my family's narrative shows, going to university is not necessarily, or explicitly, about class escape and becoming middle class. Rather than focus on class escape, I examine how university becomes a means to a class-differentiated good life for twenty-six working-class university students and graduates from Cranebrook and its surrounding suburbs in outer Western Sydney, Australia—a good life embedded in place, in Western Sydney.

Western Sydney is not conventionally associated with a good life. It's an area imagined, from the outside, to be a place of lack and stagnation, "Sydney's other half" (Powell 1993, 5). Powell (1993, xviii), writing nearly three decades ago, explains:

> The west is seen as the repository for all those social groups and cultures which are outside the prevailing cultural ideal: the poor, the working class, juvenile delinquents, single mothers, welfare recipients, public housing tenants, Aborigines, immigrants from anywhere.

Yet, for people who call Western Sydney home, the region can be a place of desire, the Australian Dream[2]. Visions of a good life are, after all, not placeless. This is something acknowledged in scholarship on suburbanism and the Australian Dream (Rowse 1978; Stretton 1975), as well as migration and mobilities (Hage 2009), but is mostly absent in scholarship on higher education where the social space tends to be privileged over the placial—except for Finn (2017a, 2017b) and Donnelly and Evans (2016). So, too, it is absent in the field of Australian youth studies which focuses on the geographical mobility (not social mobility or existential mobility) of young people from regional areas to urban environments (Farrugia 2016). Normative understandings of a good life are not normally associated with working-class culture (Skeggs and Loveday 2012), nor with working-class suburbia (Symonds 1997).

I chose to examine the experiences of students and graduates from Cranebrook and its surrounds for two reasons: (1) it's the most economically diverse suburb in the Penrith region and (2) few residents have tertiary qualifications. The class distinctions that operate in Cranebrook provided fertile ground to explore the micro-politics of class and mobility. As I elaborate in Chapter 2, class is reproduced in "webs of material and symbolic ties" (Wacquant 2013, 275). Bourdieu (1987, 5), drawing from Goffman, calls these acts of classification "a sense of one's place." Class, Bourdieu (1984 [1979], 485) explains, "is defined as much by its *being-perceived* as by its *being*, by its consumption—which need not be conspicuous in order to be symbolic—as much by its position in the relations of production." But a sense of place is not just classed but placial too. Class is, indeed, diversely emplaced, or rather place is diversely classed. Place is, thus, central to this project. I do not, however, offer an in-depth theorization of place. These debates are well rehearsed elsewhere (Agnew 2011; Tuan 1977). It is, indeed, "the concrete effects of places that matter more than remaining at the abstract level of conceptualising place" (Agnew 2011, 326). I make an argument for "homely mobility." "Homely mobility" is a term I use to describe degrees of social and existential mobility in place and the pull of place. This relation—the pull back home—can be one of goodness and violence. The homing disposition of the habitus can limit mobilities in the world, preserve the status quo, and collude with the reproduction of class inequalities (Bourdieu and Wacquant 1992).

Following Bourdieu (2008 [2004]), I use and develop the term "microcosm" to refer to Cranebrook and its surrounding suburbs. Microcosms, as I argue in Chapters 1 and 2, have elastic boundaries and various scales of existence. Cranebrook is at once a suburb, part of the Penrith Local Government Area (LGA), and Western Sydney—all of which have distinct geopolitical boundaries. Yet, "Cranebrook" also exists in several other dimensions that are not so clearly bounded and are contradictory. It is a place that is lived, experienced, and imagined, and is at once shaped by discourses that are local and proud, local and ambivalent, local and critical, outsider and critical, and tied up with discursive constructions of Penrith, Western Sydney, and social housing more broadly (as I explore in Chapter 2). Cranebrook also exists as a patchwork of pockets, pockets that, at times, may seamlessly fold into one another, and at other times, exist, or are imagined to be, distinct and bounded microcosms of their own—particularly the pocket of Housing Commission. Place names are used ambiguously in the Australian vernacular, and the Penrith LGA, itself, comprises of thirty-eight suburbs and rural townships. Penrith is one of those suburbs. So "Penrith," the place name, denotes both a suburb and a larger LGA. Being from Cranebrook, as I shall demonstrate in Chapter 2, is also about being from Penrith (the region) and—for some—being from Western Sydney (the wider region). Placial recognitions are, indeed, elastic, relational, and situated accomplishments.

Place and Experiences of Living in Western Sydney

Contextualization of Western Sydney

Western Sydney is a vast region that stretches from Parramatta in the east, to the Blue Mountains in the west, to the Hawkesbury River in the north, and to the Wollondilly region in the south. It was once known as the "Cumberland Plain," though this term is no longer used in common parlance. It is a watery region without beaches, a place of big rivers, creeks, and dams. It is Dharug, Tharawal, and Gandangara country (traditional custodians of the land) and the site of the Sydney Wars (1816) where there was fierce Aboriginal resistance to British colonization. Up until the mid-twentieth century, Western Sydney was sparsely populated and predominantly a pastoral and agricultural region. Sectarian conflict was rife in the early colony, and Irish-Catholics tended to settle on the Cumberland Plain, where farming land was cheaper, whereas Protestants dominated the more exclusive suburbs of Sydney's north (Gwyther 2008a). In the postwar period, however, the region changed dramatically: many of its small communities rapidly suburbanized as new housing developments were built on their peripheries, wedged between orchards, poultry farms, market gardens, and bush. So, as the city reached the plain, the Cumberland Plain became an extension of Sydney, the "Western" and "South Western" suburbs of Sydney, "Western Sydney."

The Cumberland County Council was established in the postwar period to carefully plan the development of the Cumberland Plain; however, its visionary goals of greenspaces and the relocation of industry and culture to the Plain were at odds with the public housing authority, known as the NSW Housing Commission, and their brief to provide a large number of suburban houses as cheaply and quickly as possible (Gwyther 2008a). Sydney's housing shortage had intensified with the "post-war baby boom" and the arrival of migrants from the UK, Germany, the Netherlands, Poland, Malta, Italy, and the former Yugoslavia (Gwyther 2008a). The Cumberland County Council's plan was eventually abandoned in favor of sprawling development. Most housing was modest in size (averaging 4.9 rooms in 1954), owner-built, and cheaply constructed out of "fibro" cement (Gwyther 2008a). The new suburbs were either owner-built or large social housing estates (Gwyther 2008a). They initially lacked basic infrastructure, like kerbs, guttering, and sewerage, and they also lacked hospitals, schools, and public transport (Gwyther 2008a). The region, overtime, became home to Australia's most important manufacturing markets, but the government invested little in the region—services remained concentrated in Sydney's east, not west (O'Neill 2017).

Western Sydney, today, has a population of 2.5 million people (profile.id. 2018, https://profile.id.com.au). It's the fastest-growing region in Australia, and 35 percent of its residents were born overseas and speak over 100 different languages. It has the highest concentration of immigrants in Australia, particularly the newly arrived, and is also home to Australia's largest urban Indigenous community in the nation (WSU 2019). Many of its older inner suburbs have undergone at least one cycle of cultural reorganization over the last fifty years (Gwyther 2008a). Pendle Hill, for example, was an Anglo-Celtic community before the Second World War, after the war became known as "Little Malta," and today is home to a thriving Indian community who represent over 20 percent of the population (Burnley 1974; profile.id. 2018, https://profile.id.com.au). Many of Western Sydney's older inner suburbs are in need of renewal or are being remade as postwar fibro is bulldozed to make room for apartments or plot-hungry brick veneer homes, derisively known as "McMansions." "McMansion" is a derogative term used to describe oversized, cheaply constructed, and mass-produced homes (Gwyther 2008a). Western Sydney's outer suburbs, suburbs like Cranebrook, on the other hand, are dominated by English speakers and people of Anglo-Celtic ancestry (Gwyther 2008a). These outer-ring areas are experiencing a different type of change: their greenspaces are being swallowed up by private developments, known as "Master Planned Communities" (MPCs), the home of the "McMansion," and a more homogenous, wealthier, and exclusionary resident population (Gwyther 2008b).

Western Sydney is now home to a shrinking "old economy" and to some of the most disadvantaged communities in Australia (Randolph and Holloway 2005). It is a hodgepodge of moderate-income households, growing pockets of disadvantage in private housing stock, large and growing migrant communities, wealth on the urban fringe, and public housing estates with significant social disadvantage (Randolph and Tice 2014). Most of Sydney's public housing is in Western Sydney and almost all public housing residents receive welfare payments of some sort (Randolph and Tice 2014). Morgan (2006, n.p) comments that this has turned clusters of public housing into what the English call "sink estates." These are places of "social disadvantage, places struggling to develop local pride and community leadership" (Morgan 2006, n.p). Randolph and Holloway (2005) point out that shifts in government expenditure have further contributed to social polarization, with the wealthier suburbs attracting most government funding. In Cranebrook, for example, there are stark contrasts between the MPC ("Waterside") and the rundown public housing estate, which is in much need of renewal.

Perceptions of Western Sydney

The suburbs have long held an ambivalent place in Australian social commentary: they are either seen as the site of the good life—a place of freedom, privacy, and self-expression—or they are seen to be parochial and dull, a denial of civilization (Rowse 1978; Stretton 1975). Western Sydney, according to Symonds (1997), is the latter: it doesn't embody what is perceived to be good about Australian suburbia. Powell (1993, 140), however, argues that while Western Sydney is perceived to be a wasteland, there is some lure— however tenuous. The Penrith region, she writes, is sometimes represented by Sydney's media as the site of nostalgia, whiteness, lost familiarity, and community (Powell 1993, 140). It occupies a different type of difference to, say, the multicultural suburbs of Cabramatta and Parramatta, Bankstown and Blacktown (inner suburbs of Western Sydney). The lure of Cabramatta, for example, "is *difference within the familiar;* exotic people and food, and multicultural others, side by side with the dangers of class and social differences, alleged street crime, Chinese triads, gang warfare, and youth violence—but all within the boundaries of Australia, of Sydney" (Powell 1993, 134). Hage (1997, 99) has developed these ideas in his work on "cosmo-multicultural" consumption in Cabramatta. "Cosmo-multicultural" consumption is a relation to "ethnicity largely as an object of consumption." Hage (1997) suggests that Cabramatta is the exotic other for "cosmo-multiculturals" from Sydney's east who venture into Western Sydney to consume difference.

Despite more recent regional transformations—economic, cultural, and architectural—from the outside, Western Sydney and its residents ("westies") continue to attract scorn and derision. The "aspirational" came to prominence in the late 1990s to describe upwardly mobile "westies"—those sections of the Western Sydney's working class who have "made money" (Gwyther 2008a, 68). They are now one of the most despised figures in political commentary and are ridiculed for sending their children to private schools, for living in MPCs, and, indeed, for "staying put" in Western Sydney rather than moving to the supposedly leafier and more desirable suburbs of the east (Gwyther 2008a). Gwyther (2008b, 1) explains:

> Aspirationals came to prominence in the late 1990s to describe a seemingly new constituency of voters living on the urban fringes who appeared to have clawed their way out of the *real* battler class and into big cars, big houses and even bigger mortgages.

Blogs, radio programs, and newspaper articles continue to report on the contempt directed at Western Sydney and its residents. More recently, scholars from Western Sydney University, as part of a symposium on "initiating change by design," were challenged to "solve" the stigma of Western Sydney and potentially "reimagine" the region as "Riverlands, Sydney" (Pink et al. 2015, n.p). Most of the researchers hadn't considered that, for its residents, the region might be a place of pride, the site of a good life, and that a name change was neither necessary nor desired. Two participants in the working group were from Western Sydney, and, through the stories they shared, the research team realized that they had unknowingly recast the area as "problematic" and "tragic" (Pink et al. 2015, n.p).

Most scholarship on Western Sydney examines how it is "othered" from the outside, rather than the experiences of its residents from the inside. Indeed, if we look at Western Sydney from the inside out—as Pink et al.'s (2015) work suggests we should do—alternative perceptions of the region emerge. Simic (2008), for example, has examined how being a "westie" may be source of pride, not just a term of contempt. Mee (2002), too, found that residents of Western Sydney were proud of the region and perceived it to be a better place to live than elsewhere in Sydney because of its spaciousness, affordability, community spirit, natural environment, and its proximity to parks and extended family. She points out that the desirability of the natural environment is particularly important. To outsiders, the plains are flat and boring, but for those who live there, the landscape is highly valued—evidenced by the long and hard battles fought by locals over the years to protect its bushlands from developers (Mee 2002). Gwyther (2008b, n.p) has examined the desirability of Western Sydney, specifically the MPC, the haunt of the "aspirational." Her participants, who considered themselves "average Joe Blows," had relocated to MPCs from older suburbs in Western Sydney, places with high concentrations of public housing and declining government investment. The MPC, for them, offered security—monetary and social. It was a place they could live out their version of the Australian Dream.

Higher Education and Western Sydney

The Whitlam government, as previously mentioned, began a process of equalizing educational opportunities in Australia "to every child at every level from preschool to tertiary" (Whitlam 1973, 5). Whitlam's approach to education was regionally focused, and, despite popular opinion that Western Sydney's citizenry were better suited to a practical education, Whitlam promised that the next university would be established in Western Sydney. Young people coming of age in Western Sydney in Whitlam's time, people like my Mum, may have missed out on higher education, but Whitlam's policies and legacy ensured the next generation would get their chance. Whitlam (1985, 314) understood that Australia's education system was not straightforwardly a "great instrument for the promotion of equality," but that it predominantly functioned as "a weapon for perpetuating inequality and promoting privilege." And he fought vigorously for an education system that ameliorated societal inequalities, not one that entrenched and reproduced class privilege. Class, religion, and geography, Whitlam (1969, 2) argued, should place no restrictions on the educational horizons of all Australians. Education was central to Whitlam's policy platform of radical social change (along with Indigenous rights, multiculturalism, gender equality, and universal health care), and as leader of the Australian Labor Party, he initiated a series of reforms to education: he established the Australian Schools Commission and Technical and Further Education Commission, distributed funds to schools based on need, removed university and technical education tuition fees, and assumed full financial responsibility for tertiary education—which was previously a state responsibility (Whitlam 1985, 315).

Whitlam's vision for a university in Western Sydney has since been met—thanks to regional lobby groups and a state Labor government led by Neville Wran whose cabinet was dominated by MPs from Western Sydney—and Australia's higher education system is now more accessible, but the sector continues to entrench class inequalities. In Whitlam's time, Australian universities had a semi-equal status, but that changed with "Dawkins Reforms" led by a federal Labor in the 1980s. The Dawkins Reforms abandoned Whitlam's visions for higher education and transformed the operating conditions of the sector into one of wild competition for funding and students (Marginson 2007). The Dawkins Reforms also transformed some Colleges of Advanced Education (CAEs) into universities, and these newer universities have struggled to accumulate the prestige and recognition attached to Australia's much older universities, such as the Group of Eight (Watkins 2020). And according to Whitlam (2004, 1–2), the "plan to turn CAEs into universities achieved the reverse of turning too many universities into CAEs." Western Sydney University (formerly, the University of Western Sydney) is one of these newer universities. Local government representatives from Western Sydney described their new university as "bargain basement" (Hutchinson 2013, 77). And the name, one local representative argued, "would result in the university sharing the social opprobrium implied by the geographical reference in the name 'UWS'" (Hutchinson 2013, 77). Perceptions of Western Sydney as a cultural wasteland do, indeed, stick to Western Sydney University. The university is perceived, by some, to be a "bogan" university (Rossiter 2013). Western Sydney University is also understood to be the university for those who perform poorly in the Higher School Certificate ("UWS = U Went Shit").

The Group of Eight continue to attract the top students who are disproportionately from more privileged class backgrounds, and these students maintain a monopoly in elite disciplines, like medicine and law (Watkins 2020). Graduates from the Group of Eight are also more likely to secure first jobs matching their qualifications, and graduates who are employed full-time can also expect to earn 10 percent more than non–Group of Eight graduates (Norton and Cherastidtham 2014). The rewards of higher education are unevenly distributed. It matters where you go to university. It also still matters where you live. Western Sydney now has a growing population of degree holders—a quarter of Sydney's total—yet the region continues to be spatially disadvantaged, particularly in those sectors where graduates are seeking work, which are concentrated in Sydney's east, not west (O'Neill 2017). Public pressure has forced the Australian and NSW governments and their agencies to prioritize jobs growth in Western Sydney, and since 2014 there have been three major commitments to jobs generation in Western Sydney: the construction of Western Sydney Airport, the construction of an aerotropolis, and the creation of a thirty-minute city[3] in Western Sydney (O'Neill 2020). But, for O'Neill (2020), these ventures are risky and detail on job generation is lacking. He writes:

> The airport is being constructed at a time of great volatility for air travel in the near future, with a high degree of uncertainty about the nature and volume of air traffic in the longer term. The spillover effects into an aerotropolis are untested, and thereby are uncertain, by definition. Then, for Western Sydney's greenfields employment areas the capacity to generate job densities needed to make a significant contribution to the region's job total would need to change substantially from the low-density land use practices on such sites over the last decade. (O'Neill 2020, 15)

Most of the research participants attended Western Sydney University (twenty-four out of twenty-six). It is one of Australia's largest universities (48,458 students), most students are domestic (41,229), and most domestic students live in Western Sydney (34,069) (WSU Pocket Profile 2018). It has nine campuses spread throughout the region—one of which is in Penrith. Its older campuses are suburban, located on the fringes of city centers, while its newer campuses are vertical and located in the heart of its regional centers. It has a large percentage of students from low socioeconomic backgrounds (25 percent) compared to Australia's elite institutions (10.6 percent) (WSU Pocket Profile

2018). Many of its students—63 percent—are also first-generation university students—meaning, their parents are not university graduates (WSU Pocket Profile 2018). The university describes its students as "aspirational," as wanting to "make their mark in the world," and to "contribute to their communities" (WSU Securing Success 2018-2020 Strategic Plan). This is a very different use of aspiration, one without the derogatory connotations of the grown-up westie. In Chapter 5, I examine how the research participants contribute back to their communities. I specifically examine "vertical" (Hage 2000) relations of "gratitude"—of care and reciprocity for people and place, of "giving back" to Cranebrook. I examine how gratitude can have a "flow-on effect" and involve acts of reciprocation and exchange to others beyond Cranebrook. Exchange, Sennett (in Wise 2009, 226) argues, "turns people outwards."

Researching Class, Place, and Higher Education

I conducted in-depth semi-structured with six current students and twenty graduates. They were aged between eighteen and thirty-six, and provided a mixture of retrospective and in-the-moment experiences. They attended secondary school in Cranebrook or its surrounding suburbs and were first-generation university students. They can all be described as coming from "working-class" backgrounds: their parents were variously employed as tradesmen, factory workers, small business owners, retail workers, truck drivers, security guards, office workers, secretaries, postal workers, nurses, and defense force personnel. I used the terminology "first-generation university student or graduate" to recruit participants. Though the term "working class" may have attracted some participants, it also may have confused, dissuaded, and deterred others. Scholars have commented that class is something people may misrecognize or make "strenuous efforts to deny, disidentify and dissimulate" (Skeggs 1997, 94). Class, too, is something that many Australians feel uncomfortable talking about. Yet, as Australian novelist and social commentator, Tim Winton (2013–14, 27), explains:

> It's still personal and immediate; it's still a live issue. I feel it grinding away tectonically in the lives of relatives and friends who may not want to talk about class but who are subject to its force every day.

I also chose not to use the word "class" because I was interested in questions of class identity. During my first few interviews, I asked participants, "Do you see yourself as middle class or working class?." This question produced confusion and was a case of "the sociologist [asking] the respondents to be their own sociologists, by asking them directly the question he is asking himself about them" (Bourdieu 2000, 59). I then removed the question and decided to see if a language of class emerged without direct questioning.

One participant attended St. Paul's Grammar School, and another participant attended Cambridge Park High School (in a surrounding suburb). Ten participants attended Xavier College, a local Catholic school. The rest of the participants (fourteen) attended Cranebrook High School. Cranebrook High School and Cambridge Park High are government schools, St. Paul's Grammar School is a private school (yearly fees reach up to $16,000), and Xavier College is a "systemic" Catholic school. Systemic Catholic schools provide Catholic education to all Catholic students, regardless of their means (unlike "private" Catholic schools). In 2013, Cranebrook High School was ranked 643 out of the 645 schools in the state based on NSW Higher School Certificate results for 2012 (Better Education, bettereducation.com.au). Cambridge Park High School (578) and Xavier College (310) fared better. St. Paul's Grammar School does not have a ranking (most students complete the International Baccalaureate rather than the NSW Higher School Certificate), but they are well known in the local community for their academic excellence. Most participants, as mentioned, attended Western Sydney University (twenty-four out of twenty-six), and six of those participants also attended other institutions for further study or transferred to Western Sydney University from another institution. Two participants were graduates of the University of Sydney only. Almost all participants continued to live with family while studying—only one lived on campus, and out of all the participants, ten have never left Cranebrook, eight live in neighboring suburbs, and eight moved away.

I was always mildly surprised by how similar my life and history were to the research participants' lives and histories, or how many people we knew in common—what Bourdieu (1999b [1993], 610) calls "social symmetry." Penrith is, after all, a small world—though much smaller than I anticipated. I am, after all, of Penrith—although not Cranebrook. I occupy a similar position in the wider social space based on a variety of visions and divisions, such as age, class, place, education, and so on. Our positioning in the social world and our trajectories though that world are, indeed, "not singular" but "linked" to a larger "social trajectory" (Wacquant in Bourdieu and Wacquant 1992, 44). Yet, although the research participants' experiences were—mostly—familiar and recognizable, we shared differences too. I shared, for example, much in common with one participant, Jacklyn (pseudonyms used). Jacklyn mentioned that her Nan had recently passed away—mine had too—and that her Nan was once a school cleaner in Mount Druitt (a suburb of Western Sydney). My Nan also worked as a school cleaner in a neighboring suburb. Jacklyn talked about how her stepfather, who was once a diesel mechanic, had a serious workplace accident, and how has struggled to work since. My father, a tradesman, was also involved in a serious workplace accident—though he was able to return to work. The latter difference—my father's return to work and her stepfather's struggle to work—meant that our childhoods diverged. I had a childhood of financial stability, Jacklyn had one of financial hardship; my parents had a mortgage in South Penrith and later Glenbrook, Jacklyn lived in Housing Commission in Cranebrook. And as I shall detail in Chapters 2 and 5, these small-scale distinctions within a microcosm like Penrith can be experienced as radical and profound.

This project, with its embeddedness in the socially proximate and familiar—with all its micro differences and distinctions—broadly involved researching my own social world. This is what Bourdieu (Bourdieu and Wacquant 1992, 253) calls "participant objectivation." Participant objectivation involves demystifying the *illusio* or interest of one's worlds—that is, exposing the social magic that makes those worlds meaningful. Participant objectivation can reduce some forms of misrecognition produced in the research encounter, but it does not remove them, and as I shall also explain in the following text, can introduce new forms. The reduction of some forms of misrecognition can be seen throughout this book, say in my discussions with Jacklyn about McDonald's. As I shall further detail in Chapter 2, I asked Jacklyn to tell me about her brother. With some defensiveness, as revealed by a hesitation and pause, Jacklyn explained that her brother is a manager at McDonald's: "My brother [pause] . . . he um [pause] . . . he is a McDonald's manager. He wants to work his way up and actually eventually own a Maccas." Jacklyn wasn't sure how I was going to react. We then discussed McDonald's—my partner was working at McDonald's at the time (though at a different store in Penrith), we knew people in common (her best friend worked with my partner), and, importantly, I made it clear that I perceived McDonald's as a legitimate career path. We then talked about how people underestimate and misrecognize employees of McDonald's. This worked to overcome "the fear of patronizing class attitudes which, when the sociologist is perceived as socially superior, is often added to the very general, if not universal, fear of being turned into an object" (Bourdieu 1999b [1993], 613).

Yet, while social proximity and familiarity may have curtailed some forms of misrecognition, I still—several times—said the wrong thing and reacted in the wrong way. Social proximity and familiarity do not remove social distinctions. On several occasions, I misunderstood the research participants' experiences as "my own" and "the same." Peel (2003, 2) writes, "The mistake of many venturers—and the mistake that I made—is to think that you already know the story when what you must do is listen." I learnt this the hard way. Jenny, for example, spoke about a teacher who discouraged her career aspirations (discussed in detail in Chapter 2). I commented that I also had a teacher who made similar comments. My words, however, did not work to build rapport but were instead inattentive to the degrees of difference—however small—that operate between my former secondary school, McCarthy Catholic College[4], and Cranebrook High School. My comments instead worked to jar the conversation. This is what Bourdieu (1999b [1993], 610) calls the "intrusion effect." After I shared my experience with Jenny, she raised an eyebrow, paused, and said, "Really? At McCarthy? A private school?." In disbelief, she then proceeded to talk about how some people really shouldn't be teachers. For Jenny, Cranebrook High School and McCarthy Catholic College were two very different schools. I felt foolish sharing my "hard luck" story. Other participants, like Pat and Lucy, also commented that McCarthy was one of the better schools in the area, a "private school," and Pat even sent his daughter to McCarthy.

Researching the socially proximate and familiar also produced new forms of misrecognition for me—the researcher. This is because participant objectivation involves "objectifying the respondent [which] means objectifying oneself" (Bourdieu 1999b [1993], 611). This can be emotionally difficult. Bourdieu (in Bourdieu and Wacquant 1992, 63) explains, "the harshest and most brutally objectifying analyses are written with an acute awareness of the fact that they apply to he who is writing them." But, for Bourdieu, participant objectivation is conducted by the researcher who has left the world under scrutiny. It involves making use of one's knowledge of those worlds which "one has retired from" (Bourdieu in Bourdieu and Wacquant 1992, 259). Yet, I had not left my world. I still live in the Penrith region. In the Conclusion, I reflect on how my relation to the research field was too "thick and sticky" (Hage 2005) and how the familiar became both an asset and an obstacle. Participant objectivation was, for me, especially difficult because it involved objectifying not only my investments in home, but my investments, or *illusio,* in higher education, resulting in a wearing down of what Bourdieu calls a *"libido academica"* (Bourdieu in Wacquant and Bourdieu 1989, 19). Demystifying the *illusio* of one's world can be paralyzing. You need *illusio* to move through the social world like "fish in water." Researching class and processes of reproduction, too, can be particularly unnerving (Bourdieu 1988 [1984]; Hoggart 1990; Skeggs 1997).

Book Outline

In Chapter 1, I review the scholarship on class and higher education. I begin by demonstrating the significance and continuing relevance of Bourdieu and Passeron's (1979 [1964] and 1990 [1970]) work on the reproduction of symbolic power in education. To explain the logic of symbolic power, and how it works to reproduce inequalities, I review the sociological dimensions of Bourdieu's modus operandi, as well as how contemporary Bourdieusian scholars use and develop his scholarship (Bathmaker et al. 2013, 2016; Burke 2015; Lehmann 2012; Marginson 2011; Reay et al. 2009, 2010; Watkins 2020). Following Finn (2017a, 2017b), I argue that Bourdieusian scholarship on higher education demonstrates the continuing salience of class, but that this work—for the most part—is a-placial and a-mobile. There is a need to move beyond the bounds of the "field" of higher education and "social mobility" when examining experiences of higher education. I review a small and emerging body of work associated with the "mobilities turn" in higher education which argues for the importance of place and attends to alternative mobilities, such as subjective understandings of moving well (Donnelly and Evans 2016; Finn 2017a, 2017b; Finn and Holton 2019). While this scholarship is significant, I suggest that it is important to also examine how these mobilities involve relations of domination. To examine relations of symbolic power and the culturally specific ways people accumulate being, I turn toward and develop the philosophical dimensions of Bourdieu's work—which are absent in Bourdieu's own scholarship on higher education, as well as contemporary Bourdieusian scholarship on higher education. I develop my concept of homely mobility—which describes degrees of mobility in place and the social gravity of place. It is a concept that engages with the sociological and philosophical dimensions of Bourdieu's work, but also the scholarship of Hage (1997), Simmel (1950), and, to a lesser extent, Ahmed (2010).

In Chapter 2, I explore how university becomes a means to a good life—a good life that is shaped by the push and pull of "webs of material and symbolic ties" (Wacquant 2013, 275) that operate in microcosms, like Cranebrook. The research participants positioning in Cranebrook, their sense of place and the place of others in that microcosm, affects their visions of a good life and what constitutes social mobility. I demonstrate that the decision to go to university is shaped by the push and pull of family and teachers—an entanglement of social obligations and commitments, such as gratitude and faithfulness, shame and recognition. The accumulation of being is, indeed, about persevering in our being, and being is—after all—a relational accomplishment. The accumulation of our being is what Hage (1997) calls the accumulation of homeliness and is shaped by the pursuit of security, community, familiarity, and possibility. Security, specifically economic security, is a particularly important ingredient of a good life for the research participants, and desires for economic security were fueled by class realities. I argue that parents and teachers not only work to push young people toward particular futures, but they also function as representations of particular futures—representations that can create uncertainty about university as a means to a good life, and representations that can work to emplace hope in Cranebrook and the wider Penrith. Some participants talk about "the road not taken"—other post-school pathways that do not involve university, like a career at McDonald's or work as an electrician. University, I demonstrate, is not a normative means to "the" good life but is one of many means to "a" good life.

In Chapter 3, I consider the experience of feeling "at home" at university. I argue that the homogenizing notions of class habitus and institutional habitus, as well as the bounded notion of field, do not adequately capture the varied ways we come to feel recognized at university (Atkinson 2011; Watkins and Noble 2013). Following Bourdieu (2000), I examine "degrees of integration" and the micro-politics of fit and recognition. I argue that attending university in one's homely geography can afford modes of belonging at university, specifically for those students at WSUs Penrith Campuses. Our environments, the places we are most at home in the world, can operate as "elastic horizons" (Noble 2015) and provide "degrees of integration" (Bourdieu 2000) in new environments. I demonstrate that homeliness does not necessarily involve a passive withdrawal from the world, but can be about agency and self-expansion, the accumulation of being (Hage 1997). Feelings of homeliness can also provide students with the confidence to transcend their "comfort zones" and complete postgraduate study at a different university, such as the University of Sydney. There is, of course, a flipside to this goodness. Revision and transformation are never radical. The gravity of particular places can limit and define movements in the world. Placial degrees of integration, then, orient one's movements in the social world—toward particular campuses and not others, toward sameness and away from difference. This movement is, of course, one of both agency *and* domination—or rather one of homely goodness and homely violence.

In Chapter 4, I examine how the research participants differentially negotiate the labor market in the period after graduation, particularly how they remain invested in, or not, the promise of university. The transition from university into graduate employment can be lengthy and difficult, and many graduates move into an insecure buffer zone (Furlong and Cartmel 2005). I call this period of abeyance the "graduate waiting room." I examine "strategies of compensation" and how mobilities may be reconfigured in the face of "diploma inflation" (Bourdieu and Passeron 1979 [1964], 92). Some of the research participants "persevered" and eventually found work (though not necessarily in graduate roles), others "moved on" to other jobs and careers, and some remained "stuck." Those who remained "stuck" maintained what I call a "cruel attachment" to the promise of university: this form of attachment denotes a relation to an object of desire that offers very little sustenance. I argue that the experience of class mobility, for those who remain "stuck," may be reconfigured in new ways—for example, through the experience of touristic travel. This chapter demonstrates that the rewards of higher education are unevenly distributed. Working-class students are often reliant on universities for knowledge about labor markets, and this dependency—combined with limited and localized stocks of social capital—can work to reproduce classed inequalities. "Moving on" and "persevering" can involve moving very little.

In Chapter 5, I consider relations of "staying put," or being oriented back, to place—to Cranebrook and the Penrith region more generally. Working-class places, like Cranebrook, can be sites of a good life, not just places to be left behind—but places of possibility. I attend to micro-mobilities *in* place, not just mobilities between differently classed worlds. Mobilities within microcosms can be significant and may constitute forms of existential or social mobility. This is what I call "homely mobility"—a term used to describe degrees of mobility in place and the social gravity of place. I examine how one's social commitments and obligations to family and to Cranebrook shape mobilities. Relations of faithfulness and gratitude, I argue, have gravity: they can pull one back into place, give continuity and coherence to social life, and work to reorient social mobilities, or, in Pat's case, bond one to a "good life" that is a site of social tension. Indeed, "staying put" is not necessarily psychologically smooth. Nor is upward social mobility in Western Sydney a straightforwardly "happy" journey. Relations of faithfulness and gratitude, I argue, do not just involve horizontal exchanges—between people—but also vertical exchanges between people and place. I demonstrate how homely mobility is a relation of domination—not just care. It is a form of symbolic violence—albeit a "gentle" and "disguised" form of domination (Bourdieu 1990 [1980], 133). Homely mobility works to reproduce ways of being while providing room to grow, but within limits.

1

Homely Mobility
Rethinking Bourdieu

Introduction

In this chapter, I review the scholarship that informs the development of my concept "homely mobility"—a term I use to describe degrees of "existential" and "social" mobility in place, places that I call "microcosms," places that have "social gravity." This chapter is divided into four sections. The purpose of the first three sections is to demonstrate the uses and limits of the existing scholarship, and, in the final section, I develop and apply my argument through a preview of the chapters. In the first section, I begin by reviewing Bourdieu and Passeron's (1979 [1964] and 1990 [1970]) well-known work on education, reproduction, and "diploma inflation." Bourdieu and Passeron's (1979 [1964] and 1990 [1970]) sociological scholarship on class and education is central to the field of study and is indeed central to my research. Contrary to conventional ideas about the education system producing greater equality, Bourdieu and Passeron (1979 [1964] and 1990 [1970]), writing several decades ago, argued that the education system offers a mirage of change while reproducing social power through the transmission and reconversion of symbolic capital. To explain what symbolic capital is, and what it does, I discuss Bourdieu's modus operandi: his forms of capital and habitus, and their relation to fields and social spaces. As I demonstrate, Bourdieu and Passeron's (1979 [1964] and 1990 [1970]) work has ongoing relevance and salience, and scholars of education continue to develop his sociological concepts to explain enduring inequalities (Bathmaker et al. 2013, 2016; Burke 2015; Lehmann 2012; Marginson 2011; Reay et al. 2010; Watkins 2020).

Bourdieu's scholarship on higher education, along with contemporary Bourdieusian scholarship on higher education, does, however, have its limits. It does little to think outside the binaries of social mobility and immobility and working-class and middle-class "fields." This work, Finn (2017a, 2017b) argues, ignores the significance of place and other forms of mobility. In the second section, I consider a small and emerging body of work associated with the "mobilities turn" in higher education (Donnelly and Evans 2016; Finn 2017a, 2017b; Finn and Holton 2019). This scholarship explores a range of mobility practices that are informed by personal relationships and connection to place, and is important because it calls for attunement to the micro-politics of mobility and the highly differentiated ways that people move and attach meaning to their mobilities. Mobility does, after all, mean more than social mobility. This scholarship offers a significant contribution to the field of study through its emphasis on place and subjective understandings of "moving well." Following this body of work, I too argue for the importance of attending to place and to alternative mobilities in place, but I also call for an engagement with the ways these relations involve both goodness *and* domination. Indeed, while the mobilities scholarship attends to the ways people make their lives meaningful, structural constraints fade to the background—that is, the ways people make meaningful a world that makes them.

The mobilities scholarship described earlier is not Bourdieusian and moves away from Bourdieu's sociology to think about place, mobility, and relationality. I too consider place, mobility, and relationality, but I use Bourdieu to do so. In the third section, I develop the *philosophical* dimensions of Bourdieu's work. Bourdieu's work is more than a political economy of symbolic power. It is also a political economy of being (Hage in Zournazi and Hage 2002). I preview Bourdieu's philosophical work on the accumulation of being, or what Hage (in Zournazi and Hage 2002) calls the "accumulation of homeliness." Drawing from Husserl's (1983 [1913]) notion of *umwelt*, Bourdieu (1989) explains that it is important to attend to people's perceptions of what is meaningful, or what is worth pursuing, within their social worlds, not necessarily what is valued in the wider social space. Hage (2009b) calls this "existential mobility." The philosophical dimensions of Bourdieu's work are not present in his sociological scholarship on higher education and home. Bourdieu never empirically examined the ways education becomes a means to a good life, and how visions of a good life are shaped by the push and pull of home. I do. In the final section, I preview the book's argument about "homely mobility": a term used to describe degrees of mobility in place (both social and existential) and the social gravity of people and place. It is a concept that engages with not only the sociological and philosophical dimensions of Bourdieu's work but also the scholarship of Hage (1997), Simmel (1950), and, to a lesser extent, Ahmed (2010), to examine the experiences of students and graduates from Cranebrook and its surrounding suburbs.

Bourdieu, Higher Education, and Symbolic Power

To examine educational inequalities, this research engages with, and extends, the sociological dimensions of Bourdieu's work on symbolic power—what Dreyfus and Rabinow (1993, 35) call Bourdieu's "scientific theory of social meaning"—which, as I will show, has ongoing relevance. Bourdieu, in his influential book, *Distinction* (1984 [1979]), and with his collaborator, Passeron, in their equally influential books, *The Inheritors* (1979 [1964]), *Reproduction in Education, Society and Culture* (1990 [1970]), and *Academic Discourse* (1994), argue that the education system, despite being conventionally understood as a mechanism for social mobility, is instead an apparatus for social reproduction. Like their contemporaries (Bernstein 1971; Bowles and Gintis 1976; Young 1958), Bourdieu and Passeron (1979 [1964]) sought to understand the connection between the growth of mass education systems and the hardening of class inequalities. Their work, written several decades ago in France, is a critique of commonsense views of education that equate academic success or failure with natural talents. It is also a critique of celebratory political discourses that position higher education as the means to national economic success and as the means to individual success. These celebratory political discourses also attribute educational inequalities to issues of representation and the idea that inequalities can be improved by widening access to those groups previously excluded from higher education, such as the working class. These celebratory political discourses are, of course, still prevalent today and, as I discussed in the Introduction, have driven contemporary higher education policy in Australia.

Bourdieu and Passeron (1979 [1964]) argue that these commonsense views of education and celebratory political discourses together represent the dominance of human capital theory—the idea that national economic growth is fueled by well-educated or trained citizens (Becker 1964). Human capital theory, Bourdieu (1986, 244) explains, focuses too narrowly on the economic profits of education: "the profitability of educational expenditure for society as a whole, the 'social rate of return,' or the 'social gain of education as measured by its effects on national productivity.'" Human capital theory, "despite its humanistic connotations," does not, Bourdieu (1986, 244) argues, "move beyond economism." It does not consider cultural investments, particularly the ways different social classes invest different proportions of both economic and cultural resources into education, and "the differential chances of profit which the various markets offer these agents or classes as a function of the volume and composition of their assets" (Bourdieu 1986, 244). For Bourdieu and Passeron (1979 [1964], 27):

> The most effective way of serving the system while believing one is fighting it is to attribute all inequalities in educational opportunity solely to economic inequalities or to a conscious political aim. The education system can, in fact, ensure the perpetuation of privilege by the mere operation of its own internal logic.

This "internal logic" refers to the reproduction and legitimation of symbolic power, or symbolic capital. According to Wacquant (in Bourdieu and Wacquant 1992, 119), symbolic capital is one of Bourdieu's most complex ideas and his whole body of work "may be read as a hunt for its varied forms and effects."

Bourdieu and Passeron (1979 [1964]) argue that symbolic power is continuously reproduced through a social structure (or what they call a "social space") that is continuously shifting and historically fluid. Their work moves away from conventional understandings of social mobility occurring within a "fixed and stable" structure (Friedman and Savage 2017, 71) and demonstrates that shifts in the social space, such as the opening up of higher education, may offer an illusion of change, say of increased meritocracy, but that these transformations work to maintain permanence and preserve the status quo. Bourdieu (1984 [1979], 161) explains:

> Once this mechanism is understood, one perceives the futility of the abstract debates which arise from the opposition of permanence and change, structure and history, reproduction and the "production of society." The real basis of such debates is the refusal to acknowledge that social contradictions and struggles are not all, or always, in contradiction with the perpetuation

of the established order; that, beyond the antitheses of "thinking in pairs," permanence can be ensured by change and the structure perpetuated by movement.

The field of higher education, Bourdieu and Passeron (1979 [1964]) argue, reproduces symbolic power through the transmission and reconversion of symbolic forms of cultural capital.

To explain what symbolic capital is and how it works to reproduce inequalities in education, it is first necessary to explain what Bourdieu means by economic capital, social capital, cultural capital, and their specificity and relationship to habitus, field, and the social space. Economic capital refers to money or objects that can be converted into money, such as institutionalized property rights. All forms of capital can be derived from economic capital but, as Bourdieu (1986, 252) argues, "only at the cost of a more or less great effort at transformation, which is needed to produce the type of power in question." Social capital refers to one's social connections, networks of "mutual acquaintance and recognition," that can be mobilized as resources (Bourdieu 1986, 248). It is not just *who you know* but *who knows you*. Social capital requires constant work: its reproduction requires continuous, back-and-forth, exchanges of recognition. It is a relation of social obligation and commitment. Cultural capital, which Bourdieu (in Bourdieu and Wacquant 1992, 119, emphasis in original) also calls "informational capital," refers to "what you know," as opposed to "who you know." It can exist in three forms: "in the *embodied* state, i.e., in the form of long-lasting dispositions of the mind and body; in the *objectified* state, in the form of cultural goods (pictures, books, dictionaries, instruments, machines, etc.) [. . .]; and in the *institutionalized* state," such as academic qualifications and awards (Bourdieu 1986, 243).

The notion of embodied cultural capital, mentioned earlier, relates to Bourdieu's (2000) conceptualization of habitus. Bourdieu was interested in how the social world comes to be inscribed on the body. He developed the notion of habitus to describe the ways our bodies congeal and coalesce with the social world—the ways we are corporeally formed, oriented, and haunted by our experiences, histories, and environments. We have a well-adjusted habitus, or what Hage (1997, 102) calls a "well-fitted habitus," when we have accumulated the capital necessary to act efficiently in an environment, when we have internalized the "strategies" or "practical sense" of an environment

(Bourdieu in Lamaison 1986, 112). The master carpenter, working speedily and skilfully with their tools and timber, has adjusted and adapted to their environment, their workshop, their trade. They have a well-fitted habitus. The middle-class student, whose family actively engages in particular cultural practices, such as going to the theater, art gallery, or museum, possesses the practices and tastes that dispose them to feel more "at home" at university (Bourdieu and Passeron 1979 [1964], 13). Working-class students, on the other hand, are more likely to feel "out of place" at university (Bourdieu and Passeron 1979 [1964], 13). The latter example is, as I will show in the following text, much more complicated today—different universities can afford different experiences of fit.

Habitus and capital, thus, exist in relation to particular types of environments: what Bourdieu calls "fields" and "social spaces"—and, as I will later argue, *microcosms* too. A field is a *specialized* and *institutionalized* environment, "arising when a domain of action and authority becomes sufficiently demarcated, autonomized, and monopolized" (Wacquant in Wacquant and Akcaoglu 2017, 62). We know the logics of fields implicitly: we know when we can sink into place and move with ease and comfort, and we know when we are out of place, out of our comfort zones, when we are, "fish out of water" (Bourdieu in Bourdieu and Wacquant 1992, 127). This relates to Bourdieu's (1987, 5) "sense of one's place" (as discussed in the Introduction). Bourdieu (in Bourdieu and Wacquant 1992, 106) likens the notion of field to a "magnetic field" and explains that the boundaries of a field are where the magnetic pull of the field ceases to have much effect. Fields pull some people in and they push others away. Fields do transform, and they do so in a somewhat paradoxical fashion. They are at once *"systems of relations that are independent of the populations which these relations define"* (Bourdieu in Bourdieu and Wacquant 1992, 106, emphasis in original). So too, are fields the product of competition between players to establish what is worthy of accumulation in the "game" (Bourdieu in Bourdieu and Wacquant 1992, 101–6). Fields are spaces of strategy and struggle.

Fields may also consist of a series of subfields. Higher education, for example, does. Marginson (2006, 11), drawing on Bourdieu's *The Field of Cultural Production*, argues that Australia's higher education system is structured by an opposition between elite "Sandstone" universities (or the "Group of Eight") and what he calls "heteronomous vocational and regional institutions." The latter struggle and compete for students, the highest entrance scores, grants, publications, and citations (Marginson 2006). Reay et al. (2010), in their work on higher education in the UK, argue that these different types of institutions—new and old—may also afford different conditions for belonging. The feel of a new and a local university is, indeed, different from the hallowed halls of Oxbridge. The former, they argue, affords a sense of social fit for working-class students and that this sense of fit "lulls working-class students into a sense of security and symmetry, providing a comfort zone where the working-class students feel they are accepted" (Reay et al. 2010, 112). Comfort is conceptualized as the "familiar" and as being around *people like us* (Reay et al. 2010, 111). On the other hand, Reay et al. (2010) found that working-class students at prestigious universities experience a sense of social discomfort among their peers from more privileged backgrounds. For these students, the elite university represents a "middle-class bubble" rather than the "real" or "ordinary" world (Reay et al. 2009, 1111).

Not all social action, however, transpires in a field. It transpires in a social space. Wacquant (in Wacquant and Akcaoglu 2017, 62–3) explains:

> The vast majority of social action unfolds in social spaces that are just that, social spaces, that is, multidimensional distributions of socially efficient properties (capitals) stipulating a set of patterned positions from which one can intelligibly predict strategies. But they are not fields because they have no institutionalized boundaries no barriers to entry and no specialists in the elaboration of a distinctive source of authority.

A "social space" is a term that describes a more encompassing social world, like Bourdieu's France of the 1960s, a constellation of many different fields and microcosms, and allows us to map the distribution of capitals (Bourdieu 1989, 23). It is, Wacquant (in Wacquant and Akcaoglu 2017, 62) explains, "the mother-category." For Bourdieu (1984 [1979], 169), "it is an abstract representation, deliberately constructed, like a map, to give a bird's-eye view, a point of view on the [. . .] social world."

Capital has "symbolic effects," or rather can become "symbolic capital," when it has accrued legitimacy, dominance, and recognition within the wider "social space"—not just within a field. Symbolic capital is, Bourdieu (1989, 23) argues, "the power granted to those who have obtained sufficient recognition to be in a position to impose recognition." Symbolic capital is social power. It is often disguised, concealed, and rarely revealed—and this act of misrecognition is what Bourdieu (in Bourdieu and Wacquant 1992, 167) calls "symbolic violence." The symbolic violence associated with the transmission of symbolic forms of embodied cultural capital is, Bourdieu (1986, 246) argues, one of the most important strategies of reproduction:

> But the most powerful principle of the symbolic efficacy of cultural capital no doubt lies in the logic of its transmission. On the one hand, the process of appropriating objectified cultural capital and the time necessary for it to take place mainly depend on the cultural capital embodied in the whole family [. . .]. On the other hand, the initial accumulation of cultural capital, the precondition for the fast, easy accumulation of every kind of useful for cultural capital, starts at the outset, without delay, without wasted time, only for the offspring of families endowed with strong cultural capital; in this case, the accumulation period covers the whole period of socialization. It follows that the transmission of cultural capital is no doubt the best hidden form of hereditary transmission of capital, and it therefore receives proportionately greater weight in the system of reproduction strategies, as the direct, visible forms of transmission tend to be more strongly censored and controlled.

Symbolic capital is, as mentioned, unevenly distributed in the field of higher education. Not all university qualifications have symbolic effects. We live in a period of "diploma inflation" (Bourdieu and Passeron 1979 [1964], 83). Greater degrees of recognition are attached to some universities and not others, and greater degrees of recognition are attached to some disciplines and not others (Bourdieu and Passeron 1979 [1964]). Bourdieu and Passeron (1979 [1964], 78) argue:

> When class fractions who previously made little use of the school system enter the race for academic qualifications, the effect is to force the groups whose reproduction was mainly or exclusively achieved through education to step up their investments so as to maintain the relative scarcity of their qualifications and, consequently, their position in the class structure. Academic qualifications and the school system which awards them thus become one of the key stakes in an interclass competition which generates a general and continuous growth in the demand for education and an inflation of academic qualifications.

Working-class and lower-middle-class students are concentrated in less prestigious disciplines and less prestigious institutions (Bourdieu and Passeron

1979 [1964]). "The new arrivals," Bourdieu and Champagne (1999 [1993], 423) explain, are the "first victims" of "diploma inflation." The uneven distribution of symbolic capital in the field of higher education works as a form of symbolic violence, particularly for "new arrivals" who do not necessarily recognize the objective value of their degree:

> It is an *integrative* struggle, since those who enter this chase, in which they are beaten before they start as the constancy of the gap testifies, implicitly recognise the legitimacy of the goals pursued by those whom they pursue, by the mere fact of taking part. (Bourdieu and Passeron 1979 [1964], 97)

Bourdieu and Passeron's work on the uneven distribution of symbolic capital has ongoing salience in Australia (Marginson 2011; Watkins 2020). The Group of Eight, for example, attract the top students who are disproportionately of a higher socioeconomic status (SES), and these students maintain a monopoly in elite disciplines, like medicine and law: "Of those studying medicine, 91 per cent were of a high SES, and while the corresponding number for law was not as high, at 65 per cent, again those of a high SES were dominant" (Watkins 2020, 200). The concentration of Australian elites in the most prestigious institutions and faculties has profound implications—particularly in a period when graduates receive less financial benefit than in the past and they are more likely to work part-time and/or in jobs that require no tertiary qualification (Norton and Cherastidtham 2018, 76). Norton and Cherastidtham (2018, 91), in their work for *The Grattan Institute*, have shown that graduates of medicine and law can expect the biggest starting salaries. Norton and Cakitaki (2016) also found that graduates of medicine have far better employment prospects than all other graduates. Graduates from the Group of Eight are also more likely to secure first jobs matching their qualifications, and graduates who are employed full-time can also expect to earn 10 percent more than non–Group of Eight graduates (Norton and Cherastidtham 2014). Watkins (2020), in her work for the *Australian Cultural Fields* project, also found that elites maintain their advantage through the possession of postgraduate qualifications.

In addition to the transmission of symbolic forms of cultural capital, Bourdieu and Passeron (1979 [1964], 79) argue that the economic and social yield of a qualification also depends on one's accumulation of valuable economic and social capitals: "Outside the specifically scholastic market, a diploma is worth what its holder is worth, economically and socially." Those graduates who do not have valuable forms of social and economic capital at their disposal find it the most difficult to reap the rewards of a university qualification (Bourdieu and Passeron 1979 [1964]). Recent scholarship from Canada and the UK supports these findings (Bathmaker et al. 2013, 2016; Burke 2015; Lehmann 2012). Bathmaker et al. (2013, 740), for example, found that middle-class students know how to play the game: "[they] are not only dealt the better cards in a high-stakes game, but they have internalised the knowledge, through economic and cultural advantages, of when and how best to play them." They also found that middle-class students used their social networks to secure internships—and they did so without a conscious acknowledgment of their advantage. Working-class students, on the other hand, were more likely to have vague career goals and "had a pre-disposition towards trying to play a meritocratic game fairly, putting extra effort into securing a higher-class degree rather than securing an internship for instance" (Bathmaker et al. 2013, 741). Abrahams (2017) calls the latter "honourable mobility," as opposed to what the working-class students saw as "shameless entitlement." This is, of course, increasingly complex as internships become embedded within degrees.

Place and Mobilities

The Bourdieusian scholarship powerfully demonstrates the ways symbolic capital is produced, distributed, and reproduced. There are, however, limitations. These limitations relate to not only how contemporary Bourdieusian scholars engage with Bourdieu (as I shall later discuss) but also the limits of Bourdieu's own work on illuminating the experiences of working-class students in higher education. For the most part, Bourdieusian work on higher education is, indeed, a-placial: its emphasis is on bounded fields and the social space, not physical places (Donnelly and Evans 2016; Finn 2017b; Finn and Holton 2019). It also does little to move beyond the binaries of social mobility and immobility (Donnelly and Evans 2016; Finn 2017b; Finn and Holton 2019). Sociology, Sheller (2014) argues, has a preoccupation with social mobility. Mobility does, however, mean more than social mobility (Sheller and Urry 2006; Sheller 2014). The "mobilities turn" in social, cultural, and geographical research, led by Urry, has, indeed, called for attention to alternative ways of thinking about mobility and attention to the diverse forms that mobility may take (Sheller and Urry 2006; Sheller 2014). There is a small and emerging body of work associated with the "mobilities turn" that examines the diverse mobilities of university students and graduates in the UK (Finn 2015, 2017a, 2017b; Henderson 2020; Holton 2015; Holton and Finn 2018a, 2018b; Finn and Holton 2019).

Finn (2017b, 746), for example, explores a range of mobility practices that are informed by personal relationships—both loose and dense, "for better or for worse, and not simply as a means of capital exchange and/or for the purposes of social mobility." Quoting Adey (2006), Finn (2017b, 755) explains that university-related mobility is a "highly differentiated activity where many different people move in many different ways." In her work on young women at university, Finn (2017b) describes the experiences of one student, "Ashley," who was White British and the first in her family to attend university (an elite university located in a different city). When Ashley began university, she continued to visit home regularly and struggled to develop friendships at university. As a way to overcome loneliness, Ashley worked on a casual basis for an employment agency at various places around her new city. Working for the employment agency enabled her to develop new friendships and a deeper familiarity with the city, as well as become financially independent. Ashley's experiences, Finn (2017b, 752) argues, are "complex and agentic" not simply representative of working-class immobility. She writes:

> This is an example of mobility capital put to use in different ways and to different ends. Ashley benefited significantly from both her actual and potential mobility—her "motility" [. . .]—not only in terms of the extra money she earned from her agency work and the social networks she accessed there, but also in the accumulation of emotional capital "on the move" between fields that boosted her self-esteem and emotional wellbeing. Thus, mobility capital should not be merely understood as inherited familial resources, which specifically take students away from home; but, rather, as a dynamic matrix of access, competence and appropriation of mobility that may form links with, and may be exchanged for, other forms of capital. (Finn 2017b, 753)

Finn's work, then, moves within and across different social fields to examine student and graduate mobilities as embedded within wider experiences of personal life—not just the field of higher education. This approach is a "relational" one (2017a, 419). Finn (2017a, 421) writes:

> Relationality posits that actions, identities and values are fundamentally embedded within webs of relationships. These may be enriching and sustaining; however, they can be equally difficult, mundane, and even toxic. Thus relationality [. . .] offers a fluid framework for theorising the broad range of relationships that matter to people.

This scholarship also calls attention to the significance of place, particularly the pull of home. Donnelly and Evans (2016), for example, have examined how university choice processes are shaped by place and kinship relations. Finn (2017a), and in her recent work with Holton (Finn and Holton 2019), has examined how graduate mobilities may be shaped by proximate relations that are embedded in place—relations that pull one back to home. This collective focus on place, diverse mobilities, and relationality is important—it helps to shift a focus away from a-placial and a-mobile Bourdieusian scholarship on reproduction and provides an alternative way of thinking about student and graduate mobilities beyond the accumulation of symbolic capital, of social power, of inequality. Yet, in the process, this scholarship unintentionally backgrounds the significance of structural inequalities. Recent scholarship from Henderson (2020), however, calls for an attunement to both place and class. The pull of home is, indeed, a relation of domination. It is important to attend to the ways people make their lives meaningful, but so too is it important to attend to the ways people make meaningful a world that makes them. Structural inequalities are, indeed, an embodied dimension of social being and action. To do this, I call for a deeper engagement with Bourdieu's notion of habitus. Finn (2015) and Donnelly and Evans (2016) are both critical of Bourdieu's conceptualization of habitus. Finn (2015, 28), for example, writes:

> Whereas habitus implies habitual and unthought responses, relationality posits that social action, and the identities this gives rise to, emerges in and through active, intentional and often emotionally demanding negotiations with others to whom we feel a sense of connection. This includes families but extends also to colleagues, peers, housemates and so on. These negotiations reflect, reinforce and also complicate power relations and they are saturated with moral significance.

A focus on the relational aspects of experience is important but habitus is not merely the "habitual" or the "familiar"—it is, I argue, relational, both in its formation and ongoing enactment and accumulation. Donnelly and Evans (2016), too, argue that habitus "does not capture the non-classed elements of space." However, habitus, as I argue in the next section, is *both* placial and classed.

On the Accumulation of Being: The Philosophical Dimensions of Bourdieu's Work

To examine subjective understandings of "moving well," and their very emplacement in Cranebrook and the wider Penrith, I turn toward and develop the *philosophical*, not just sociological, dimensions of Bourdieu's modus operandi—or what Dreyfus and Rabinow (1993, 35) call Bourdieu's "empirical existential analytics." Bourdieu's work is more than a theory of the uneven production, distribution, and reproduction of symbolic capital—of social inequality (Threadgold 2020). Bourdieu is, after all, a philosopher among the sociologists (or a sociologist amongst the philosophers). He was originally trained in philosophy, and later transformed into an anthropologist and then a sociologist—but he always saw himself as engaged in "fieldwork in philosophy" (Hage 2013, 79). Hage (2013, 79) writes that for Bourdieu:

> Philosophy asks the most complex and intellectually demanding questions about the world. Bourdieu, however, sees it as ill-equipped to produce answers to the questions it asks. This is because the richest answers to its questions come out of empirical research that socially contextualizes the production of knowledge.

For me, however, this process was reversed. Through my interviews and engagement with my empirical material, I developed questions that the sociological dimensions of Bourdieu's work alone could not answer. I thus came to Bourdieu's philosophy through my fieldwork. My fieldwork, as discussed in the Introduction, opened up questions about a good life and place, and the philosophical dimensions of Bourdieu's work provided ways to think about how university becomes a means to a good life, a class-differentiated good life, and one embedded in place (as I shall detail in the following section).

Bourdieu (1989) argues for a weaving together of what he calls social physics and social phenomenology. Bourdieu's approach, Wacquant (in Bourdieu and Wacquant 1992, 11) writes, should both "construct the objective structures (spaces of *positions*), the distribution of socially efficient resources that define the external constraints bearing on interactions and representations" (social physics) and "reintroduce the immediate, lived experience of agents in order to explicate the categories of perception and appreciation (*dispositions*) that structure action from inside" (social phenomenology). Drawing from Husserl's (1983 [1913]) notion on *umwelt*, Bourdieu (1989) explains that sociology must attend to people's perceptions of what is meaningful, or what is worth pursuing, within their social worlds, not necessarily what is valued in the wider social space. It is for this reason that Hage (2013, 79) describes Bourdieu's work as *a political economy of being*: "It is a critical mode of understanding the production and circulation of culturally specific ways of perceiving 'being' (that is, whatever is contextually sensed as a 'good,' fulfilling, satisfying, viable, etc., life)."

Attending to the research participants' experiences and the different ways they accumulate being involves moving beyond the field of higher education to explore what is meaningful within their microcosms. The accumulation of being is, indeed, about accumulating a sense of "being at home" in one's environment (Bourdieu 2000). This is, Bourdieu (2000) argues, the homing disposition of the habitus. Bourdieu (2000, 143) writes, "He feels at home in the world because the world is also in him, in the form of habitus, a virtue made of necessity which implies a form of love of necessity, *amor fati*." This love of home is a relation of *conatus*, "of a tendency to perpetuate themselves in their being, to reproduce themselves in that which constitutes their existence and their identity" (Bourdieu 1993, 274). This notion of *conatus* is important. It allows us to think about the pull of home, not just the trope of flight (say, class escape, escape from Western Sydney). This pull is what Hage (2011, 90) calls social gravity: "it is the very intensity of one's interest in the social world that makes for the meaningfulness and intensity of the world."

This *interest*, Hage's (2011) social gravity, is what Bourdieu (2000) also variously calls *libido* or *illusio*—terms used to describe the way we are engrossed and enveloped by the social world and driven by something in it that gives our lives meaning. Bourdieu (2000, 135) writes, "*Illusio* is that way of *being* in the world, of being occupied by the world." It describes the logic of our action, our drive, the chase. Bourdieu (2000) argues that the very act of being oriented toward objects, of being occupied, of having *illusio*, provides sustenance, the accumulation of being, what Hage (2009, 97) calls "existential mobility." To have no *illusio* is to experience a lightness of being (Bourdieu 2000; Hage 2009; Threadgold 2020). *Illusio* pulls us into the social world and connects us to others. Drawing from Pascal, Bourdieu (2000, 240) explains:

> Through the social games it offers, the social world provides something more and other than the apparent stakes: the chase, Pascal reminds us, counts as much as, if not more than, the quarry, and there is happiness in activity which exceeds the visible profits—wage, prize or reward—and which consists in the fact of emerging from indifference (or depression), being occupied, projected towards goals, and feeling oneself objectively, and therefore subjectively, endowed with a social mission. To be expected, solicited, overwhelmed with obligations and commitments is not only to be snatched from solitude or insignificance, but also to experience, in the most continuous and concrete way, the feeling of counting for others, being *important* for them, and therefore in oneself, and finding in the permanent plebiscite of testimonies of interest—requests, expectations, invitations—a kind of continuous justification for existing.

The objects we chase are objects that promise a good and happy life. This is an affective orientation to the world. Bourdieu (2000, 211), in *Pascalian Meditations*, again quotes Pascal at length:

> Interest takes the form of an encounter with the objectivity of things "full of interest". We are [. . .] full of things which take us out of ourselves. Our instinct makes us feel that we must seek happiness outside ourselves. Our passions impel us outside, even when no objects present themselves to excite them. External objects tempt us of themselves, and call to us, even when we are not thinking of them. And thus philosophers have said in vain: "Retire within yourselves, you will find your good there." We do not believe them, and those who believe them are the most empty and the most foolish.

University is one such object. Cranebrook and the wider Penrith is another. University, as I argue in this book, is an object that promises happiness and a good life, and Cranebrook and the wider Penrith are sites of this good life.

On Homely Mobility: Domus and Domunis

The philosophical dimensions of Bourdieu's work described earlier are absent in scholarship on higher education—in both Bourdieu's own work and Bourdieusian-inspired scholarship. Indeed, despite Bourdieu's philosophical work on home and the accumulation of being, he never empirically examined the pull of home as an embodiment of structural inequalities embedded in the practical dimensions of everyday life. In Bourdieu's (1970) empirical work on home, particularly in his ethnography of the Kabyle in Algeria, home is just a place of socialization. And in Bourdieu's empirical work on reproduction, specifically his work on the French education system, cultural capital and habitus are used to examine processes of reproduction. Bourdieu, in his work on home or education, does not examine the ways education becomes a means to a good life, and how visions of a good life are shaped by the push and pull of home. Contemporary Bourdieusian scholarship has examined why working-class students go to university—for a better life, financial betterment, to become middle class. However, what exactly constitutes a good life (or the better life beyond financial betterment) and the ways a good life is class differentiated remain implicit and underexplored (Bathmaker et al. 2016; Lehmann 2009a, 2009b; Loveday 2015; O'Shea et al. 2017). And, as discussed, Finn (2017a, 2017b) and Donnelly and Evans (2016) have examined the pull of people and place, but not how these relations may involve processes of reproduction. I do both, and, in doing so, I examine classed and placial processes of reproduction: how social worlds are reproduced and transformed through working-class people's participation in higher education.

I use Hage's (in Zournazi and Hage 2002) work on "homeliness" to provide a way forward. Hage (in Zournazi and Hage 2002, 160) suggests that we think about the accumulation of being as the "accumulation of homeliness":

> Immediately when you speak about the pursuit of homeliness, even though we are still into fuzzy, vague terms, we've come down a bit more tangibly from the pursuit of being—and suddenly the imagination starts working on something more concrete depending on the image.

The accumulation of homeliness is about the pursuit of homely feelings (either one of the following or in combination): security, familiarity, community, and possibility (Hage 1997, 102). "Security" refers to a sense of safety and the absence of threats, and, importantly, a degree of wilfulness in one's environment. Hage (1997, 102, emphasis in original) explains, "A deeper sense of security and homeliness emanates from the space where we not only have but where *we feel empowered to seek* the satisfaction of our needs and to remove or exclude threatening otherness." "Familiarity" refers to our spatial knowledge of an environment. To have feelings of familiarity is to have a "well-fitted habitus" (Hage 1997, 102). Familiarity is linked to security: to have spatial and practical control is to feel secure. "Community" is particularly important—feeling like you are part of a community provides a powerful sense of "objective and subjective gratification" (Hage in Zournazi and Hage 2002, 162)[1]. Hage (in Zournazi and Hage 2002, 162) describes a sense of community as, "a sense of articulation to others, concretely speaking—the feeling of connection, of sharing, or recognition." Finally, a sense of "possibility" involves having hope and opportunities for betterment. Homeliness, then, is not "claustrophobic"— it involves possibilities for growth and self-expansion, but within the limited resources of a given environment (Hage 1997, 103).

I move beyond the field of higher education to explore what is meaningful within the research participants' "microcosms." As discussed in the Introduction, I use the term "microcosm" to describe geographical places, specifically Cranebrook and its surrounding suburbs. Social spaces and fields are, after all, embedded in physical places. They overlap, entangle, and bleed into one another. We are, after all, "not *atopos*, placeless, as Plato said of Socrates" (Bourdieu 2000, 131). Bourdieu (1999e [1993], 123–4) explains:

> As bodies (and biological individuals), and in the same way that things are, human beings are situated in a site (they are not endowed with the ubiquity that would allow them to be in several places at once), and they occupy a place. The *site (le lieu)* can be defined absolutely as the point in *physical space* where an agent or thing is situated, "takes place," exists: that is to say, either as a *localization* or, from a relational viewpoint, as a *position*, a rank in an order. The *place* occupied may be defined as the extent, surface and volume that an individual or thing occupies in the physical space.

Bourdieu (2008 [2004], 86) did use the term "microcosm" in his later work— for example, he uses it to refer to his hometown, but Bourdieu does not develop the term *analytically*. According to Wacquant (in Wacquant and Akcaoglu 2017, 67), Bourdieu did, indeed, draft a book by the same title, but it remains unpublished. Microcosms, I argue, have elastic geographical boundaries and various scales of existence. Cranebrook, as I will detail in Chapter 2, is at once a suburb and at other times a place with different pockets, and it sometimes collapses into the wider Penrith region and Western Sydney more broadly (even the Penrith Campus of Western Sydney University)—all of which have distinct geopolitical boundaries, but also exist in a number of other dimensions that are not so clearly bounded.

I make an argument for "homely mobility"—a term I use to describe degrees of existential and social mobility within the microcosm of Cranebrook and the wider Penrith region. Existential mobility may coexist with social mobility— the acquisition of symbolic capital—but it may not. The two forms of mobility do "tend to coincide in a number of social situations" but "they are not the same thing" (Hage 2009, 99). Hage (2009, 99) explains, "One can be in a job and climbing the social ladder within that job yet still feel stuck in it." The homing disposition of the habitus allows us to emplace visions of the good life. The suburban life, in what is perceived to be a less-desirable geography and a place of stagnation, can be a place of desire. Visions of a good life are, after all, not placeless. This is something acknowledged in work on migration and mobilities—Hage's body of work is a key example—but is something strangely absent in most work on higher education where the social space tends to be privileged over the geographical, or where questions of the good life are neglected. Normative understandings of a good life are not normally associated with working-class culture, as Skeggs and Loveday (2012) have pointed out. Nor are they associated with working-class places (Allen and Hollingsworth 2013; Henderson 2020), or with Western Sydney (Symonds 1997).

The notion of homely mobility moves away from dualistic narratives of social mobility between worlds marked as working class and worlds marked as middle class (Bourdieu 2008 [2004]; Friedman and Savage 2017; Hoggart 2009 [1957]; Lawler 1999; Munt 2000). Hoggart (2009 [1957], 264), for example, describes the educationally successful working-class lad, the "scholarship boy." It is a story of those who are "emotionally uprooted from their class" and "who, for a number of years, perhaps for a very long time, have a sense of no longer really belonging to any group" (Hoggart 2009 [1957], 263). Some scholarship boys, Hoggart (2009 [1957], 264) writes, find themselves "at home" in their new world, but most find themselves "chafing" (264) between "two worlds" (267). The scholarship boy is "at the friction-point of two cultures" (Hoggart 2009 [1957], 264). Lawler (1999) has written about the social mobility experiences of middle-class women from working-class backgrounds. Like Hoggart, these women experienced a sense of discomfort, shame, and pain. Lawler (1999) explains that they refuse to be working class, but at times experience a "disrupted habitus": moments when they do not pass as middle class, or when they fear not passing as middle class—when their working-class habitus resurfaces and disturbs. Friedman and Savage (2017), too, have written about movement between classed worlds and argue that it produces a "hysteresis" effect, which, as Friedman (2016, 131) suggests, citing Bourdieu and Passeron, is generated when "the environment with which they are objectively confronted is too distant from that in which they are objectively fitted." It describes a lag between habitus and field.

This book, too, moves away from Friedman (2015, 2016) and Friedman and Savage's (2017) argument that slow-speed, short-range mobility is "largely psychologically smooth." Short-range mobility refers to class changes into "modest" and "intermediate" occupations—although what constitutes *modest* or *intermediate* occupations is unclear (Friedman 2016, 136). They use this typology to describe their participants who continued to live in their geographical area of origin, were in relationships with people from similar backgrounds, and were proud of their working-class identity. Friedman (2016, 137–8) argues that they "rebuff[ed] change," which at times meant "actively stunting one's own upward trajectory," to avoid "a confrontation between dispositions formed in primary socialization and those demanded by their destination." Their habitus, Friedman (2016, 137) writes, "functioned to protect respondents, psychologically, from the potential dislocation of social mobility." An emphasis on "rebuffing change," however, ignores the changes already experienced by these participants—they are upwardly mobile, after all. "Rebuffing change" also falls back onto a binary model of mobility from working-class to middle-class worlds. "Stunting," too, implies a failed transition. Rebuffing change and stunting together, then, ignore the weight of micromovements and degrees of social mobility *within* microcosms.

This book instead examines degrees of mobility within Cranebrook and the wider Penrith area which may be quite significant, socially, emotionally, and relationally. As Bourdieu (1999a and 2008 [2004]) argues, we need to stay attuned to a sense of uprooting, hierarchy, and movement within microcosms. He calls this "positional suffering" (Bourdieu in Bourdieu et al. 1999a, 3–5). Bourdieu (2008 [2004], 86) has written about his father's mobility within the peasant world of Bearn. Bourdieu's (2008 [2004], 86) father was the son of a "peasant sharecropper," who, when around thirty years-old, became a postman and later the clerk of the village post office in Bearn. This was a job that separated him from his peasant friends, some of whom were "better-off" economically (2008 [2004], 86), but still made "wounding insults and aggressive jokes" (85) against *"lous emplegats,* clerks 'with white hands'" (84–85). Bourdieu (2008 [2004], 86) writes, "my father never spoke without some fury about his experience of social differences as they asserted themselves in the village microcosm". Postal work also alienated Bourdieu's father from his own father and brother who had "stayed on the farm" (Bourdieu 2008 [2004], 85). This was something that "pained him" and "he would lend a hand when they were most busy and he had some leave" (Bourdieu 2008 [2004], 85). This book also engages with Bourdieu's notion of a "sense of one's place": the idea that class is produced through processes of distinction embedded in microcosms that may, indeed, be experienced as more profound and simultaneously work to mask larger-class inequalities and differences.

It calls for a rethinking of the notion of social mobility and attention to the *social gravity,* or *illusio,* of one's microcosm. The accumulation of being may involve "staying put." Staying put may involve relations of "getting out and getting away" (Lawler 1999) within place, as I will explore in Chapters 2 and 5. Staying put may also involve honoring social obligations and commitments, such as the sacrifice of migration, or reciprocating the care given by a teacher, or giving back to one's community (Pearce et al. 2008). *Illusio,* or rather the chase, after all, involves social obligations and commitments (Bourdieu 2000). Social obligations and commitments, I argue, involve relations of faithfulness and gratitude. Faithfulness and gratitude, Simmel (1950, 395) writes, belong to "among those 'microscopic,' but infinitely tough, threads which tie one element of society to another, and thus eventually all of them together in a stable collective life." Faithfulness refers to perseverance of a relationship long after it started. Faithfulness, then, expands the idea of "the chase" to think about other ways we are enveloped by the social world while still pursuing homely mobility. Simmel (1950) writes that every relationship begins with interest and that over time this interest turns into faithfulness. Gratitude is about opening oneself up to the world and reciprocating an offering—not necessarily to the person who initiated the act of giving. Simmel (1950, 388) explains that it is about "throw[ing] a new bridge to the other." These relations, I demonstrate, can involve both vertical and horizontal recognitions: between an individual and Cranebrook, or between individuals (Hage 2000).

Following Bourdieu and Passeron (1979 [1964]), I explore how the promise of higher education is unevenly distributed. Not everyone has access to the rewards associated with a university qualification. There may not always be a correspondence between *illusio* and the chances (or *lusiones*) one has of realizing their interests. Some graduates are left waiting. I call this period of abeyance the "graduate waiting room." The old education system, Bourdieu and Passeron (1979 [1964], 91–2) explain, had strongly marked boundaries and strict processes of "elimination" through examination that led to sudden "disinvestment" by groups of students—the working class and the lower middle class. The new system, while it "fobs off" many students who graduate with less valuable qualifications, does not, however, lead to sudden "disinvestments" (Bourdieu and Passeron 1979 [1964], 92). The social hierarchy in the new system is fuzzy and blurry. To paraphrase Hage[2] (in Zournazi and Hage 2002), *the rewards of a university degree work like an imaginary bank account that you have but you cannot access, but you are happy to have this bank account because ultimately you think that you can access it*. This idea of remaining invested in an object whose realization is impossible but is perceived to be a possibility—an attachment that provides sustenance—is akin to Berlant's (2011) notion of "cruel optimism." Indeed, scholars have described the education system as being one of "cruel optimism" for working-class students (Bunn et al. 2019; Reay 2017; Sellar 2013).

Bourdieu and Passeron (1979 [1964, 92]) explain that if people do "disinvest" from their aspirations, they are likely to experience "personal criticism and crisis" (Bourdieu and Passeron 1979 [1964], 92). The blame is on them, the individual, rather than society itself. This is, they argue, because the effects of devaluation are often masked by the value one might bestow on their qualification, a value which is not necessarily "objectively acknowledged" (Bourdieu and Passeron 1979 [1964], 82). Bourdieu and Passeron (1979 [1964], 90) argue that "the strategies people employ to rebuild the interrupted path of a hoped-for trajectory, are [. . .] one of the most important factors in the transformation of social structure." These actions are what Bourdieu and Passeron (1979 [1964], 90) call "compensatory strategies." Following Bourdieu and Passeron, I examine strategies of compensation as the research participants reconfigure stalled mobilities: some "persevere" with their aspirations, others "move on," and some feel stuck—unable to move on or retrain. The latter maintain what I call a "cruel attachment" to the promise of university: it denotes an ambivalent and critical relation to the promise of university, Western Sydney University. I also examine how, in the absence of a permanent job in a desired career, social mobility may be reconfigured in new ways. As I will demonstrate in Chapter 4, one may feel at once both socially and existentially mobile *and* immobile in relation to proximate others.

I also consider how the "rewards"—that job, that life—are class differentiated and class differentiating. As Bourdieu (2000, 217) has argued, our habitus influences what we chase and desire: "One is always surprised to see how much people's wills adjust to their possibilities, their desires to the capacity to satisfy them; and to discover that, contrary to all received ideas, *pleonexia*, the desire always to have more, as Plato called it, is the exception." What we chase may be valued in our microcosm, but what we value in our microcosm may not be valued in the wider social space. Bourdieu (1984 [1979]) calls this an act of distinction. This is about the domination of some microcosms over others. The homing disposition of the habitus can limit our mobilities in the world, preserve the status quo, and collude with the reproduction of class inequalities (Bourdieu and Wacquant 1992). This type of relation, for example, has been explored by Willis (1977) in his influential work on the "counter-culture" of British working-class "lads" who remain deeply invested in their milieu, resist the school system, and ultimately reproduce a dominated position in society. Willis's analysis, of course, is not Bourdieusian but, as Berger (in Bourdieu and Wacquant 1992, 80), argues Willis, "describes ethnographically the interpenetration of 'habitus' and 'action' that Bourdieu outlines so persuasively in theoretical terms."

The violence of homeliness not only involves contradictions—contradictions related to the uneven distribution of symbolic capital—but also involves ambivalent feelings. Following Ahmed's (2010, 6) work on the promise of happiness, I examine how "ordinary attachments to the very idea of a good life are also sites of ambivalence, involving the confusion rather than separation of good and bad feelings." Like Bourdieu, Ahmed (2008, 2010) has examined how attachments to objects that promise a good life, what she terms "happy objects," may involve social pressures and obligations. Ahmed (2008) calls this "sociable happiness." Ahmed (2008, 2010) in particular examines how these social pressures and obligations can involve bad feeling. I use Ahmed's work, along with Simmel's (1950), to examine how gratitude to people and place can also be tinged with bad feeling. Gratitude, as I will demonstrate in Chapter 5, can have a "taste of bondage" (Simmel 1950, 393). Simmel (1950, 393) writes, "A service, a sacrifice, a benefit, once accepted, may engender an inner relation which can never be eliminated, because gratitude is perhaps the only feeling which, under all circumstances, can be morally demanded and rendered."

I also use Ahmed's (2010) work to examine how the good life, for those who are living the life they wished for, can be a site of disappointment. One can be "affectively alienated" from the promise of happiness (Ahmed 2010, 49). Ahmed (2010, 31) writes, "Desire is both what promises us something, what gives us energy, and also what is lacking, even in the very moment of its apparent realisation. There can be nothing more terrifying than getting what you want, because it is at this moment that you face what you want." She argues that you never really know what it is that you want, and what you want is "not simply 'ready' as an object" (Ahmed 2010, 31). Happy objects, in these instances, can become sites of "personal and social tension" (Ahmed 2010, 31). Disappointment does not necessarily lead to reorientation. Gratitude and faithfulness, as I will argue in Chapter 5, can bind one to the scene of disappointment, to the wished-for good life, to happy objects. Social ties, I will also argue, can mean that small-scale changes within one's microcosm—becoming different from friends and family—can be quite significant and can produce feelings of disappointment and alienation. Bourdieu (1990 [1980, 137]) writes, "Minimum objective distance in social space can coincide with maximum subjective distance."

Homely mobility, thus, involves degrees of goodness and violence, good feeling and bad feeling, care and domination. Homely mobility is contradictory. Hage (2017, 91–2), drawing from the work of Benveniste, the French linguist and semiotician, points out that the etymological roots for home, or *domus* (Latin), shares its roots with *dominus* (Latin). According to Benveniste (1973 [1969], 248), "The personage called *dominus* has authority over the *domus*; he represents and incarnates it." The *dominus* dominates. Both words—*domus* and *dominus*—come from the root word *doma*: "to do violence; to tame" (1973 [1969], 251). Homeliness ("domus"), then, is entangled with domination ("domunis") (Hage 2016). Hage (2017, 92) argues, "the aggressive affects associated with 'domination' are often thought of in opposition to the gentle and cuddly affects associated with the home" (Hage 2017, 92). This is, of course, a dimension of Bourdieu's (1990 [1980]) notion of symbolic violence. Symbolic violence is, after all, what he calls the "gentle" and "disguised" form of violence (Bourdieu 1990 [1980], 133). Symbolic violence, as mentioned previously, is the violence exercised with complicity (Bourdieu 2000, 241). Its cruelty lies in its goodness.

Conclusions

In this chapter, I have reviewed the scholarship that informs the concept of "homely mobility"—the term I use to describe the social gravity of people and place, and the accumulation of being, both social and existential, in place. I began by demonstrating the significance and continuing relevance of Bourdieu and Passeron's (1979 [1964] and 1990 [1970]) work on the reproduction of symbolic power in education, culture, and society. Their empirical research, published in the 1960s, revealed how the education system reproduces class inequalities, in contrast to conventional ideas about the education system being a mechanism for greater equality. To explain the logic of symbolic power, I then reviewed the sociological dimensions of Bourdieu's modus operandi: capital, habitus, field, and social space—as well as how they relate to one another, how they relate to the reproduction of inequality in higher education, and how contemporary Bourdieusian scholars have used and developed them (Bathmaker et al. 2013, 2016; Burke 2015; Lehmann 2012; Marginson 2011; Reay et al. 2010; Watkins 2020). Following Finn (2017a, 2017b), I argued that Bourdieu's sociology of higher education, as well as contemporary Bourdieusian scholarship on higher education, powerfully demonstrates the salience of class but that this work—for the most part—is a-placial and a-mobile. Its focus is on social mobility and its analytical boundaries are those of a field—a university.

I then reviewed a small and emerging body of work associated with the "mobilities turn" in higher education (Donnelly and Evans 2016; Finn 2017a, 2017b; Finn and Holton 2019). This work moves beyond the bounds of Bourdieu's field, as well as a preoccupation with social mobility, to examine alternative mobilities and how people make sense of their movements—that is, their subjective understandings of moving well. This work draws attention to the significance of place and the significance of people in those places. It, thus, provides an alternative and important way of theorizing experiences of higher education. Yet, while significant, I argued that it engages little with the ways these alternative mobilities—the pull back home, for example—are classed and involve relations of domination. To examine relations of symbolic power and the culturally specific ways people accumulate being, I turned toward and developed the philosophical dimensions of Bourdieu's work—which are absent in his own scholarship on higher education, as well as contemporary Bourdieusian scholarship on higher education. I used Bourdieu's sociology and philosophy, along with Hage's work on homeliness, Simmel's work on faithfulness and gratitude, and Ahmed's work on the ambivalence of a good life, to develop my concept of "homely mobility"—a concept which allows me to understand the ways students and graduates make meaningful a world that makes them.

2

University and the Promise of a Good Life

Introduction

In 2015, an advertisement for Western Sydney University went viral.[1] Ali (2015), journaling for the *Independent* in the UK, wrote, "Western Sydney University's powerful refugee student recruitment advert takes the internet by storm." The advertisement has since accrued 2,935,492 views on YouTube (July 3, 2021). It's a hero story: one of suffering, transformation, and redemption. It's the story of Deng Adut and his journey from child soldier in war-torn Sudan, to refugee in Western Sydney, to human rights lawyer for refugees in Western Sydney. The moving montage of clips shows a younger Deng being forcefully taken from his mother, fighting in a warzone, recovering from a bullet wound, being smuggled out of Sudan by the UN, and traveling on a plane bound for Australia. "Western Sydney took him in"—the place, the people, and the university. This statement hovers over images of Western Sydney's streets. It could be Rooty Hill or Wentworthville (suburbs in Western Sydney). The housing is iconic to the region: a mixture of the prewar weatherboard, postwar fibro, and contemporary brick veneer, divided by color bond, redbrick, and hedging. The clip shows Deng being bundled into a blanket by an Anglo-Celtic-Australian-looking woman. It also shows Deng riding his BMX bike past another string of fibro homes. He is at home. He is comfortable. He is on the move. The place and the fibro congeal to represent possibility and opportunity.

"At fifteen, he taught himself to read." "A free man he chose to live in his car." He is the self-made and independent man. He is the "deserving" migrant who has reciprocated the initial offering and has given back and continues to give back. "A law degree enables him to protect others." "Deng continues to fight."

There's a shot of Deng in court, shaking hands with a client, they've just won their case. He gives back to those in the most need—with his success he helps those in his community, refugees in Western Sydney. Importantly, however, Deng did not achieve what he did by himself. He was cared for by Western Sydney—again, the place, the people, and the university. This advertisement, then, mediates between collectivism (the Western Sydney that cares for Deng, and the Western Sydney that is cared for by Deng) and individualism (the man who taught himself to read). Interestingly, and again importantly, Deng continues to live and work in Blacktown, the epicenter of Western Sydney. This advertisement emplaces hope in Western Sydney—a region not conventionally seen to be the site of a good life. A good life is seen to be elsewhere. Deng's story, then, is a different type of hero's story, a different type of story about place. It's one of escape, but it's not about escaping Western Sydney. It involves "staying put" in Western Sydney. There's possibility in Western Sydney.

In this chapter, I examine how university becomes a means to a good life, and how Cranebrook and the wider Penrith region may be sites of that good life. As discussed in the Introduction, education has become a dominant way hope for a good life is produced and distributed. The Australian government, for example, positions higher education as a means to national economic success and as a means to individual success (DEEWR 2009). Young people, particularly those from working-class backgrounds, are encouraged to *raise* their aspirations and participate in higher education (DEEWR 2009). Education is seen to be liberatory, meritocratic, and emancipatory for all, which, as we know from Bourdieu and Passeron (1979 [1964] and 1990 [1970]), represents the dominance of economic theory and masks the reproduction of class inequalities. It also marks a move away from a "politics of expectation" associated with Keynesian governance toward the neoliberal agenda of "aspirational citizenship" (Raco 2009, 438). No longer can people expect the government to provide them with a sense of security, but they are instead encouraged to be self-sufficient and entrepreneurial through their investment in education (Raco 2009). Unemployment has become a "phenomenon to be governed" (Rose 1999, 162). The ideal subject is middle class and the ideal life is middle class. This represents what Raco (2009, 437) calls an "existential politics."

Empirical research, as also previously discussed, has found that working-class students internalize these government policy assumptions about the importance of higher education (Allen 2014; Byrom and Lightfoot 2013; Christie 2009; Lehmann 2009a, 2009b, 2015; Zipin et al. 2015). This research also demonstrates how parents and teachers play a key role in *pushing* working-class students toward university. Parental hopes and desires, in particular, create strong incentives for "change and transformation, rather than social reproduction" (Lehmann 2015, 25). This is what Lehmann (2009b, 643) calls the "social mobility project"—that is, "the ultimate goal of [. . .] working-class students [. . .] is to actually enter the ranks of the middle class." The "social mobility project," he argues, is about a "wish to escape" working-class life (Lehmann 2009b, 643). But, as Lehmann (2013) points out, a focus on class escape can unwittingly pathologize working-class lives. Indeed, the trope of class escape doesn't leave much space for the possibilities of attachment to working-class lives and places. Allen and Hollingsworth (2013) have examined attachments to working-class places, but in their scholarship the *pull* of people and place forecloses aspirations—working-class places outside urban centers are places devoid of possibility.

I instead examine how "working-class places" may be more than sites of stagnation and may indeed be sites of a good life. Out of the twenty-six research participants, only two talked about leaving Cranebrook and the wider Penrith region. I begin by discussing Cranebrook. I explain where Cranebrook is located, who lives there, as well as the research participants' perceptions of Cranebrook and its various pockets. I then examine how the research participants' positioning in the world, their imaginings of a good life, and their imagining of university as a means to a good life are shaped by an awareness of class realities, and processes of class distinction that operate in Cranebrook and the wider Penrith region. I also discuss how the research participants' imaginings of university as a means to a good life are shaped by the push and pull of social obligations and commitments. I specifically examine the role parents play in pushing working-class students toward university. I also discuss the support teachers offered, mainly "Miss Harris" (a teacher from Cranebrook High School and a resident of Cranebrook), who emplaced hope in Cranebrook, and, in doing so, did not just push her students toward university, or toward other possible futures, but also *pulled* her students back to Cranebrook. Lastly, I examine how imaginings of a good life also involve doubts and ambivalence. The research participants talked about other post-school pathways, pathways that did not involve university as a means to an end but involved other forms of employment, such as working at McDonald's and becoming an electrician. University, I argue, is not a normative means to "the" good life, but one of many means to "a" good life.

Emplacing Visions of a Good Life

Cranebrook, NSW, Australia, 2749, Population 15,759

Cranebrook is nestled in the far western fringes of metropolitan Sydney, 50 or so kilometers away from the GPO, on the edge of the Cumberland Plain, in the north of Penrith, within the Penrith Local Government Area (LGA). It's at the crossroads of the Mulgowie (Mulgoa people of the Dharug Nation), the Wianamattagal (South Creek people of the Dharug Nation), and the Boorooborongal (Richmond people of the Dharug Nation). A paleo-archeological study of the "Cranebrook Terrace," "probably the most intensively studied stratigraphy and thoroughly dated alluvium of any terrace in Australia" (Nanson et al. 1987, 76), found that Aboriginal Australians have lived in Cranebrook and its surrounds (and by extension the Sydney basin) for at least 45,000 years. Many of the Dharug succumbed to colonial violence, starvation, and disease—an all-too-familiar, unsettling, settlement story. The Dharug called the area Muru-Murak, or "mountain pathway." Its colonial name comes from James McCarthy's farm, "Cranebrook House," presumably to describe the water birds of the region—the Mulgoa's namesake. McCarthy's farm was established in 1794 on the Mulgoa's yam farms, just six years after the First Fleeters landed in Sydney Cove. McCarthy, an Irish Catholic, has gone down in local legend for providing secret Catholic masses, refuge to outlawed Irish-Catholic priests, and establishing the first Catholic cemetery in New South Wales. My secondary school, McCarthy Catholic College, was named in his honor.

Cranebrook is bounded, on its western side, by the "Lapstone Monocline," a geological term used to describe a eucalypt-covered escarpment that looks blue from a distance, what we call the Blue Mountains. The Nepean River (or Yandhai) and the partly human-made "Penrith Lakes Scheme"—a series of rehabilitated quarries which once supplied the gravel and sand to almost all of Sydney's construction industry—sit at the foot of the Mountains. The Lakes is home to Penrith's Whitewater Stadium and Regatta Centre, where athletes competed for gold, silver, and bronze at the 2000 Sydney Olympic Games. The River and the Lakes watery estuaries weave their way through Cranebrook. It's part floodplain country, part rolling hills, escarpment meets escarpment. Cranebrook was, until recently, bounded on its eastern side by the old Australian Defence Force (ADI) site—the location of a Second World War munitions factory situated on a vast stretch of rare and endangered woodlands, home to the last wild emus and kangaroos of the Cumberland Plain, numerous endangered species, and significant Dharug archeological sites. Large parts of the ADI have recently, and controversially, been developed for housing but a significant part of the bushland remains, just. It is now known as Wianamatta Regional Park.

Cranebrook is not just bordered by bushland or what remains of the ADI. Wianamatta Nature Reserve sits smack-bang in the middle of Cranebrook. In 2016, a bushfire tore through the dense scrubland and some properties and vehicles parked on its rugged peripheries were lost. You get a sense of wilderness in Cranebrook and its surrounding suburbs. You're in Sydney, but you're outside of Sydney. You get a sense of space, big space, and big skies. Gumtrees abound, and when it is summer, their grayish-brownish bark sparkles with cicada shells, "that like [. . .] my fondest memory from when we moved here" (Laura, graduate). Sporting fields and green spaces snake their way through the suburban subdivisions: Grey Gums Oval, Mountain View Reserve, Andromeda Drive Reserve, Cranebrook Park, Cranebrook Dog Park, and so on. Amber talked about the park nearest her home: it collected, connected, and ensured the continuity of school-based friendships. She said:

> And we used to go to the park every afternoon, like the majority of our year would go there from school and just play and hang out. Um, and that kept going up until high school as well. [. . .] We went to Xavier or Cranebrook, but we'd all get back together at the park and play soccer or footy in the afternoon.

Cranebrook's green spaces are shrinking to make way for housing. As mentioned, the ADI site is now home to two large (and manicured) housing developments: Jordan Springs (on the Cranebrook side) and Ropes Crossing (on the Mt Druitt/St. Marys side). These developments consist of small to very large houses built on very small blocks of land. Another, and more exclusive, housing estate, "Waterside," sits within Cranebrook's southern boundary. The developers of Waterside rehabilitated a series of waterways and landscaped its parks, boulevards, and pathways with trees, grasses, and shrubs local to the Cumberland Plain. Like the developments in the ADI site, the blocks of land are much smaller. These newer housing developments enclose a hodgepodge of older ones: a pocket of former military housing clad in 1970s brick veneer, a pocket of rundown Radburn-style social housing in much need of renewal, and various pockets of privately built suburban homes, some large, some small, mostly on bigger blocks of land and constructed out of brick. Older colonial buildings are scattered mostly around Cranebrook's western boundaries and hark back to Cranebrook's not-so-distant pastoral past. Rural properties and market gardens can be found in the north. Nick (graduate and student), who lives in the north of Cranebrook, said:

> It's more spacious, so it's not really dense housing, which I quite like. I like having a quarter of an acre backyard [laughs]. We've got chooks, we've got a piece of the Cumberland Plain in the backyard [laughs]. Like it's, like it's . . . yeah. So, I quite like that. I like having space and I mean, we've . . . and to be able to do things. I mean, you walk around and there's very few streetlights where we are because of . . . so you can go out at night and actually see the stars, and it gives. . . . As much as I didn't spend a lot of time growing up on rural property and mum and dad did, it gives us a piece of that to still hold onto and to still look after it and to enjoy.

As Nick's comments show, Cranebrook is desirable and spacious. It embodies the quarter-acre block fantasy of suburbia (Stretton 1975)—a pro amid all the cons that cloud perceptions of Western Sydney. But it's not just the spaciousness of the quarter-acre block, but its proximity to bush—to even bigger open spaces—that adds to its desirability, which, as I explained in the Introduction, is cited as one of the reasons residents enjoy living in the region (Mee 2002). This spaciousness is agentic and, as Nick says, affords room *to be able to do things*, or, rather, it provides room to grow.

A Statistical Portrait of Cranebrook

Cranebrook, unlike other areas in Western Sydney—a region known as the multicultural heartland of the nation—is, on the contrary, "whiter" than the Greater Sydney average. Powell (1993, 140), as discussed in the Introduction, commented that Penrith: "harks back to an earlier era of

'Australian identity." It is, she argued, the site of nostalgia, Britishness, lost familiarity, and community spirit, centered around its rugby league club, the Penrith Panthers. It occupies a different type of difference to the more multicultural suburbs of Western Sydney that have undergone multiple cycles of cultural reorganization in the postwar period (Gwyther 2008a). Powell's comments on the "Britishness" (or more appropriately, the "Anglo-Celticness") of Penrith have ongoing relevance: most residents in Cranebrook speak English only (86.1 percent compared to the Greater Sydney average of 58.4 percent), and 42.6per cent identify as having Australian ancestry,[2] 38.5 percent as English, 11.2 percent as Irish, and 8 percent as Scottish (profile.i d. 2018, https://profile.id.com.au).[3] Around 4.5 percent of residents identify as Maltese and 5.2 percent of the population identify as Aboriginal or Torres Strait Islander (compared to a Greater Sydney median of 1.5 percent). Those who identify as Aboriginal or Torres Strait Islander are concentrated in the Housing Commission estate where they represent around 20 percent of the population. Cranebrook, then, is both whiter *and* blacker than the Greater Sydney average.[4]

Migration flows into the Penrith region come from other Local Government Areas (LGAs) in Western Sydney, such as Parramatta, Cumberland, Fairfield, and Blacktown. Like other parts of Western Sydney, out-migration is concentrated to the Blue Mountains (a tree-change), or South-East Queensland and the Central Coast (a sea-change).[5] The latter has been dubbed "Mt Druitt by the Sea" or "Parramatta by the Sea" because of its high concentration of "westies" who have made "the Coast" their home.[6] People in the Penrith region do, however, tend to stay put, and 57 percent of the population did not change their address over a five-year period, which is slightly higher than the Australia-wide median of 52 percent. While 15 percent of those who moved, moved within Penrith itself. Out of the twenty-six research participants I interviewed, twenty continue to live in Penrith, and only six now live beyond the LGA's borders. Three live close by in neighboring LGAs: the Blue Mountains, the Hawkesbury, and Liverpool. Three live further afield in the Hunter Valley of NSW, Brisbane, and London. The participant living in the Hawkesbury talked about spending most of his time at his partner's house in Cranebrook, the participants living in London and Liverpool spoke about a return to Penrith, and the participant who moved to Logan in Brisbane said, "Logan is the Penrith of Brisbane [laughs]"—by which she means Logan is also a predominantly working-class suburb on the fringes on a major city.

Cranebrook's socioeconomic profile, based on census data, is both ordinary and atypical. Its Socio-Economic Index for Area (SEIFA) percentile is ordinary. The percentile indicates the approximate ranking of suburbs and localities in relation to one another and gives an indication of where the area sits in relation to the whole nation. The higher the score, the greater is the advantage, and the lower the score, the greater is the disadvantage. Cranebrook's score is 53, compared to Greater Sydney's percentile of 77. This means that 53 percent of Australian suburbs are more disadvantaged than Cranebrook. More residents live in social housing—7.5 percent—compared to the Greater Sydney average of 4.6 percent. Around 48 percent of households in Cranebrook have a mortgage, and the median weekly mortgage repayment is $463 compared to the Greater Sydney average of $495 and the Penrith average of $466. This is significantly more than the median weekly rental payment of $383 (Greater Sydney's average is $447, and Penrith's average is $374). The socioeconomic differences between the housing pockets is stark, particularly between "Waterside" in the west and the Housing Commission estate in the east. Waterside has a median weekly combined household income is $2,349—so, hypothetically, in a two-person household, that's each person earning around $32 an hour for a thirty-six-hour workweek. In the social housing pocket, on the other hand, 34.6 percent of households have a combined income of less than $650 per week. Nick said:

> You drive from one side of Cranebrook to the other and I think you see a bit of everything. It's yeah, right through from someone who owns a Lamborghini through to someone who can't even afford to register their Commodore[7] that's sitting on the front lawn.

The three most common occupational groups in Cranebrook are: clerical and administrative (17.8 percent compared to the Greater Sydney average of 14.6 percent), technicians and trade workers (15.7 percent compared to the Greater Sydney average of 11.7 percent), and professional (15.4 percent compared to the Greater Sydney average of 26.3 percent). Residents of Cranebrook are more likely to have no qualifications (45.3 percent compared to the Greater Sydney average of 37.7 percent) or vocational qualifications (25.4 percent compared to the Greater Sydney average of 15.1 percent) rather than university degrees (12.9 percent compared to the Greater Sydney average of 28.3 percent).

Cranebrook, Class, and Distinction

This statistical portrait of Cranebrook gives the impression that there is little social or geographical mobility in Cranebrook—economic accumulations of capital are average, or below average, and most residents do not have access to valuable forms of cultural capital, such as university qualifications, either. As discussed in Chapter 1, class is not, however, just about mapping the unequal distribution of economic and cultural resources, what Bourdieu (1990 [1980], 140) calls "social physics." Bourdieu (1987, 2) has famously stated, "agents are both classified and classifiers, but they classify according to (or depending upon) their positions within classifications." Class exists twice: in the objective and the subjective (Bourdieu 1987). That is, class also involves symbolic dimensions. It is produced and reproduced through processes of distinction that are affective, relational, positional, and, as discussed in Chapter 1, embedded within microcosms. Processes of class distinction, Bourdieu (1990 [1980], 137) argues, are often experienced as more profound within microcosms:

> Contrary to the physicalist self-evidence which assumes that, in the case of continuous distribution, difference diminishes as proximity in the distribution grows, perceived differences are not objective differences, and social neighbourhood, [. . .] has every chance of also being the point of greatest tension.

The research participants' location in Cranebrook, and their relations to the different pockets of Cranebrook, the wider Penrith, Western Sydney, and Greater Sydney, within a "plurality of visions and divisions" (Bourdieu 1987, 11), affected their self-perceptions of class and place, self-perceptions that were shifty and slippery.

The research participants often positioned themselves in relation to the Housing Commission estate. Jacklyn, for example, grew up in the Housing Commission estate. She described herself as "scum" and "lower class," specifically in relation to the privately owned pockets of Cranebrook, pockets she described as "working class, middle class, they're kinda the same thing." Jacklyn defined working class and middle class as having a job. She said, "I think it's cause that's how we were grown up. Like that was part of the thing. You're like, 'Oh ya [pause], you're scum, you're not working class.'" Scum is associated with dirt and marks particular bodies and objects as disgusting, as "matter out of place" (Douglas 2001 [1966], 36). Disgust is fundamental to power relations—it mediates social class and marks difference (Lawler 2005; Miller 1997; Rossiter 2013; Tyler 2008). It works to classify spaces and bodies that are seen to be lower, bodies and spaces that are seen to be beneath.

Those participants who lived in pockets outside the social housing estate mostly saw themselves as "ordinary," "middle class," "normal," or "average." Their self-perceptions involved a sideways glance to the Housing Commission estate, their friends, and their family. Rachael said:

> I always felt like I was sort of middle rung. Like we weren't, we didn't have to live in the Housing Commission, but you know, I couldn't go to a lot of social things because my parents didn't have enough money. I felt a bit like all my friends were coming with phones to school and new things and I was like, "Well, I can't afford that." You're not cool if you don't have Adidas runners and Adidas pants. And like even your uniform, you could just have a plain yellow shirt. The cool kids had their Nike yellow shirt. I used to come in my Lowes, Big W,[8] yellow shirt. People would be like, "That's Lowes."

Some participants explained that the Housing Commission estate becomes a metonym for Cranebrook, despite its diversity, and, through this association, Cranebrook is seen to be the not-so-desirable patch of Penrith, what Alice calls "the lower class." Adrijana said, "I think, yeah, there was definitely a lot of culture of, 'It's Housing Commission, it's a tough area, you know.'" Most participants also talked about the area being known as "Crimebrook"—a pseudonym designated by others in the Penrith region, but also self-deprecating and self-characterized, and one not straightforwardly about, or productive of, class disgust and shame, nor pride and pleasure. Indeed, Rossiter (2013) argues for attunement to the very ordinariness and ambiguity of flows of class distinction, particularly in Australia. In her work on the cultural figure of the "bogan," she writes that the affective value that accumulates around the "bogan"[9] is slippery, mobile, and fluid, and "pulls in more than one direction" (Rossiter 2013, 90). It "works to sting and stick, but [also] to dissolve as a joke or be met with scorn or pride" (Rossiter 2013, 87).

Alice, for example, talked about how her boyfriend often compared Cranebrook to Glenmore Park. Alice said that he "makes jokes about [Cranebrook] all the time," jokes that involve not-so-neighborly hierarchization, jokes met with playful resistance, defensiveness, and deflection. Glenmore Park is located on Penrith's southern fringes and is the largest housing development in Penrith. It is also one of the more affluent suburbs in the area. Like other "Master Planned Communities" (MPCs) in Western Sydney, its residents have been ridiculed, by outsiders, as "aspirationals" and "cashed-up bogans" (Gwyther 2008a). Within Penrith, however, Glenmore Park is perceived to be a very desirable place to live. Alice explained:

> And [my boyfriend's] like, "Yeah but Glenmore Park's better. Everybody knows that Glenmore Park is better." And I'm like, "Really? Because there was something that I was reading that says there are more drug busts in Glenmore Park than there are in Cranebrook." And I said that to him and he's like, "No that's not true." But then he's like, "That's because all the smart drug dealers live in Glenmore Park and they sell their drugs to the people in Cranebrook." And I'm like, "Well they can't be that smart if they're getting busted, can they?" [Laughs].

Glenmore Park, here, becomes implicated as a site of crime; it is not just "Crimebrook" the police visit, "the lower class of Penrith" (Alice), the joke's on Glenmore Park, "the upper class of Penrith" (Alice).

Other participants also resisted Cranebrook as "Crimebrook," and this resistance also involved comparing crime in Cranebrook to crime in other nearby areas, like Glenmore Park. Jenny, who grew up in Cranebrook, moved to Glenmore Park, and then back to Cranebrook, said:

> [Cranebrook] is what it is. [. . .] Like Glenmore Park, maybe drive through there, and it's got graffiti everywhere, and you know the backyards are so small that the kids are forced out onto the street. Whereas in Cranebrook you still get a backyard. The kids have got room to play. You've got room to put a pool in.

Jenny, here, simultaneously positions Cranebrook as a site of the Australian Dream, and the Australian Dream—of a big backyard—is understood to reduce crime. Shannon also talked about "brushing past the stigma" of "Crimebrook." She said, "It's a great area. I love Cranebrook." Her dad grew up in what she described as a tough pocket of Western Sydney, and his childhood stories made Shannon all the more appreciative of life in Cranebrook. She described the sense of community in Cranebrook, "we used to have like street parties [. . .] and we've always grown up together [. . .]. Yeah, a huge sense of community. Everyone knows everyone." Shannon talked about her desire to stay put: "I think you stick here for a while. Like I've been here my whole life. And I don't see myself leaving at any time."

Cranebrook as Crimebrook, as a site of crime, not a good life, was not just deflected, but subversively embraced. Rossiter (2013, 90) calls this "the pleasures in contempt"—a contempt that may involve an "upwards" gaze. Adrijana talked about Cranebrook High School being known as "Crimebrook High." She laughed that her peers enjoyed being the "tough" school—it was particularly handy and made for amusing sledging when competing against other local schools. Adrijana said, "I remember those kids [Cranebrook High School football team] used to make up lies to say [both laughing] to the kids from St Dom's [another local Catholic school] that like there, there was a stabbing and then like you know ... hardcore drugs or something." Adrijana, like two other participants, also talked about her peers embracing being "boganny" at the Rock Eisteddfod Challenge (a dance and drama competition between secondary schools in NSW):

> Adrijana: We did Rock Eisteddfod. And that was a really–
> Alex: Yeah, your school was always in the paper for Rock Eisteddfod–
> Adrijana: Yeah that was a really big thing and made it look really good. And um I remember whenever we'd go there, you know Cranbrook?–
> Alex: The all-boys school? Oh, that really posh school in the city?–
> [...]
> Adrijana: It's super posh, like I think it's totally independent, private. And I remember they would always mispronounce our school's name and say [speaks with a posh accent], "Cranbrook High School." And we would get like you know a little bit boganny. [Speaks with a broad Australian accent] "Not Cranbrook—it's pronounced Cranebrook!"–
> [Both laugh]
> Adrijana: You know because we were in the like audience up the top when like everything is done and they're announcing the awards and like the whole of the school is like, "Yeah!"–
> [Both laugh]
> Adrijana: Just yelling, yeah–
> Alex: That's funny–
> Adrijana: But I think that was like a little thing, like cause somebody eventually somehow realised that that was a private all-boys school and so, they, you know, would get really uppity, like, "We're not a private all-boys school!!" We got offended!

Cranbrook is an elite independent school in Point Piper,[10] a place regarded as the most expensive suburb in Australia. The pleasure and pride in being from

Cranebrook, *not* Cranbrook, and the pleasure and pride in being and speaking a "little bit boganny" are made all the more enjoyable from the nosebleed section, and in the context of the awards ceremony where Cranebrook High School snatched the winnings from Cranbrook School, a school used to topping the league boards.

Being from Cranebrook, for some, was not always embraced but elided. Being seen to be "boganny" can produce a mixture of amusement and discomfort. Skeggs (1997, 94–5), in her ethnography of working-class women in Britain, has written about how her participants, "made strenuous efforts to deny, disidentify and dissimulate" from positions marked as working class. Nick talked about how Penrith's other soccer clubs perceived his club, Cranebrook United Soccer Club, and, in doing so, distanced himself from residents of the social housing estate:

> It's funny actually, you can play soccer in the Nepean district, which is the district Cranebrook plays in. And probably about a third of our team are from the social housing background, *but* they're all nice guys. I mean, one or two of them you would call massive bogans, but they're still nice guys and . . . neither of them a . . . none of them are particularly violent or anything like that, which is good. But you verse some of the other teams, like I can think of an example last year when we were versing a club, Penrith Football Club, Penrith FC, and they insisted that we were all bogans and social housing bums [laughs].

Nick's comment *but they're all nice guys* works to counter the perception that the *guys* from Housing Commission are rough, violent even, and also subtlety works to differentiate Nick from those *guys*.

Pat talked about the classed discomfort that fueled a series of name changes in Cranebrook. He said, "It was Cranebrook. Then the private area people complained that [. . .] the percentage of public housing tenants was too great and dragging down the price, so they split the suburb in two: to be Cranebrook and Mount Pleasant." Most private housing was located in Cranebrook, and all public housing in Mount Pleasant. According to Pat, Mount Pleasant's homeowners campaigned to have the boundaries shifted so that they became part of Cranebrook, not Mount Pleasant.[11] Mount Pleasant attracted much notoriety in the local community and became known as "Mount Peasant." After some time, Penrith Council decided to drop the name Mount Pleasant, and the various pockets once again became "Cranebrook." Pat joked, "Crimebrook, Mount Peasant, back to Crimebrook."

Some participants explained that they would avoid saying they were from Cranebrook in certain contexts. Sheree sometimes tells people she's from Penrith. At one point, she said, "not because I'm ashamed of where I live, but people have never really heard of Cranebrook." Later in the interview, she also said, "I usually just say I'm from Penrith. Not Cranebrook specifically [laughs]. Yeah because there's sorta like a bit of a stigma attached to it. Where they're like, 'Oh derro Cranebrook'. Like, it's a bit of a Mount Druitt thing." Mount Druitt, where Sheree's mother grew up, and where her Nan still lives ("she likes it there"), is perhaps one of the most stigmatized suburbs in Western Sydney—something her mother makes self-deprecating jokes about "all the time [laughs]." Saying you are from Penrith, however, has no guarantees. As Pat said, when outsiders think about Penrith, they think about Penrith at its worst, which, Pat said, is the Housing Commission estate in Cranebrook, where he is from. Sheree said, "But I mean Penrith's sort of considered a bit daggy, or derro, or whatever, as is most of Western Sydney." Emma said she learned to avoid saying she was from Penrith and would tell people she was from Cronulla,[12] "I remember when I used to go out clubbing, and when I was single, people would say, they'd be like, 'Where are you from?,' and you'd be like, 'Penrith,' and they'd be like, 'Eww!'"

Class, then, is produced and reproduced in and by relations, in "webs of material *and* symbolic ties" (Wacquant 2013, 275, emphasis my own), misrecognitions and recognitions, that operate in microcosms, as well as the wider social space, which, as I will later argue, make possible micro-mobilities within place, or degrees of mobility. Class is diversely emplaced, or rather place is diversely classed. The classed differences that operate within Cranebrook, within the wider Penrith region, and Western Sydney more broadly, point to the elasticity of microcosms and their various scales of existence. As discussed in the Introduction and Chapter 1, Cranebrook is at once a suburb, part of the Penrith LGA, and Greater Western Sydney—all of which have distinct geopolitical boundaries. Yet, "Cranebrook" also exists in several other dimensions that are not so clearly bounded and are contradictory. It is a place that is lived, experienced, and imagined, and is at once shaped by discourses that are local and proud, local and ambivalent, local and critical, outsider and critical, and is tied up with discursive constructions of Penrith, Western Sydney, and social housing more broadly. Cranebrook also exists as a patchwork of pockets that, at times, seamlessly fold into one another and, at other times, exist, or are imagined to be, distinct and bounded environs—particularly the social housing estate.

University and a Good Life to Come

The research participants' positioning in the world, their imaginings of a good life, and their imaginings of university as a means to that good life are shaped not only by the classificatory practices described earlier but also by the push and pull of social commitments. Visions of a good life are, indeed, entangled with our obligations to others. The accumulation of being is a relational accomplishment. As Bourdieu (2000, 240) argues, "the feeling of counting for others, being *important* for them, and therefore in oneself, and finding in the permanent plebiscite of testimonies of interest—requests, expectations, invitations—[offers] a kind of continuous justification for existing." This sense of "of connection, of sharing, of recognition" (Hage in Zournazi and Hage 2002, 162) is one of Hage's homely feelings (community) that structure aspirations for a good life. As discussed in Chapter 1, the accumulation of homeliness is Hage's (in Zournazi and Hage 2002, 160) attempt to make "tangible" and "concrete" the accumulation of being. The accumulation of homeliness is not just shaped by a sense of community but also shaped (variously) by aspirations for security, familiarity, and possibility (or hope) (Hage 1997). I will now examine how university becomes a means to a good life for the research participants and how these visions of a good life are emplaced and shaped by an enmeshment of homely feelings, particularly community—our affective relations to others, our social obligations and commitments.

Family, Place, and the Desire for Economic Security

As mentioned, research has shown how the decision to go to university, for working-class students, is one shaped by parental circumstances and parental aspirations for a better life—a life of economic security and comfort, and one devoid of class injury and struggle (Lehmann 2015). A report from the Longitudinal Surveys of Australian Youth (Gemici et al. 2014) found that students whose parents expected them to attend university were eleven times more likely to do so. Adrijana's (university graduate) parents, for example, played a key role in her decision to go to university. Adrijana was born in Serbia and along with her family emigrated to Australia in the late 1980s. Adrijana's father is a fitter (like my father) and found work in a local factory as a machinist. Her mother was a beautician in Serbia (my mother was once a beautician) but her qualification wasn't recognized in Australia. She also found work in a local factory. Adrijana described the factory work as physically taxing, insecure, and poorly paid. Adrijana's father is employed on a casual basis and relies on overtime to make ends meet. Her mother recently retired after developing carpal tunnel from years on the factory floor.

Adrijana's parents wanted her to have a well-paid and secure job and one that was kind to her body, unlike theirs. The pursuit of a good life, here, is one structured by embodied class realities, aspirations for economic security, and the possibility of upward social mobility. Adrijana said:

> Yeah, my parents always [. . .] because my dad was you know a fitter, you know so he was always doing hard, you know physically hard work. My mum was working in factories [. . .] and um so over the years she developed carpal tunnel and you know just aging and stuff, so they were always saying, "Go to university, get a good job, don't get an um, I guess a blue collared job. Don't get, you know, an odd job where you have to work really hard for a little bit of money."

Adrijana's decision to go to university was also structured by the "sacrifice" of migration. Ahmed (2010, 33) argues, "Happiness can involve a gesture of deferral, as a deferral that is imagined simultaneously as a sacrifice and gift: for some, the happiness that they give up becomes what they give." Adrijana said, "And I think like, I guess the sacrifice of them leaving their family was always a big, big influence for me. They left, you know, their parents. They weren't able to be there for their parents' funerals. Like, oh I'd better do something really good. University seems to be [laughs] a good option." Australia—a "mythical," "exotic," and "capitalist" country—was a place where social mobility was possible, and Adrijana felt compelled to make the most of this opportunity. University was not just a means to a better future for Adrijana, but also a means to a "nice life" for Adrijana's parents. Adrijana said, "Like I remember we'd go shopping and there was like, yeah I don't know, like a blazer or something, and mum's like, 'You're going to wear one of those.

That's the kind of job you need so you can live a nice life and you can look after me when I'm old."

These sacrifices—of labor, family, and migration—together produced feelings of indebtedness, an indebtedness entangled with affective relations of faithfulness and gratitude. Simmel (1950, 379) writes that faithfulness is a "second"-order affective tie, one that comes after interest, after the originary coming together of a relationship, and is concerned with, "the preservation of the *relationship* to the other. It does not engender this relationship; therefore, unlike these other affects, it cannot be pre-sociological: it pervades the relation once it exists and, as its inner self-preservation, makes the individuals-in-relation hold fast to one another." Faithfulness is related to our morality; it is what Simmel (1950, 380) calls the "inertia of the soul," and it is what gives meaning and value to life. It also gives continuity to the social world: "Without this inertia of existing sociations, society as a whole would constantly collapse, or change in an unimaginable fashion" (Simmel 1950, 381). Gratitude, Simmel (1950) argues, is the feeling that "sinks into the soul" when one receives a gift (Simmel 1950, 388). Gratitude is the feeling that one cannot fully reciprocate the initial offering. It is the "moral memory of mankind" (Simmel 1950, 388) and "produces an atmosphere of generalised obligation" (Simmel 1950, 395). This atmosphere of generalized obligation can produce a pressure to follow parental desires. Adrijana said:

> Mum was more emotionally invested in me going to uni and stuff than my dad. And I, I guess I felt like . . . yeah, a bit of pressure, but also like not necessarily like a bad pressure, cause they you know they never, like it wasn't like it wasn't good for me, like for me to get a good job, for me to have, live a better life. But yeah always very aware.

This pressure, for Adrijana, involves both good feeling and bad feeling—it is a relation of both sustenance (for herself and her parents) and acquiescence.

Jacklyn's (university graduate) decision to go to university was also structured by parental circumstances, embodied class realities, aspirations for economic security, and the possibility of upward social mobility. However, Jacklyn's story is not one of migration, like Adrijana's is, but is one of extreme poverty and struggle. Jacklyn grew up living in Cranebrook's pocket of Housing Commission with her mother, stepfather, and younger siblings. She said, "The reason why we were there was because we couldn't afford anything else." Jacklyn's mother left high school early and was a "screen printer by trade" and became a "stay at home mum" after having children. Jacklyn's mother has found it difficult to transition back into the workforce. Jacklyn said, "She found it really hard to get a job again, um and through Centrelink,[13] she found a job doing mushroom picking. Just before Christmas, and they let her go [. . .]. Yeah and then they had to let her go cause they didn't have work. And now she's looking for a job again." Jacklyn's stepfather was a diesel mechanic, but after a serious workplace injury can no longer perform the heavy manual work necessary for the job. He has dabbled in several computer courses and has only recently secured a job at a fast-food restaurant. Work is difficult as "he really struggles [. . .] just to get through the pain."

As mentioned previously, Jacklyn described being seen as "scum" and "lower class": of feeling like an outsider in Cranebrook because she lived in Cranebrook's pocket of Housing Commission. But she also described feeling "out of place" within the Housing Commission estate itself. She said, "We were like the really bad people. Everyone hated us, and they'd call the police on my family all the time." This shame amplified when Jacklyn and her family were evicted from their home and became homeless. She said:

> We got evicted. Like my parents hit the drugs pretty hard a lot later. And when they split up my mum wasn't coping very well. And I didn't realise that she wasn't paying rent even though I was giving her money to pay rent. And then we got evicted from there. So, we were homeless for a little while. And that was embarrassing, and it was hard, and everybody seen our shit on the front lawn.

Probyn (2005), drawing on the work of Tomkins, pairs shame with interest. This is a shame-interest continuum. Interest, Probyn (2005, 13) explains, "constitutes lines of connection between people and ideas. It describes a kind of affective investment we have in others. When, for different reasons, that investment is questioned and interest is interrupted, we feel deprived. Crucially, that's when we feel shame." Shame, then, emerges from feeling out of place and disconnected when one desires connection. Shame can be experienced when a habitus is out of place, or is a "fish out of water," to use a Bourdieusian turn of phrase. Probyn (2005) writes that shame in the habitus can produce self-reflection and self-evaluation, which in turn can produce a radical shift in dispositions: "Through feeling shame, the body inaugurates an alternative way of being in the world. Shame, as the body's reflection on itself, may reorder the composition of the habitus, which in turn may allow for quite different choices." Probyn (2005) argues that this is something missed by Bourdieu. She explains that Bourdieu's habitus does not allow for the ways the feeling body can generate alternatives to the inevitable—alternatives to the reproduction of self and circumstance. Bourdieu, Probyn (2005, 53) argues, only thinks about the ways shame works to contain and to shut down possibilities, and how it "acts as a metonym for the wider structures of social domination."

Jacklyn desired affective recognition: to be someone other than "scum," a site of shame, of overexposure. She said, "Like living in Housing Commission, it was a big goal to get out of it and achieve something." This involved having a secure job—becoming a nurse—and living elsewhere in Cranebrook, not in the social housing pocket (I will come back to this in Chapter 5). This literal desire for homeliness feeds into her mother's imagining of a good life as one of homeownership, the "Australian Dream." Jacklyn said:

> [My mother] just wishes that she had gone and to school and studied and she wishes that she had owned her own home cause she's never owned a home. Where her brothers and sisters have owned a home and they own quite nice homes and she said if she could change a little bit she would.

Having a job and living elsewhere in Cranebrook was a desired form of invisibility. Noble (2009, 883) argues that invisibility, not visibility, and the "ordinariness it offers" is a form of recognition. "Feigned indifference," he writes, "acknowledges the others' right to be there as a legitimate participant" (Noble 2009, 883). Shame, then, shakes up Jacklyn's habitus and produces another way of being in the world. Yet, this other way of being in the world is not straightforwardly "other." It is normative in terms of being a response to neoliberal discourses of what constitutes achievement and the ideal citizen: not living in Housing Commission, homeownership, not being on unemployment benefits, being a responsible and nondependent citizen. Shame, then, can work as a form of governance, even if it propels one out of their circumstances. The accumulation of our being is, thus, relational and social, and mediated by the norms of one's family, class distinctions in Cranebrook, and societal norms more broadly. The parental push toward university, then, does not necessarily involve a radical push away from life in Cranebrook, but a pull back to Cranebrook too.

School, "Miss Harris," and Hope in Place

Teachers, as Lehmann (2015, 21) has shown, also play a central role in *pushing* working-class students toward university. Lehmann (2015, 21, emphasis my own) writes, "Although it is often argued that teachers, consciously or not, tend to contribute to the stunting of working-class students' ambition, by confusing appearance with ability [. . .], they can also assume *enabling roles*." Danielja (student and graduate) said, "there are people that are like, well, 'You know we just go to Cranebrook, like we're not going to amount to anything'. But the teachers there are just willing to help you." Danielja talked about one teacher who pushed her to go to university. This teacher encouraged her to apply for a teaching scholarship. Danielja said, "[The teacher] basically said, 'Go do this,' instead of, 'Oh this is an option for you'. She was like, 'This will change your life.'" Donelle (graduate) also talked about the support she received from teachers. Donelle attended Cranebrook High School until Year 10 and then moved to St. Marys Senior High School.[14] She fell pregnant during Year 12 and almost left school. She said, "My boyfriend at the time wanted me out of school because I was pregnant, and he wasn't dealing with the attention well." Her teachers, she said, "Were like, no, no, no. Your education!" They connected her to the school counsellor, gave her a quiet study refuge, and helped her apply for university.

Several participants talked about "Miss Harris" from Cranebrook High School. Miss Harris was proud of her students and invested in their futures. Jessica (graduate) said, "Certainly she encouraged everybody to do their best [. . .]. She gave the same support to the academic kids as she did to the, I guess, the kids that other teachers would have written off as troublemakers." Miss Harris was also proud of the area, had an ethic of care for her students, and, importantly, nurtured a sense of belonging to place. She made university tangible but, in doing so, she did not push her students in certain directions or privilege certain pathways over others. She made her students aware of different possibilities and fostered an emplaced sense of hope—that there was possibility in Cranebrook. Adrijana said:

> She was very proud of the area and she made sure that we were proud of the area [. . .]. And she lived in Cranebrook. I think she still lives in Cranebrook. She was just super proud of the area. Super proud of her students. Really wanted to . . . really, really . . . and she did, she made a difference. And she

used to talk to us about her uni experience, you know? It was like, "oh." It just normalised it in a way. Whereas if she didn't . . . I don't know if . . . I don't know if some of us would have been aware of anything.

Miss Harris, then, did not just push her students toward university, or toward other possible futures; she also *pulled* her students back to Cranebrook. Jacklyn described running into Miss Harris, "Like, she lives near me. And like, I've seen her. And walking my dog and she said, 'Hello'. And all that stuff and outside of school. And I have her on Facebook and she always asks me like, 'How are you going and how's nursing?'. And all that. And she's just a great teacher." Miss Harris, then, was a locally emplaced university-educated subject and representation of possible futures. Cranebrook was not just a site of stagnation, a dead end. Miss Harris nurtured the idea that Cranebrook was a site where one could accumulate being. It was a "suitable launching pad for their social and existential self" (Hage 2009, 98). In Chapter 5, I examine relations of reciprocity and argue that Adrijana's decision to become a teacher and work at Cranebrook High School reciprocates the gift of care she received from Miss Harris.

Not all teachers, however, were like Miss Harris. Jenny (graduate) talked about one teacher who discouraged her from going to university to study law. This teacher was what Ahmed (2010, 49) calls an "affect alien": "The affect alien is one who converts good feeling into bad, who as it were 'kills' the joy."

    Jenny: I mean, I did have one teacher and she–
    Alex: Mmm–
    Jenny: But in Year 11 I dropped her class because I was picking up 3-unit something for Year 12. And she pulled me aside and she said to me, "Jen, what are you doing? You need this. What do you want to do when you leave school?." And I said, "Well, I'm going to go do my law degree and I'm going to become a lawyer." And she turned around and she said to me, "Don't you realise, number one, you're from Cranebrook High? You're never going to go anywhere. And number two, you're, you're a girl. You're from Western Sydney. You really think you're going to be a lawyer?"–
    Alex: She said that to you?–
    Jenny: Yeah–
    Alex: A teacher?–
    Jenny: A teacher and she was a bitch. Don't get me wrong, but I actually think that was probably one of the best things–

Alex: Yep–
Jenny: Because it made me go, "Fuck you"–
Alex: Good on you, yeah.

Jenny's teacher, who taught home economics, believed that the practical skill of cooking was far more suitable for a young woman from Western Sydney. Jenny's "fuck you" was a defiant *I can do this, and Cranebrook can do this*. Going to university, for Jenny, was about accruing recognition for Cranebrook and about transforming what it means to be from Cranebrook. It emerged out of a faithfulness to people and place. I also come back to Jenny in Chapter 5 to explore relations of reciprocity, gratitude, and giving back to people and place. Jenny did, however, have supportive teachers too, "there were a lot of teachers there through the years which were really good." Indeed, immediately after her conversation with her home economics teacher, she walked straight into her year advisor's office, "And I'm like, 'What fucking shit is this? Like, seriously'. And he said, 'Don't take any notice of her. You know what she's like.'" Teachers, then, can play a crucial role in shaping (or limiting) classed and gendered aspirations. They can nurture a sense of belonging to place and emplace a sense of hope in Cranebrook, and they can also produce a defiant sense of belonging to place and a desire to accumulate recognition for Cranebrook. Hope, as I have demonstrated here, is not just relational and social, but emplaced too.

Ambivalence, Alternatives, and a Good Life

Visions of a good life also involve ruminations on the "road not taken." The research participants talked about other post-school pathways, pathways that bypassed university and the lives they might have had. Ahmed (2010, 6) argues, "ordinary attachments to the very idea of the good life are also sites of ambivalence, involving the confusion rather than separation of good and bad feelings." Desire, she writes, is entangled with anxiety. This is because "the orientation toward the good becomes a form of pressure in a world where the good cannot exhaust the realm of possibility" (Ahmed 2010, 31). Jacklyn, for example, talked about turning away from other possibilities, such as pursuing a career at McDonald's. Jacklyn worked part-time at her local McDonald's while studying, and she was "very liked there," but because she was committed to nursing, and management knew this, she thwarted her progression within the company. Her brother, on the other hand, was committed to staying at the franchise for the long term. Jacklyn said:

> They didn't push anything with me. Where [as him] they're like, "Oh yeah, this is what he wants." And they build him up quite fast. And he's done all these certificates that cost you heaps to go to uni. And he gets them all for free.

The Charlie Bell School of Management, the training college for McDonalds' employees, offers several certificates in hospitality and retail. Jacklyn does not perceive a bachelor's degree (Level 7 in the Australian Qualifications Framework) as being of greater value than these certificates (Levels 1-4). These certificates are seen to be equal to a university qualification, and in some ways better than, because they do not involve the accumulation of student debt.

McDonald's, for Jacklyn, is a misunderstood career path. I said to Jacklyn, "Yeah never . . . when people underestimate McDonald's," and Jacklyn firmly replied, "Well they do." We had a conversation about the people we know who have "made it" at McDonald's. My partner's sister has worked her way up from flipping burgers on the shop floor to managing a suite of McDonald's stores—she has accumulated greater economic wealth than anyone I know under the age of thirty-five (university graduates included). McDonald's offers economic comfort and security, like nursing. It, too, offers another type of existential and social mobility—leisurely travel. Jacklyn said:

> Jacklyn: Well their bosses take them away on a holiday for two weeks. They go to Hawaii. He shouts them at the club like drinks, for like Christmas and all that stuff. Like if they do well, like only if they do well, they get big rewards. So, my brother pushes himself, and he does come first in a lot of things, and then they get money bonuses. Or they get holidays to Hawaii or nice holidays. Oh, I wish I'd stayed there [laughs] and worked my way up–
> Alex: So, if your brother buys a Macca's eventually–
> Jacklyn: Oh yeah! That's what I said! I'll stay at nursing casually and then I'll go to Macca's cause it's something that I haven't. . . . I reckon I could get behind there and I could pick it up again quite fast because I knew everything. I was front area, back area, café. I knew it all.

Travel, for Jacklyn, is a marker of economic comfort. It's a form of enjoyment and adventure. Work travel, in particular, is a luxury. Hawaii is, of course, a popular and affordable holiday destination for many people in Penrith (along with Bali and Thailand) and is not a symbolic marker of middle classness (in the way that "adventure" travel beyond the Holiday Inn is), though it is a marker of success for Jacklyn. McDonald's hovers in Jacklyn's horizon of possibilities but is tinged with the displeasure of regret.

This ambivalence, or uneasiness, was present in other interviews. Nick (student and graduate), who works at his local bank, inside a shopping mall, and is at the bottom of a large corporate food chain (I will come back to Nick's career trajectory in Chapter 4), originally considered following his father's footsteps to become an electrician. At the beginning of our interview, he said:

> I weighed up the options of leaving school and becoming an electrician, which would have been following very similar to my father's footsteps [laughter]. I decided not to, like, I actually regret that decision a little bit, I-I think- I- I look back now and I think I'd be [pause] a little bit happier if I was an electrician.

He later repeated this comment, "I think I would have been a little bit happier being an electrician because I could spend some time out, out in the sun, and I could run my own business." Nick perceived electrical work as a pathway to economic comfort and freedom. Nick's father, who began "his trade in the signals corps" in the Australian Defence Force, has had a very successful career: he left the army after completing his trade and then worked his way up into a senior position for a large international telecommunications company. Nick said, "My father is very intelligent, very switched on [...]. I think part of it was luck in that he did see an opportunity in mobile phones, and that he looked at that opportunity and went, 'That's the way to go.'" Being outdoors, out in the sun, was also a recurring theme. Nick spoke fondly about his grandparents who were all farmers, and he talked about the pleasures of spending his school holidays on their farms, outside, helping them here and there.

Nick's parents encouraged him to go to university but they were also "firm believers in a strong work ethic, and if you're having trouble finding employment, it means you're being too picky. Yeah, at the end of the day you need to put bread on the table and keep a roof over your head." They changed their tune about prioritizing university as a means to a good life when their youngest son, Nick's brother, left school—he wasn't as academically competent, and they instead encouraged him to become a carpenter. His brother has been very successful: "I mean he's far beyond carpentry these days, he does all the foreman work." Nick's brother has purchased multiple properties in the local area and is under the age of twenty-five. Nick, the eldest of four, is building his first home, a townhouse in neighboring Kingswood—an impressive accomplishment in itself, but one overshadowed by his younger brother's achievements. Nick's brother's success, combined with his father's entrepreneurialism, fuel his ambivalence about university as a means to a good life. Parents, then, can both push their children toward university and—along with siblings—provide a representation of other possible futures, or good lives, that circumvent university.

Adrijana was also ambivalent about university as a means, or the only means, to a good life. Adrijana said:

> I think I always would have done alright no matter what I did. [. . .] I think I just tend to sort of like go with the flow a bit more, but I think that if I didn't have my parents pushing me, I don't think I would of . . . . I just don't think I would have thought to go to uni. Like I think I would have gone, "Okay well, you know, I'll get a job." And then I guess I just would've I dunno have been happy to plod along wherever.

"Plod along" and "flow" still imply a sense of movement, the accumulation of being, albeit a slower-and-less intense form of accumulation to the feverish imperative directed by her parents. Adrijana was at home with her life. The gravity of her milieu was strong, and the life she was living was already good. But Adrijana was also able to access "good" jobs that required no qualification, unlike her mother. Indeed, throughout university, Adrijana was able to find steady work at a local retail store and a large bank, and she spoke about the bank's efforts to retain her. University, then, is not a normative means to "the" good life, but one of many means to "a" good life, and attachments to the idea of "a" good life do not just involve "good feeling" but ambivalence too.

Conclusions

Visions of a good life and university as a means to that life are shaped by the push and pull of "webs of material and symbolic ties" (Wacquant 2013, 275) that operate in microcosms, like Cranebrook. Microcosms have elastic boundaries and various scales of existence. The research participants' positioning in Cranebrook, in the wider Penrith region, and in the wider Western Sydney, and their self-perceptions of place and class, affected their visions of a good life and social mobility. Their decisions to go to university were also shaped by the push and pull of family, teachers, and place—an entanglement of embodied class realities and social obligations and commitments, such as gratitude and faithfulness, shame and recognition. The accumulation of being is, indeed, intimately tied up with our relations to others. This is Hage's (in Zournazi and Hage 2002, 162) homely feeling of "community," the sense of "of connection, of sharing, of recognition." The accumulation of our being, what Hage (1997) calls the accumulation of homeliness, is, as discussed, also shaped by the pursuit of security, familiarity, and possibility. Security, specifically economic security, was a particularly important ingredient of a good life, and desires for economic security were fueled by class realities, such as injury, homelessness, and the desire for homeownership.

University, I argued, is not a normative means to "the" good life but is "a" means to "a" good life. University, I also demonstrated, is not "the" standard pathway, nor is a desire for "class escape" the norm. Indeed, the binary notion of "class escape"—of mobility from the working class into the middle class—misses the relationality of our sociality and the class distinctions that operate in microcosms (I will explore this in Chapter 5). The notion of class escape, thus, doesn't leave room for attachments to place, working-class places like Cranebrook, and ambivalent feelings toward place, a good life, and university as a means to a good life. Social commitments and obligations to family and teachers, I argued, not only work to push and pull participants toward different futures, but family and teachers themselves function as representations of possible futures—representations that can work to fuel ambivalence toward university, and can also work to emplace hope in Cranebrook and the wider Penrith region. Our social obligations and commitments can, of course, work to reproduce class inequalities. In the subsequent chapters, I develop the goodness and violence of these affective relations through my concept of "homely mobility."

3

Feeling "At Home" at University

Introduction

What does it mean to feel "at home" and "recognized" at university? In this chapter, I examine different logics of recognition at university—at the level of the setting, microcosm (Penrith), subfield (Western Sydney University), and wider field of higher education. Contemporary sociological work on being and belonging at university has demonstrated that the transition from school to university is a difficult one for all students, but that it is particularly difficult for working-class students (Baik et al. 2015; Bathmaker et al. 2016). Studies inspired by Bourdieu have explored the experiences of working-class students at university (Abrahams and Ingram 2013; Bathmaker et al. 2016; Mallman 2017). These scholars focus on how one's "class habitus" shapes experiences of belonging within the middle-class "field" of higher education, as well as the different strategies students use to feel "at home" at university, such as making use of their social networks on campus (Birani and Lehmann 2013). This work, for the most part, argues that working-class students are "fish out of water," to paraphrase Bourdieu (in Bourdieu and Wacquant 1992, 147). Reay et al. (2010) have also examined how different institutions can afford different experiences of belonging. They argue for the importance of attending to "institutional habitus" (what I call a "subfield"—habitus is embodied, not disembodied) and explain that newer universities provide a sense of social familiarity and comfort for working-class students, while more prestigious universities do not. They also found that working-class students at newer universities lack academic confidence and don't develop "learner identities." These notions of class habitus, institutional habitus, and field do not, however, adequately capture heterogeneity and the varied experiences of socialization and varied capacities to act in particular settings (Atkinson 2011; Watkins and Noble 2013).

I begin this chapter by making a case for the importance of attending to placial "degrees of integration" (Bourdieu 2000, 160) when examining experiences of belonging at university. Habitus, Bourdieu (2000, 160) explains, "is not necessarily adapted to its situation nor necessarily coherent. It has degrees of integration." I describe how feeling "at home" in the microcosm of Penrith affords degrees of fit at the Penrith Campuses. That is, feelings of homeliness in Penrith become a resource for homemaking at university. Placial degrees of integration involve both the embodiment of place, or one's "placial bearing" (Casey 2001, 410), and a recognition of the people in that place as one's own. Homeliness does not, however, involve a passive withdrawal from the world—as it does in Reay et al.'s (2010) work—and in the second section I argue that being a student at the Penrith Campuses can involve agency and self-expansion, the accumulation of being, both scholarly and social. Sometimes the research participants articulate this expansion in terms of meeting people from ethnically diverse backgrounds. This is what Hage (1997, 136) calls "cultural enrichment." Places of comfort, like the Penrith Campuses, can also have "elastic horizons" (Noble 2015, 43)—they provide a nurturing space where one can develop and later transcend. But, as I will show in the final section, there are limits to transformation and transcendence. Placial bearing has gravity. Throughout this chapter, I argue that recognition is a precarious accomplishment—a logic recognition is, indeed, temporal, relational, and situated within settings, microcosms, and the symbolic economy of fields.

Most of the research participants attended the Penrith Campus of Western Sydney University (fourteen out of twenty-six). The Penrith Campus has three sites: Werrington North, Werrington South, and Kingswood. The campuses are suburban, wedged in-between housing, a school, creeks, and bush—and, until recently, a patch of market gardens. The green spaces on each campus are vast—the lawns of Werrington North, for example, are strewn with mobs of kangaroos. It's Western Sydney University's second-largest campus by population (after Parramatta), enrolling 7,900 students (WSU Pocket Profile 2018). It's notably "whiter" than some of the University's other campuses, such as the Bankstown and Parramatta campuses which attract students from more diverse backgrounds. Penrith (the region) is, as discussed in the previous chapter, whiter than the Greater Sydney average, and indeed whiter than the

Western Sydney average. Bankstown (the region), on the other hand, has more residents who have Lebanese ancestry (15.1 percent) than the Greater Sydney average (3.3 percent), and fewer who have Australian ancestry (14.2 percent) compared to the Greater Sydney average (23.5 percent) (profile.id. 2018, https://profile.id.com.au). The buildings on Western Sydney University's campuses are mostly brick, a hodgepodge of modern architecture mixed with colonial (Parramatta and Hawkesbury)—a contrast to the Gothic and Tudor Revival style architecture of the University of Sydney's Camperdown Campus. The Camperdown Campus is located in downtown Sydney is urban rather than suburban, and—as discussed in the Introduction—has fewer students from low socioeconomic backgrounds than Western Sydney University.

The "More Homely Feel": Placial Degrees of Integration

The logic of cognition-recognition-misrecognition, as discussed in Chapter 1, is central to how we come to feel at home in the world (Bourdieu 2000). We internalize our place in the world, we recognize others who belong in our world, we misrecognize those who do not belong, and we are in turn recognized and misrecognized by others. We are "both classified and classifiers" but we "classify according to (or depending upon) [our] position within classifications" (Bourdieu 1987, 2). Every act of recognition is also an act of misrecognition (Wacquant 2013). This is Bourdieu's (1987, 5) take on Goffman's "sense of one's place":

> The dispositions acquired in the position occupied involve an adjustment to this position—what Erving Goffman calls the "sense of one's place." It is this sense of one's place which, in a situation of interaction, prompts those whom we call in French *les gens humbles*, literally "humble people"—perhaps "common folks" in English—to remain "humbly" in their place, and which prompts the others to "keep their distance," or to "keep their station in life." It should be said in passing that these strategies may be totally unconscious and take the form of timidity or arrogance. In fact, these social distances are inscribed in the body. It follows that objective distances tend to reproduce themselves in the subjective experience of distance, remoteness in space being associated with a form of aversion or lack of understanding, while nearness is lived as a more or less unconscious form of complicity.

Bourdieu is, of course, referring to a sense of one's place in the social space, but a sense of one's place is also physical, geographical, and placial. Bourdieu, in his early work, does not explicitly refer to "place" or the ways that place is embodied in his theorizations of habitus. Habitus is mostly invoked in relation to "field" (Bourdieu 1977 [1972]). The emphasis is on social embodiment, not placial embodiment. Place is, however, omnipresent in Bourdieu's (1999a [1993], 2000) later discussions of habitus. Bourdieu (2000, 131), as discussed in Chapter 1, explains, "As a body and a biological individual, I am, in the way that things are, situated in place; I occupy a position in physical space and social space. I am not *atopos*, placeless, as Plato said of Socrates." The social space and the physical space are, indeed, inseparable. We are, Bourdieu (2000, 141) writes, shaped by our "affective transactions with the environment," and these affective transactions shape how we come to feel at home in the world. This comfort between habitus and environment, or "the quasi-perfect coincidence between habitus and habitat," produces a sense of "being at home" (Bourdieu 2000, 147). This relation between habitus and environment—what I call microcosm—points to the emplacement of the habitus itself, to its "placial bearing" (Casey 2001, 410). Place is, indeed, a principle of social visions and divisions.

For some of the research participants, their sense of "being at home" in Cranebrook, and the wider Penrith—their microcosm—produced placial degrees of integration at university, specifically at Western Sydney University's Penrith Campuses, which were a short drive from their homes. Adrijana (graduate), for example, was based at the Kingswood Campus. She said, "I was still at home." The campus was "welcoming," "comfortable," and "familiar little Penrith." The campus loosely folds into Penrith, Penrith loosely folds into the campus, and together they form "home." Adrijana enjoyed the suburban feel of the campus, and she described her favorite spot: a nook in the old Allen Library that overlooked the eucalypt and grassy banks of Werrington Creek. She said, "It's so peaceful and beautiful and quiet." "Peaceful" and "quiet" suggest the absence of a "harmful threatening otherness" (Hage 1997, 102). "Comfortable" suggests a "well-fitted habitus" (Hage 1997, 102). Home, here, is an ensemble of affective states—Hage's (1997) "homely feelings" of familiarity and security. Home, then, becomes a resource for homemaking at university—that is, a sense of feeling at home in Penrith shapes how Adrijana comes to feel at home in other places in that microcosm, the Kingswood Campus, which is at once located within the microcosm of Penrith and within the broader field of higher education.

Shannon (student) also talked about architectural and geographical "fit" on campus, specifically in relation to the differences between the Kingswood Campus and the University of Sydney's Camperdown Campus. Shannon, who was a first-year university student of mixed heritage (Italian, Anglo-Celtic, and Aboriginal), participated in a weeklong program at the University of Sydney when she was in Year 12. The aim of the program was to encourage Aboriginal students to enroll in a course at the University of Sydney:

> Shannon: They had, um, like an Aboriginal event, like you spent a week there, stayed in the dorms–
> Alex: Wow!–
> Shannon: I just, I don't know, I just found it such an intimidating university. I was like, "Oh, that's like . . ."–
> Alex: Yeah, like for what reasons?–
> Shannon: Um, I think, I don't know. I just didn't really feel comfortable there. I don't know why. It just was like, "This feels really weird." It was like so close to the city and I was just like–
> Alex: Yeah–
> Shannon: Just didn't feel right. I ended up leaving early. I ended up getting sick then–
> Alex: Yeah–
> Shannon: And I was just like, "I think I want to go to UWS." And Mum was like, "Okay." I don't know, because it was so huge and it was such an old building, which I love, like I thought it was such a pretty uni, but I was just like, and it was so big as well.

The University of Sydney's "old building" and location produced feelings of disequilibrium and discomfort. The social space, Bourdieu (1999e [1993], 126) explains, "is inscribed at once in spatial structures and in the mental structures that are partly produced by the incorporation of these structures, space is one of the sites where power is asserted and exercised, and, no doubt in its subtlest form, as symbolic violence that goes unperceived as violence."

Placial degrees of integration are also dependent on recognizing the people who populate a place as "one's own." The placial is, indeed, classed, raced, and gendered, and so on. Shannon, for example, described the people at the University of Sydney as being "different":

> Shannon: Um, well, I went to the uni, like everyone, you know, they grew up around the city and were like, I don't know, just things, like act different and you know–
>
> Alex: Yeah–
>
> Shannon: I don't know, I just thought like the people were different and you know, they were like talking about all different things and it was like, "Oh, you know about this, this, this?". I was just like, "I have no idea what you're talking about but okay"–
>
> Alex: Yeah, yeah–
>
> Shannon: Yeah, we just grew up, you know, so different it was just like [laughs], "All right"–
>
> Alex: Yeah. Did they know that, um, did they know where Cranebrook was or anything?–
>
> Shannon: No, no, they had no idea. It was like, "I live in Cranebrook" and they were just like, "Where's that?". And I was like, "Oh, in Penrith." And they're like, "Where's that?". I was like–
>
> Alex: They didn't know where Penrith–
>
> Shannon: Yeah, I was like "Western Sydney." They were like, "Oh, okay." And I was like "All right" [laughs].

The event was intended to recognize, welcome, and orient Aboriginal students toward the University of Sydney but, for Shannon, it did the opposite. Categorical forms of recognition, here, give way to an entanglement of visions and divisions that are placial, classed, and perhaps racial—but not categorically so. Interestingly, Shannon did not make any reference to racial fit, but another participant, Ashley (student and graduate), commented that there were few Aboriginal students at the University of Sydney—Ashley described a strange tutorial experience where she "learnt about Aboriginals." Ashley's peers then commented that they had never met "an Aboriginal before." This was something Ashley found odd—many of her school friends at Cranebrook High School were, like Shannon, Indigenous (both Aboriginal and Torres Strait Islander[1]).

Placial degrees of integration involve both processes of inclusion and exclusion. This is the dual logic of recognition-misrecognition: it is about struggling for, and turning toward, what is homely, and effacing difference (what we are not, where we do not belong, the unhomely). Our social being and social identities are, indeed, "defined and asserted through difference" (Bourdieu 1984 [1979], 171–2). Shannon instead described feeling more "comfortable" at the Kingswood Campus:

I think UWS just feels more homely, like I feel really comfortable there. And like Sydney Uni, it looks like a great uni, but I don't know, it just seems like really prestigious and like really like top-notch to me, and I was like, "Oh, I'm not really into that." I like the more homely feel. Like, you know, I can wake up and I go, "Okay, yeah, I'm just going to head off to uni and then come back home." And there's people there who've grown up, you know, in the same area, the same ways as us.

The "more homely feel," thus, also involves geographical proximity, a seamlessness between home and university, and a classed and placial sense of integration with other students who are from *the same area,* who embody the same places—who have the same "placial bearing" (Casey 2001, 410). This expression and persistence of place in the body, or in the habitus, is what Casey (2001, 415) calls "idiolocality." Idiolocality, Casey (2001, 415) explains, "invokes the subject who incorporates and expresses a particular place, its *idios,* what is peculiar in both senses of this Greek word."

Danielja (student and graduate) also described the Kingswood Campus as being a place of homeliness in comparison to the University of Sydney:

> Danielja: Yeah, it's great. It's really casual. It's, you don't feel stressed being at campus either. Like I remember when I went to University of Sydney for one of their Open Days, you just felt so overwhelmed there and you felt like you couldn't stand in the wrong spot because something would happen sort of thing. Whereas at uni [Kingswood Campus], you know, you feel really comfortable even though there's so many people there and whatever. So, no, it's good–
> Alex: And so, that's interesting about the Sydney Uni Open Day–
> Danielja: Yeah–
> Alex: Yeah, so that turned you off going to Sydney Uni?–
> Danielja: Yeah, yeah. Um, yeah. So, it was just, um, you know, they took us like through to their museum and all that sort of stuff and they were all fantastic things, but you know, I just felt, for me, I wouldn't fit in there. Like, you go to UWS and people wear thongs and stuff like that. Could not do that at like USYD at all, like.

Danielja could sink into place at Kingswood, a sensory satisfaction embodied in the image of thongs (flip-flops). It was a place she felt she had spatial and practical control, unlike at the University of Sydney, where, as she says, *you couldn't stand in the wrong spot because something would happen*—which, again, implies a "harmful threatening otherness" (Hage 1997, 102). This, too, is a twofold process of symbolic violence and exclusion, and a turn toward the homely. Turning toward the familiar, Clayton et al. (2009, 162) argue, is one of the main strategies working-class students employ as they attempt to minimize the "threatening outside" of the higher education system.

Placial degrees of integration may involve more than "horizontal" logics of recognition between individuals in place but may also involve "vertical" logics of recognition between individuals and place. Elise (graduate), who attended the Werrington Campus, "loved" university. She talked about being "local, homegrown," and commented that the university nurtures the talent of Western Sydney. She said, "Isn't that why Gough Whitlam and stuff started it? Because it gave Western Sydney an opportunity? And there's so much talent out here." Gough Whitlam, as discussed in the Introduction, was the prime minister of Australia from 1972 to 1975, and he led the push for a university in Western Sydney. Placial recognition, here, is not just about bodily fit in places where people embody similar places but also about broader forms of placial recognition: of Western Sydney as *talented* and worthy of a university. This form of recognition from the state, from the prime minister himself, is perhaps one of the most powerful forms of recognition. The state, Bourdieu (1987) explains, has monopoly over the production and distribution of symbolic capital, the power to grant official and legitimate recognition. The state has "*worldmaking* power" (Bourdieu 1987, 13). Yet, representations of the social world always involve struggle, "a degree of indeterminacy and fuzziness" (Bourdieu 1987, 13), and as I will show later in this chapter, antagonistic visions of Western Sydney University—which are classed, racial, and placial—always threaten the recognition offered by Whitlam.

"Homegrown": The Accumulation of Academic Capacities

Feeling at home at university not only involves placial degrees of integration but also involves the accumulation of practical efficiencies, such as the accumulation of academic capacities and dispositions. As Elise's comment "homegrown" indicates, the expansion of one's "scholarly habitus" (Watkins and Noble 2013) may also be central to feeling "at home" at university. For Elise, accumulating academic capacities provided feelings of recognition: "I feel really good about myself." She felt socially and existentially mobile (Hage

2009). Elise also described the academic staff as supportive: they helped develop her skills as a marketing professional, and they continue to support her—even after graduation. She said, "I'm like friends with them on Facebook. We chat, like each other's photos, comment. Like they know so much about like my life and progression, and yeah they're amazing." The academic staff produced ongoing forms of recognition through the accumulation of Facebook "likes" and "comments," but they also functioned as proof that her university experience was valuable: "Really, really good talent. Like Jane Caro [one of Australia's public intellectuals], she's on Sunrise for advertising segments. When I tell people in my industry that she was my teacher, they're just like, 'What?! That's really good'. Yeah, she's amazing."

Tom (student) also talked about accumulating academic capacities. He said that when he first started university, he "did quite poorly" and "I took six months off and I kind of said to myself, did I want to be there?." After six months, he came back to university and "put in a bit of effort, then kind of gradually over two or three semesters I picked up my effort and my marks improved quite a lot." Tom then decided to study medicine. He talked about being a better student, "the second time around [laughs]." This involved, "putting in the extra effort from the, you know, day dot." He decided to start sitting in the front row in lecture theaters, laboratories, and classrooms. This is because, "you take a lot of distractions out of your face because there's nothing between you and the lecturer. [. . .] And then you can engage more like a conversation." Acquiring the academic capacities to succeed at university affords a sense of "competence." Competence, Noble (2009, 882) writes, is

> A fundamental aspect of processes of recognition [. . .] rarely explored. By competence I do not just mean whether we are good at something, as important as this is, but insofar as we are seen to be legitimate participants in a specific situation or event.

Feelings of competence are central to feelings at home in a given situation. To be a competent social actor is to be a legitimate participant, and in the case of the research participants, a legitimate student—not an inferior one.

The resources used to accumulate academic capacities are, of course, classed and may involve a turn to the homely: to Cranebrook High School or to family. Processes of accumulation are regulated and limited by placial constraints. Two participants talked about going back to Cranebrook High School: they asked their schoolteachers for assistance, and their schoolteachers enthusiastically offered their support. Shannon commented that her former schoolteachers would say:

> "[Shannon], oh, do you need help with your Uni work?". It's like, "I've got it covered," but you know it's good when you like get stuck. Like, I got stuck on one of my thesis points on one of the main essays and I just went up to English Department and I was like, "I don't know how to word it." And he's like, "Oh, you do it like this." And I was, "Oh, okay. Yeah." So, it's good to sort to have the help if you need it.

Similarly, Jacklyn (graduate) talked about the support she received from her science teachers:

> Jacklyn: Um sometimes I would go back, and I'd ask my health teacher or my biology teacher–
> Alex: Yeah–
> Jacklyn: For a bit of advice when, yeah at the very start when I first started cause they help with some of the stuff cause some of it actually did like what I'd learn about in health or biology–
> Alex: Yep–
> Jacklyn: Um, and then and that, I'd just go back to say, "hello" to the teachers and just be like, "How you going?" But there was only two teachers that I could really–
> Alex: Could ask for help with?–
> Jacklyn: Yeah and then as it got more advanced, they couldn't help cause they didn't understand it.

Jacklyn also described receiving support from her stepfather:

> Yeah, but my dad would proofread, like he's very smart and all that stuff, so he would proofread my essays and all that before I handed it in, make sure I had commas and all that and if I'd missed anything. Because, you know, you read it sometimes and you still miss a comma or a full stop. Yeah, and like to you that sentence made sense and you'd read it and read it, and then my dad would look at it and he'd be like, "What does this even mean? What are you saying?". And you're like, "Oh it made sense two seconds ago" [laughs]. And then he'd be like, "Oh reword it."

These participants, then, access what limited cultural and social resources they can. Clayton et al. (2009) have written about the ways working-class students maintain connections to home and the familiar (their friends and family) to overcome feelings of social alienation at university. The familiar, they argue, is a "spatial resource" (Clayton et al. 2009, 157). Here, for the research participants, home too is a spatial resource—but, in this context, an academic one.

These resources—the school and family—do, of course, have limits. Clayton et al. (2009, 167) explain, "These networks do not result in the transmission of high status or dominant cultural capital," even though they provide an "essential support system." As Jacklyn's comment indicates, her schoolteachers were unable to help once her course content became more advanced and specific, and her stepfather provided what assistance he could—proofreading. An awareness of these limits produced ambivalent feelings related to competency. Jacklyn said:

> Because I'm not very . . . like, I know people are like, "Oh you are smart because you've been to uni," but I don't feel like I'm that smart. Like, I'm not smart with words and all that. [. . .] I wasn't very clever at putting big nice words together that you needed in uni and I think that's one thing that Cranebrook downfall was, was that we weren't taught all that stuff properly, like how to do essays properly and the proper structure.

Unlike Mallman's (2017, 236) participants who view the limits of their academic capabilities as "deriving from inherent individual deficiencies," Jacklyn recognizes the structural barriers she faces—the limitations of Cranebrook High School, though she is grateful for what it can and does offer. Again, the microcosm of Cranebrook and the wider Penrith shapes how these participants come to feel at home at university.

Precarious Recognitions: Settings and Symbolic Violence

Recognition, as discussed, is twofold: it also involves processes of misrecognition. For the research participants, the recognitions associated with being a student at Western Sydney University were, at times, interrupted. Tom, for example, described moments of misrecognition. Tom said his parents were proud of his achievements, but equally frustrated by all the time he spent studying. They would say, "It's a nice day. You should be outside." He would reply, "You know, it's a nice day, but I need to study." Tom said, "I think it's just there's not quite understanding there, and like, you know, especially when you're striving, you know, I was striving for the top mark." Tom's parents, then, were invested in Tom becoming a doctor, but did not understand his investments, or *illusio*, in the scholastic—in the very process of becoming a doctor. Tom also talked about other "pressures" and "distractions" that interrupt what he describes as a "fulfilling" experience. His father, for example, pushes him to transfer to a more prestigious university:

> He goes, "Oh it's like, you know, you should try and, you know, transfer to one of the other universities." Because, he goes, like, "Employers are more impressed when they see a degree from, you know, University of Sydney, and there's more connections there and what not."

Tom also talked about how friends would make negative comments about the university. He said, "Other students from other universities write you off. It doesn't matter how good your marks are. But it doesn't matter. You're at UWS." He spoke about one friend:

> Well, he made a lot of comments about, um, about being at Wollongong and how it's a better uni. You know how people get. You know, like, you know it depends on your teachers, it depends on the effort you put in. You know, if you're getting 50s at Wollongong, you're not better than me who's getting 90-odd at, you know, University of Western Sydney. You know, you're not learning more because you're at, you know, a better university.

Emma (student), too, described an experience of misrecognition that similarly undermined Western Sydney University and her legitimacy as a university student. She talked about one tutor who made a series of comments about Western Sydney University:

> His face would give you that look like, "You're an idiot." [. . .] And he told us like, oh, he did his study at Sydney Uni, um, and Alex, it was so bad. And he made like a comment about Western Sydney. [. . .] Like the standards of our learn—[. . .]. And he was like made a few comments sometimes about like, you know, "UWS is a lot under. Like it's proven. Like there's articles on it," blah, blah, blah. [. . .] Like saying our students aren't up to standard of what we should be. [. . .] Yeah, he was terrible. [. . .] He only did that on one instance, but I wouldn't forget something like that because I think, well, all of us were like, "Oh, okay."

These acts of misrecognition—from Tom's father and friend, and Emma's tutor—are perhaps not a-placial either and may feed into classed perceptions of Western Sydney as a cultural wasteland (Powell 1993). They may also feed into past political tussles over the university's very establishment. Western Sydney, as discussed in the Introduction, was perceived by some politicians and bureaucrats as unworthy of a university—an institution of practical and technical education was perceived to be better suited to the needs, abilities, and aspirations of its people (Hutchinson 2013). This is quite different to Elise's comments about Gough Whitlam's gift of recognition to Western Sydney. Bourdieu (1987, 13) argues that objects in the social world

> Always involve a degree of indeterminacy and fuzziness, and thus, present a definite degree of semantic elasticity. This element of uncertainty, is what provides a ground for differing or antagonistic perceptions and constructions which confront each other and which can be objectivised in the form of durable institutions. One of the major stakes in these struggles is the definition of the boundaries between groups, that is to say, the very definition of the groups.

Western Sydney University does not have the symbolic legitimacy that its other Sydney rivals have, namely the University of Sydney, the University of New South Wales, the University of Technology, Macquarie University, and the Australian Catholic University. Western Sydney University, as the research participants' comments show, is always dangerously close to being misrecognized as an illegitimate institution within the wider field of higher education.

Emma and Tom's comments also draw attention to the situatedness of recognition—in a university classroom or at home, for example—and demonstrate, as Noble (2009) has argued, the importance of attending to the specificity of "settings." Indeed, degrees of integration at university do not just occur within the loose ensemble of a microcosm, or within the bounds of a "field," or a "social space," but within the confines of particular "settings" too—a setting embedded within a microcosm, subfield, field, and social space. "Setting," as Goffman (1990 [1959], 32) uses it, refers to the scenic backdrop of a particular social interaction. This is Goffman's (1990 [1959]) "sense of one's place." Fit, then, is a precarious accomplishment: one may experience placial degrees of integration within a particular setting, microcosm, or subfield, but be misrecognized within the broader field of higher education. Goffman's (1990 [1959]) "sense of one's place" in a "setting" highlights the temporality and contextuality of recognition, but, as Emma and Tom's comments also show, it must be paired with Bourdieu's (2000, 241) "sense of one's place"—within a wider political economy of symbolic power:

> Conversely, there is no worse dispossession, no worse privation, perhaps, than that of the losers in the symbolic struggle for recognition, for access to a socially recognized social being, in a word, to humanity. This struggle is not reducible to a Goffmanian battle to present a favourable representation of oneself: it is competition for a power that can only be won from others competing for the same power, a power over others that derives its existence from others, from their perception and appreciation [. . .], and therefore a power over a desire for power and over the object of this desire.

Feelings of homeliness at university—in all its degrees—is hard won. Recognition is, indeed, a precarious accomplishment.

Multicultural "Enrichment"

As mentioned earlier, fitting in may involve processes of accumulation—of accumulating academic capacities, recognition, and so on. Being a student at a new university, then, can be an expansive process—it's not necessarily a passive withdrawal from the world, as it is in Reay et al.'s (2010) work. For the research participants, this process of accumulation was sometimes narrated in terms of meeting students whose ethnicities were different to their own. Annie (student and graduate), who described Kingswood (the neighbourhood) as very white and very Catholic, spoke about the pleasures of meeting people who were neither white nor Catholic on campus (in Kingswood). Western Sydney, as discussed in the Introduction, is Australia's multicultural heartland. Some pockets in the region are extremely diverse, while others, like Penrith, are more ethnically homogenous. I asked Annie if university has changed her in any way, and she responded, "I've got more friends in different parts of Sydney and Western Sydney and a lot more diversity with my friends." Annie also talked about going along to the "Queer Room" on campus, and said she tried the "Churchy group but it ended up not being for me." Annie talked about becoming more accepting:

> It's basically . . . yeah . . . because at uni is when you're exposed to the . . . well, I was exposed to everyone of different races, different religious backgrounds, and all those sorts of things. Um, I think that's what made me more accepting.

This self-assessment involved an inward glance, an evaluation of the past and present self, but it also involved turning toward her family: to her father and aunty. Annie's new friendships, specifically her friendships with Muslim women who wear a hijab, have made them particularly uncomfortable. Annie's proximity to "a Muslim" is shocking:

> Like um, dad got really weird when it was . . . . I was doing a group assignment with two of, with three people, three other people, and dad was picking me up and he was like, "Oh, you know, we can drop, um, her off on the way," and everything. Like, this was on the phone. I'm like, "Okay, yeah, okay, we're good." And I'm thinking, "Okay, okay, thanks, dad. Yeah, pick us up or whatever." And then after dad, like, dropped her off and then, like, we drove down the road. He's like, he stopped the car and turned to me, "You never told me your friend was a Muslim?!". And I'm like, "How is that a problem?!" And he's like, "It's not. I just wasn't expecting it . . ." [Laughs]. I, I, I didn't even think of it because it's, like, she's a friend.

Annie also described how her aunty said: "Your friends are all Muslims. They all wear the burka!". Annie explained that her friends did not wear a burka, that they wore a hijab instead, and that her family had many misconceptions about Islam. Annie's words point to how an embrace of the "other" can be expansive. This is not, however, a form of "cultural enrichment" associated with "cosmo-multiculturalism"—a relation to "ethnicity largely as an object of consumption" rather than an experiential subject (Hage 1997, 99). Annie's embrace of the "other" is about a multiculturalism of "intercultural interaction," the development of *friendships* that cut across ethnic differences (Hage 1997, 100). This process affords feelings of existential mobility, the feeling that one is moving well (Hage 2009). Annie's words also point to how these processes of accumulation involve practical work on one's relationships: not just between Annie and her new friends, but between Annie and her family.

Annie's words, of course, cannot tell us much about how her Muslim friends feel at Kingswood (the campus and the broader suburb), or at Western Sydney University's other campuses. Annie's story—and the racialized (and gendered) discomfort of others (her father and aunty)—suggests that belonging at the Kingswood Campus is precarious for some, for students who wear a hijab. For them, perhaps, Kingswood is not so homely. Idriss (2014), who has written about the experiences of young Muslim men from Bankstown at inner-city universities, similarly found that the young men's ethnicity, combined with their class and what I would call placial bearing (after Casey 2001), together produced a sense of alienation from their whiter and more affluent peers. Yet, Annie's words do tell us that her father and aunty felt threatened by her friends' *difference*. This racialized discomfort toward Muslims emerged in another interview. Sheree (graduate), for example, described the Bankstown Campus as having: "a lot of Muslims. I think because of the area. Bankstown's obviously heavily populated with Muslims."[2] Sheree was hesitant at first to utter the word "Muslim" and then admitted that it is seen to be a bad word "these days." This is perhaps because the Arabic "other" is perceived to be the enemy or folk devil in contemporary Australian society (Idriss 2014; Noble 2005). As Sheree's words indicate, she did not feel "at home" at the Bankstown Campus: each campus, indeed, affords different degrees of fit that cut across various visions and divisions of difference. Sheree's words, too, point to the fragility of homeliness: particularly for working-class students from Arabic-speaking backgrounds. Do these students feel at home at Western Sydney University? And do they feel more at home on the Bankstown Campus?

"Cocoons" and "Comfort Zones": Desiring Discomfort

For some of the research participants, the Penrith Campuses constituted what Hage (2009, 98) calls a "suitable launching pad for their social and existential self" and provided them with the confidence to move out of their "comfort zones." Noble (2015, 36) writes that an "at homeness" with the things around us "is central to both a sense of self and to the possibility for future action." This echoes Winnicott's (in Honneth 1995, 99) conceptualization of the mother-child relation: to be cared for, or rather to *be held*, and thus recognized, can provide a nurturing and comforting space from which one can expand and develop, and later transcend. "Some boundaries," Noble (2015, 43) writes, "are not borders but elastic horizons." This notion of transcendence is important. According to Hage (1997, 103), a homely space is only a homely space if it is "a space open for opportunities." He argues, "Most theorisations of the home emphasise it as a shelter but, like a mother's lap it is only a shelter that we use to rest and then spring into action [. . .]. A space which is only like a shelter becomes, like the lap of the possessive mother [or father!], a claustrophobic space that loses its homely character" (Hage 1997, 103).

Adrijana, for example, talked about the Kingswood Campus as being a nurturing space, a "cocoon." She completed a bachelor of arts with a major in art history and talked about *becoming* "comfortable with being a student." She acquired an "at homeness" at university, socially and academically, and this "at homeness" constituted "the physical *and* social agency to move beyond that ensemble" (Noble 2015, 37). Adrijana then decided to enroll in a master of art curatorship at the University of Sydney. This was a move she described in terms of leaving her cocoon: "Sydney University was just such a big scary place because I'd just stepped out of my cocoon that was you know comfortable, familiar, little Penrith. I mean I was working in the Plaza[3], so I was, you know, Penrith was my life." Stepping out of one's "cocoon" can be a difficult experience: it involves adjusting to new environments, and this adjustment may transform the way one sees oneself and the world. Adrijana talked about becoming more attuned to class and placial differences, particularly after the University of Sydney offered her a "HECS Equity Place," or "reduced fees," because she attended Cranebrook High School. Adrijana said:

> That was the first time I really thought about where I grew up cause I thought, like I always knew obviously it's a [Cranebrook] working-class area, you know. I never thought that I lived in like a particularly wealthy area, but I didn't think that it was such a low socio, like I didn't realise that it was seen that way that it was gonna be targeted for . . . something like that. Because that's a fair bit of money. I don't know how many students were given that though. Like I've got no idea. I didn't, I don't know how I was targeted. I just sort of got a letter. I didn't understand what it meant [laughs]. I went to the Student Centre to ask [. . .]. I think that was the first time I really started thinking about it because I think for my undergrad I was at Kingswood, so I was still at home. So, I never really thought about

socio-economic differences because like, "We've got a university. What do you mean?" [laughs].

Adrijana then began to notice that some of her peers came from "very wealthy backgrounds" and "the Eastern Suburbs." She described the typical student as having a father who "had a collection or something of artworks." Adrijana also described the difficulties she had developing friendships. She said: "The art crowd was definitely a bit more . . . and they all sort of like went to each other's, you know, wherever who worked and at which gallery or whatever, and they all seemed to meet, you know, I don't know, like grow, or grew up together and stuff so, yeah." Adrijana felt like a newcomer. She talked about one incident as being emblematic of her experiences at the University of Sydney:

> I remember one day [speaks with laughter] I didn't, I don't know, I guess I just didn't really . . . it was still sort of warm and I don't know, it was like, I don't know if it was autumn or if it was spring, I can't remember. It was just sort of like in-between the weather. And I think I was either wanting to get the last little bit of wearing a dress in or the first you know bit of wearing a dress in. And I wore this dress. It was purple. Like a light purple, I think. It was some sort of print or something. It was like a flowy sort of you know sundress or whatever. And then I got there, and everybody was wearing black or grey, or black and white, and mostly black. And I just remembered thinking like, "I didn't get the memo. Why is everyone wearing black?" [. . .]. I was like, [speaks with laughter] "What?! Are you guys trying to tell me something?."

Entangled in Adrijana's descriptions is a politics of discomfort based on affective experiences of misfit in her new material and social environments, a habitus out of place. Adrijana did make one good friend: he was also an alumnus of Western Sydney University and lived in Mulgoa, on the fringes of Penrith. Like her "Eastern Suburbs" peers, who Adrijana describes as being "familiar" with one another, she also developed a friendship with someone from *her* familiar. Adrijana did not develop an "at homeness" with her peers, although she described learning to feel comfortable: "I'd become comfortable, you know, towards the end of it all."

Adrijana talked about becoming comfortable with discomfort—but particular types of discomfort: scholarly and placial. Indeed, Adrijana talked about her experiences at the University of Sydney as being difficult, but in *hindsight*, she was glad she *stepped out of her cocoon*. She said, "As uncomfortable as I may have felt at, you know, Sydney, feeling sort of out of the way, I guess, like, it forced me to step out of my comfort a little bit." The "gap" between habitus and environment, between expectations and experience, produced a sense of satisfaction. Bourdieu (2000, 149) explains:

> If it is accepted that the principle of the transformation of habitus lies in the gap, experienced as a positive or negative surprise, between expectations and experience, one must suppose that the extent of this gap and the significance attributed to it depend on habitus: one person's disappointment may be another's unexpected satisfaction, with the corresponding effects of reinforcement or inhibition.

Stepping out of her cocoon was not initially a conscious aim, but over time it became one—within limits. Bourdieu (2000, 207), drawing from Husserl, makes a distinction between these conscious and unconscious relations to the future:

> Husserl did indeed clearly establish that the *project* as a conscious aiming at the future in its reality as a contingent future must not be conflated with *protention*, a prereflexive aiming at a forthcoming which offers as quasi-present in the visible, like the hidden faces of a cube, with the same belief status (the same doxic modality) as what is directly perceived; and that it is only when it is retrieved in scholastic reflection that it can appear, retrospectively, as a project, which it is not in practice

Adrijana said that she now finds herself "pushing things a little bit more." Discomfort became a project. She talked about her decision to attend a summer school at the University of Cambridge. Like Western Sydney University, the University of Sydney functioned as a launching pad into another institution outside her comfort zone. She said:

> I was doing the art history thing and then I realised, "Oh you know, university's not that bigger, scarier place after all." And I went to do, like I went to Europe and I thought, "Oh, wouldn't it be awesome to like go to Cambridge or something." So, I did summer school there. It's a two-week summer school course.

Adrijana did not say a lot about her time at Cambridge except that it was "beautiful," and I regret not asking her to elaborate on her experience.

Yet, there are limits: while Adrijana railed against some forms of comfort, she continued to desire a classed sense of fit—the latter was something she never felt at the University of Sydney or in the art world. As I will show in the following chapters, Adrijana later secured work at an auction house, but then decided to retrain as a teacher in Western Sydney: "I felt like I was making the decision to go back into the real world. I guess because it really felt like it was like just this little niche pocket where I didn't belong." This decision was also rooted in a desire for a job with more stability but also a desire to be where she felt most at home in the world: "UWS is more peaceful. That's why I came back for the teaching one." *Peaceful* implies the absence of conflict and struggle. *The real world*, Penrith, is a microcosm endowed with meaning and interest. Like Shannon, classed feelings of discomfort, not feeling at home in the world, ultimately work to contain Adrijana's movements. Thus, there are limits to the elasticity of horizons and limits to habitus transformation. The "parents" homely embrace, then, is both possessive *and* provides possibilities for transcendence, or rather possibilities to "spring into action." This ambivalence, I argue, is captured in the word the "spring"—the parents' embrace can work to push one forward but can pull one back, forcefully. In Chapter 5, I examine the social relations that work to pull some research participants back to place, to Cranebrook and its surrounds.

Emma, who I introduced earlier, also actively sought out some experiences of discomfort. She anticipated discomfort and worked to maintain a momentum of discomfort followed by comfort—a discomfort-comfort continuum. Emma did not want to live a life of regret, and she associated regret with existential and social "stuckedness" (Hage 2009), remaining in one's "comfort zone." Emma was one of only two participants who spoke about leaving the Penrith region and her father's life weighed heavily on her own: "Sometimes he's like, 'Oh, you know, I should have done this, should have done that,' and I feel like he should have progressed more in his career where he has kind of been in the same spot, in his comfort zone, and I don't think he is truly happy in that." Emma spoke about going to Western Sydney University as getting out of her "comfort zone," particularly because she was a mature-aged student (mid-twenties) and never completed the Higher School Certificate (HSC)—what you chase is, of course, determined by your circumstances. Going to university was a space where Emma could acquire academic capacities and credentials to increase her social power and thus career prospects, and so avoid *being stuck in the same spot*. Being a student and acquiring skills provided Emma with a sense of accomplishment:

Emma: I feel like I've got more status–

Alex: Oh, really?–

Emma: And-and I don't mean that in an arrogant way but–

Alex: Yeah–

Emma: I do feel in a way that I do feel like I'm in a bit more of a–

Alex: Yeah–

Emma: Even though I haven't finished uni, but I just feel like a bit more accomplished that I'm trying to do more in my life, do you know what I mean?–

Alex: Yeah–

Emma: And not in a like–

Alex: Yeah, I know what you mean–

Emma: Do you know, yeah?–

Alex: Yeah–

Emma: Yeah. No, but I do. I feel quite content. Yeah–

Alex: Yeah–

Emma: I feel good. Even at work, for example, no-one's done a uni degree. I sort of like, you know, I kind of feel–

Alex: Yeah–

Emma: Good in that aspect, you know–

Alex: Yeah–

Emma: But not in an arrogant and like "Oh, I've got a uni degree," like–

Alex: Mm-hmm–

Emma: But just it makes you feel good–

Alex: Yeah–

Emma: Like you're doing something, you're learning more, and you know?

Emma compared her accomplishments to those of her work colleagues—she did not turn her gaze toward other students at more prestigious institutions.

For Emma, moving out of her comfort zone also involved moving from the Kingswood Campus to the Parramatta Campus at Western Sydney University. Emma described Kingswood as being homely but commented that the Parramatta Campus "had a totally different atmosphere. Strange isn't it? I feel like there's more different ethnicities here and less in Penrith." For Emma, Parramatta, because of its cultural diversity, felt radically different—unhomely, outside her "comfort zone," and less like "high school." Rather than complete her classes at the Kingswood Campus (which was only a five-minute drive from her home), Emma later opted to complete her classes at Parramatta. Like Annie, Emma enjoyed opening herself up to new experiences and meeting people from diverse backgrounds. She said, "I don't want to be comfortable. I like pushing myself." Yet, some comfort was desired. Emma's decision to complete her subjects at Parramatta was also fueled by a desire to form meaningful friendships with other students—moving between two campuses, combined with being a part-time mature-aged student, making it difficult to get to know other students:

> Emma: You know what I found hardest? Being a mature-aged part-time student–
> Alex: Yeah–
> Emma: Far out. Like, it's hard because it's harder to make friends when you're studying part-time, and I was going between Parramatta and Kingswood Campus, so one unit in Parramatta, one in Kingswood–
> Alex: Yeah–
> Emma: So, there was a mixture of people. And I've noticed in today's society as well, people aren't as friendly. Like you know, I've noticed in classes, some classes you go to the first time everyone sits separately and you kind of like hide. Like, oh, you know, it's really, it's so sad. And it's . . . I've struggled. I feel like I'm a social person, but I've struggled to make a friend at Uni–
> Alex: Yeah–
> Emma: I've made like one, you know–
> Alex: Yeah–
> Emma: But the others, they're acquaintances. Like, you'll talk to them in class but no, you know, "Oh, let's go to coffee" or I feel like it's quite, it's-it's strange. Like I've struggled to . . . like in the sense like I was hoping like full-time uni I would make some new friends, you know, blah, blah, blah. It hasn't been that easy. Like it's not . . . it's hard to explain but it's–
> Alex: No, I know exactly what you mean–
> Emma: People are very . . . it's-I think it's just how people are now. Like very off-p—what's . . . I don't know what I'm trying to say. Stand-offish.

Emma's desire for meaningful friendships at university, and their relative impossibility, *everyone sits separately and you kind of like hide*, points not just to the importance of thinking about fit in terms of habitus and its degrees of integration, but, indeed, also to the lean and mean university pedagogies that structure Australia's field of higher education and afford limited time for students to get to know their peers. Being a student in Australia, as survey data discussed previously shows (Baik et al. 2015), is a particularly lonely affair—for all students, from all backgrounds. Adrijana and Emma's comments, combined with earlier comments from Shannon and Danielja, demonstrate that fit is, indeed, precarious. It does not just involve being around people who one recognizes and feels recognized by but involves the formation of concrete and meaningful friendships—which, according to Emma, are particularly elusive at university.

Conclusions

In this chapter, I examined different logics of recognition and misrecognition at university. I argued that the homogenizing notions of class habitus and institutional habitus, as well as the bounded notion of field, do not adequately capture the varied ways we come to feel "at home" and recognized at university (Atkinson 2011; Watkins and Noble 2013). Following Bourdieu's (2000) notion of "degrees of integration," I argued for the importance of attending to the placial dimensions of the habitus. Attending university in one's microcosm—Penrith—can afford modes of belonging at university, specifically at Western Sydney University's Penrith Campuses. Our environments, the places we are most at home in the world, can operate as "elastic horizons" (Noble 2015) and provide "degrees of integration" (Bourdieu 2000) in new environments. Home is, indeed, a resource for homemaking at university. This is not, as I demonstrated, necessarily a passive withdrawal from the world, but can involve agency and self-expansion, the accumulation of being and recognition—of academic capacities and new friendships that cut across ethnic differences. Recognition is, of course, precarious. What is valued within a setting, microcosm, or subfield might not be recognized within the wider symbolic economy of a field. For some participants, the recognition that came with being a student at Western Sydney University was always dangerously close to being misrecognized.

I argued that the Penrith Campuses, for some participants, constituted what Hage (2009, 98) calls a "suitable launching pad for [the] social and existential self"—it provided them with the confidence to move out of their "comfort zones." For those participants, comfort was experienced ambiguously and ambivalently, desired and railed against, a *project* and *protention*. A gap between expectations and experience, and the associated feelings of discomfort, produced a sense of satisfaction—the feeling that one was "moving well." There are, however, limits. Revision and transformation are never radical. The pull of place can limit, orient, and define movements in the world—toward particular campuses and not others, toward sameness and away from difference. The pull of place, here, produces a tension between the idea of Western Sydney University taking its students *somewhere,* and the research participants' reliance on the homely as a resource and anchor. This movement is, of course, one of both agency *and* domination:

> For agency is itself socially structured: the acts of classification that guide the choices of individuals are systematically oriented by the mental and corporeal schemata resulting from the internalization of the objective patterns of their extant social environment. The preferences, habits and inclinations of persons are embodied social structures which transcribe within their organism the organised influences and forces of their milieu. Structural determinism is thus lodged at the very heart of agency and is indistinguishable from it. (Wacquant 1993, 4)

This is, indeed, a dimension of the symbolic violence of homely mobility.

4

The Graduate Waiting Room[1]

Introduction

A few years ago, I attended my university's "strategy day"—a symposium of decadal planning attended by the Board of Trustees and members of its subcommittees. The day before the strategy day, we all attended the opening of our university's newest campus in Liverpool, a suburb in outer Western Sydney that shares some boundaries with Penrith. The mayor of Liverpool said a few moving words. She came to university, Western Sydney University, as a single mother with four young children. For her, university opened doors and radically changed the course of her life. She was the girl from Liverpool who was now the mayor of Liverpool. A colleague, not from Western Sydney, turned to me and said, "I've always been sympathetic of the 'underdog'. That's why I'm here." The next day, the strategy day, we listened to a presentation on the future of higher education delivered by a well-known economist, Andrew Charlton. Charlton asked, "Is higher education still the golden ticket for young Australians?." The answer was, "No, education is no longer a golden ticket for all Australians." The rewards of a university degree are unevenly distributed. I knew this. A handful of others in the room knew this too. For most of the room though, the presentation was unsettling, radical perhaps, a divergence from the mayor of Liverpool's success story.

A senior member of staff went into damage control. In his review of the day, he pointed out that young people today "choose" the alternative to permanent employment. See, he recently had lunch with ten public servants he hired a decade or so ago. They were, at the time, the cream of the crop and employed in one of the government's most prestigious graduate programs. Yet, as he revealed, only three were still working in the public service. The others had chosen the alternative: insecure and flexible forms of employment over secure and permanent forms of employment. One, for example, had opted for something else entirely: she now worked as a yoga instructor. Most of the room laughed. The seriousness of the public service was, indeed, a contrast to yoga. The laughter, too, seemed to laugh off the seriousness of the economist's words. University was once again a golden ticket, and the gig economy was a "choice". I didn't laugh though. In this chapter, I attend to the experiences of those graduates who struggled to find graduate employment in the immediate period after graduation. While seven participants successfully found graduate positions in nursing, teaching, communications, human resources, law, and research, eight participants struggled to secure employment in their preferred careers.

We live in a period of "diploma inflation" where the rewards of higher education are unevenly distributed (Bourdieu and Passeron 1979 [1964]; Watkins 2020), and for graduates of Western Sydney this difficulty is compounded by spatial inequalities—graduate employment opportunities are concentrated in Sydney's east, not west (O'Neill 2017). Following Finn and Holton (2019), I turn my attention to the graduate experience of "waiting." Finn and Holton (2019) have examined the experience of "waithood," which refers to a period of purposeful deceleration and stepping back from pressures to find graduate employment, and I instead examine the experience of "waiting" as a period of forced suspension between graduation and securing desired forms of employment. I call this period of abeyance the "graduate waiting room." The transition from university into graduate employment can, indeed, be prolonged and protracted. Waiting is a condition where "we anticipate the future as too slow in coming, as if in order to hasten its course" (Pascal in Bourdieu 2000, 209). It is a relation that describes the "breaking of the tacit collusion" between *illusio* and *lusiones* (Bourdieu 2000, 208).

Bourdieu and Passeron (1979 [1964]), many decades ago, argued that victims of diploma inflation—those graduates who are left waiting—either remain invested in the promise of university or disinvest from its promise and experience a personal crisis. The former mode of attachment is similar to Berlant's (2011) notion of "cruel optimism"—which describes an investment in an object whose realization is impossible, but is considered to be a possibility. Scholars have likened the contemporary education system to one of cruel optimism (Reay 2017; Sellar 2013). Bourdieu and Passeron (1979 [1964], 90) call these investments and disinvestments "compensatory strategies." They write, "The strategies which one group employs to try to escape downclassing and to return to their class trajectory, and which the other group employs to rebuild the interrupted path of a hoped-for trajectory, are today one of the most important factors in the transformation of social structure" (Bourdieu and Passeron 1979 [1964], 90). I examine how the research participants in this study invest or disinvest from the promise of university, but argue that not all attachments to the promise of university are relations of cruel optimism, nor do all disinvestments lead to personal crisis.

I begin by examining three different ways the "graduate waiting room" is negotiated: some research participants "persevered" with their aspirations, others "moved on," and some felt stuck—unable to move on or retrain. The latter, those who were stuck, maintain what I call a "cruel attachment" to the promise of university. It is a relation that offers very little sustenance and very little hope. It is a relation of regret—of missed employment opportunities. I then discuss how "waiting" and a corresponding sense of social and existential immobility may be reconfigured in new ways that involve an assessment of one's proximal relations. To do this, I examine Courtney's complex self-assessment about how a two-month Contiki holiday made her "feel middle class," despite questioning if she is "worse off" going to university. University, for the research participants, was, indeed, a utilitarian investment, or what Lehmann (2019, 354) calls a "vocational education." These compensatory strategies are similar to the "proximate relationalities" of first-generation university graduates in Finn's (2017a, 426) study. Having "proximate relationalities," for her participants, involved "changing course"—that is, letting go of career ambitions and finding work locally in nongraduate roles, such as aged care and administration. Her middle-class participants, on the other hand, tended to be geographically mobile and had what she calls "elastic relationalities." While my participants' mobilities are proximate too, their attachments to the promise of university—as outlined earlier—involve more than "changing course," but persevering and cruel attachments too.

"Compensatory Strategies"

Persevering

Two participants described finding it difficult to secure graduate employment in the initial period after graduation, but persevered in the face of setback and disappointment and eventually secured work. Jessica (first degree awarded over ten years ago), for example, completed a bachelor of health science with a major in play therapy at Western Sydney University. She expected university to be a launching pad into a career in play therapy. The program originally had links with the Sydney Children's Hospital, but late into Jessica's degree the hospital disaffiliated from the program: "The Children's Hospital that had been part of designing the degree said that they actually didn't need the graduates." Along with her peers, she was offered the opportunity to switch programs, but decided to complete the specialization. The program, however, was niche, "like most narrow segment of occupational therapy," and Jessica found it difficult to find work after graduating. She said:

> I sort of spent eight or nine months continuing to work in um food retail, which had been something I'd worked in, um during uni, and sort of couldn't find a job. Applied for loads but because it was such as obscure degree, people were like, "Oh no sorry. That's not what we're after."

Only one of Jessica's peers found work as a play therapist. Two others left the profession: one is now a midwife and the other works in childcare. She said she felt jilted: "I'm just quite grateful that somebody is doing [a study of graduates] and sort of particularly around the whole getting a degree that's a bit useless for want of a better word at the end of it."

Jessica eventually found work with the NSW government working in child safety: "It wasn't in a therapeutic role. I was as a child protection caseworker. So, um it was really a case of the main prerequisite for that was to have a degree um in a like in a health or related field so." Jessica was only twenty-one, the job was emotionally difficult, and she "burnt out inside of 18 months." Jessica then moved to Queensland and decided to enroll in a master of occupational therapy—something she saw as essential to securing work as an occupational therapist. Indeed, "diploma inflation" has meant that postgraduate qualifications are increasingly used to gain an advantage in the labor market (Watkins 2020). Jessica now works as an occupational therapist for the Queensland government. The effects of devaluation were, however, placed into sharp relief when she compared her salary to her husband's (who works in retail). She said: "He out earns me. So, I feel like a tool [laughs] for spending six years at uni not earning any money while he was quite happily earning money. I don't like, I think my longer-term earning potential is a little bit higher for going to uni but." The "graduate premium" in Australia does remain large, though not all graduates gain a premium from attending university (Norton and Cherastidtham 2018, 92). Jessica's relation to the "promise of university" was, then, ambivalent and her ambivalence was shaped by her partner's economic success—which he achieved without a university degree.

Sheree (degree awarded under five years ago) also found it difficult to find work after completing a bachelor of psychology from Western Sydney University: "I thought I would get a job like straight away, which didn't happen. I thought I'd be on like massive money. Didn't happen [laughs]." Sheree waited over twelve months to find work, and for a long time she felt like she had made a mistake going to university: "My first thought was just like, 'I've just wasted four years of my life when, you know, all my friends are out doing, you know, reception jobs and stuff and they've all got money and they've all got brand new cars and stuff.'" Sheree experienced regret, and, like Jessica, this regret involved a glance to her immediate social networks. Sheree said she applied for "hundreds of jobs" and "all different sorts of jobs" and that "I just sort of gave up after a while. [. . .] You're just like, 'Why do I bother even sending out those applications if no one even you know gets back to me.'" She said that "no one wanted me because I didn't have experience." She then decided to volunteer with a women and children's support group once a week for six months, and "after I'd put that I'd been volunteering on my resume and um I ended up landing the job that I have now."

Sheree said that she "needed some sort of qualification" for her job in social work, but that a university degree was not essential—some of her colleagues had TAFE diplomas and some were still university students. Sheree, however, still felt that she was "moving well," that she was socially mobile, particularly when she compared her new job to her previous role in a supermarket:

> I hated it. I hated the hours. Like you have to work Thursday nights and weekends all the time. And stuff like that. [. . .] Like I'll occasionally do a weekend but it's not like late-night finishes and I don't have to work, you know, Christmas Eve till late and New Year's Eve and all that sort of stuff till heaps late at night.

She also enjoyed her new job and she found it both interesting and challenging: "Like interacting with the kids is a big thing. Um and I feel like in a way I'm um sorta like protecting them or helping to protect them from, you know, child abuse and drugs and alcohol and all that, like domestic violence and all that sort of stuff." For Sheree, then, the effects of devaluation are masked by small-scale degrees of mobility that involve an assessment of past working conditions, but also by feelings of existential mobility: of the accumulation of being that her new job offers. What is interesting, then, is that aspirations and their fulfillment are not only unevenly distributed, but chasing one's aspirations, or persevering with one's aspirations, can involve the perseverance of one's being, or the perseverance of one's class position. Thus, the promise of university and what constitutes its fulfillment is class differentiated and can also work to reproduce class differences. Aspirations, though associated with chance and uncertainty, are "a limited, and in a sense, regulated uncertainty" (Bourdieu 2000, 213).

Moving On

Some of the research participants who did not secure the positions they hoped for discussed making meaning from an alternative route to somewhere else—a readjustment that involved a reorientation toward the more feasible and the less ambitious. These participants expected a swift, specific, and straight path into their hoped-for careers, and when their aspirations did not transpire, they speedily moved on. They did not wait around. Nick (degree awarded over five years ago), for example, hoped to become an "agri-economist," but now works in customer service at a local bank. As discussed in Chapter 2, Nick completed a bachelor of agriculture with a major in agricultural economics. He applied for a myriad of graduate roles but was unsuccessful:

> So, when I first finished my degree I did apply just about to everywhere. Everywhere from Elders [stock and station agents] to the Department of Primary Industries through to places like ABARE, the Australian Bureau of Agriculture Resource and Economics, who handles a lot of statistics. Because my degree majored in agri-economics, and I did do a little bit of statistics, that's more where I wanted to go. But yeah, I wasn't very successful in finding a job. I found it extremely hard.

Science graduates, as the statistics reveal, have great difficulty securing graduate employment and have some of the poorest graduate outcomes. For example, in 2017, over 40 percent of science graduates were still seeking work three years after graduation (Norton and Cherastidtham 2018, 78). The Graduate

Outcomes Survey (DET 2018, vi–vii) indicates that 41.6 percent of "agriculture and environmental science" graduates are employed in full-time roles that do not fully use their skills and qualifications, and of those 41.6 percent, 35.3 percent indicated that there were "no jobs in (their) area of expertise."

Nick questioned why he was unsuccessful: he was, after all, a high-achieving student, had years of customer service experience under his belt, including some management responsibilities, and spent his school holidays working on his grandparents' farm. I am not sure if Nick was aware of the specific difficulties faced by science graduates. He did not say. He did not, however, experience "personal criticism and crisis," like Bourdieu and Passeron's participants (1979 [1964], 92). Nick did not blame himself and was particularly critical of Western Sydney University, like Jessica. Despite completing a specialization, and his faculty's long history teaching agriculture,[2] he described his degree as subpar. He said, "It was a scattergun shot at trying to teach a little bit of everything and was specifically about nothing." He compared his degree to other universities that are also well known for their agricultural colleges: Charles Sturt University and the University of Sydney. These universities, Nick argued, taught their students "specific" skills. Nick also argued that Western Sydney University lacked prestige. Nick discussed applying for a graduate position, and he "got the feeling" that being a graduate of Western Sydney University was a disadvantage:

> When I was applying for work within the Department of Primary Industries, there was a particular individual who was doing the interviews [. . .]. And the particular individual was . . . when she read that I was from UWS, I got the feeling as soon as she read that, I wasn't going to get the job.

Data from the "Quality Indicators for Teaching and Learning" (www.qilt.edu.au, accessed July 21, 2019), or QILT survey, indicates that graduates from Charles Sturt University (82.6 percent) and the University of Sydney (80.4 percent) do have more success securing full-time employment than graduates from Western Sydney University (71.4 percent)—though these statistics refer to full-time employment only, and these roles are not necessarily graduate ones.

Nick also talked about employers wanting a more experienced candidate:

> They didn't want someone fresh out of uni, they wanted someone that was two years out of uni, or three years out of uni, that had been working in that

field all that time. And I was sort of like, well, I mean [...]. How do you get that experience? And you basically ask that question, and they go, "Well, it's not our concern" [laughs]. And it really is like that, like it's very, very brutal sometimes.

In a competitive graduate labor market, graduates are expected to have "experience" and traineeships, and unpaid internships are increasingly required for entry into most forms of graduate employment. Nick did not attempt to gain more "experience." He did not know how to. Nor did Nick know how to translate the experience he already had into a narrative of employability. Bathmaker et al. (2016), in their work on university students nearing course completion, found that many working-class students end up as "drifters." Drifters were students who had vague career goals or were unsure of what they needed to do to reach their goal. Working-class students, they argue, may end up as drifters because they do not have the "insider knowledge" nor the social capital needed to navigate the graduate labor market (Bathmaker et al. 2016, 117). Morgan and Nelligan (2018) make a similar point about creative aspirants from working-class backgrounds. They argue that the rapidity of deindustrialization has meant that there is a disjuncture between the occupational experience of parents and their children and that this limits the ability of working-class parents to mentor their children in the new economy.

By the time Nick graduated, he had already started working at his local bank:

> You start applying for jobs six months before you even finish the course, and by the time you've graduated, it's four to six months after you've actually finished your degree. So, it's about 12 months since I've actually started applying for jobs and I virtually found nothing. By the time I'd graduated I'd started at the bank. And I was, yeah, quite happy with that, but obviously, it's got nothing to do with my degree. My degree did not help me get the job or anything like that, it was purely based on my previous customer service experience, and the fact that I had really good references from previous jobs that were very, very strong references. Always had a good work ethic and stuff like that so I had no issues getting work, it was just, yeah, getting it with that degree was, yeah.

Again, Nick did not blame himself, but he was critical of his degree. Nick was keen to emphasize his customer service experience—indeed, at one point he was the "top salesman in the country" for a retail store specializing in electronics. He said, "I'm a massive introvert at home, but once I get to work, I can turn it like a switch and all of a sudden I can talk to a fence post!" Having a "good work ethic" was a recurring theme. As discussed in Chapter 2, having a good work ethic was about sucking it up, so to speak: "My parents have always been firm believers in a strong work ethic, and if you're having trouble finding employment, it means you're being too picky. Yeah, at the end of the day you need to put bread on the table and keep a roof over your head." Morgan and Nelligan (2018) argue that working-class graduates cannot afford to tread water and wait, or indeed work in unpaid roles to accrue experience, but that they must find whatever work they can. A "good" transition, then, involves moving into full-time employment, not necessarily graduate employment—though graduate employment is desirable. Waiting around for graduate employment is not. This work ethic is, indeed, classed: pickiness and waiting around, not getting stuck into work, is dishonorable for Nick. It is also gendered: Nick must be able to provide. Providing, no matter how humble the pay check, is more honorable than not providing at all.

Nick was proud of himself for moving on, for not waiting around, even though his job at the bank requires no qualification. There is agency here, despite its apparent absence. Hage (2009, 100–1) calls this the "heroism of stuckedness": "asserting some agency over the fact that one has no agency by not succumbing and becoming a mere victim and an object of circumstances that are conspiring to make a total agentless victim and object out of you." Nick endures the situation he has found himself in. Yet, while Nick accepts the present, he is also hopeful. Nick is now studying commerce at Macquarie University and talked about becoming a "Branch Manager" in the future. He said that the bank was "full of opportunities": "like we employ more people than the Australian Defence Force." Nick's comments, then, mediate between older models of liberal citizenship that value "self-reliance, autonomy and independence as the underpinning of self-respect, self-esteem, self-worth and self-advancement," and the neoliberal self which co-opts these values through the notion of "enterprise, seeking to enhance and capitalise on itself through calculated acts and investments" (Rose 1999, 164). The latter is what Morgan and Nelligan (2018, 85) call "labile labour." Graduates, they argue, must now be "mobile, spontaneous, malleable and capable of being aroused by new vocational possibilities. They must also present as eager and ambitious, but, paradoxically, this ambition must be diffuse."

James (degree awarded under five years ago), like Nick, expected a sure-fire path from university into a job, specifically from his policing degree at Western Sydney University into the Australian Federal Police (AFP):

> There was a couple of jobs in the AFP that were pretty appealing to me, so I thought well I'll get the degree, the degree on like the description says that it's a good pathway to get into the AFP. I thought that'd be sweet, so I'll do that, and I'll get into AFP and I can worry about all that stuff later, yeah. How hard could it be?

James thought that academic staff would help him secure a graduate role with the AFP and was disappointed when they did not: "'Look, we're almost done. How do we go about getting our foot in the door with AFP?'. [Staff member] basically just said, 'Well that's up to you now. Give you something to think about.'" Like Nick, James attempted to understand why he was unable to seamlessly move from university into his hoped-for career. He argued that there was a rivalry between the AFP and the NSW Police Force, and because his course was affiliated with the NSW Police Force, staff were "anti-AFP." James also argued that the AFP were not helpful either: they instructed him to join a mailing list for advertised jobs. He waited months and months in the lead up to graduation and never received a single job alert. A cursory "google" of the search terms "AFP Graduate Program" does, however, bring up a wealth of information. The AFP's website has detailed instructions for applicants. Like Nick, James appears to be a "drifter" (Bathmaker et al. 2016)—unable to successfully navigate the graduate labor market. And, again, like Nick, James felt let down by the University, "I've really felt ripped off with the degree because at the start of it, it said it's a perfect gateway into AFP and it really wasn't. They had no intention of helping us get that position, they had no affiliation, they had no links. So yeah, that was a bit frustrating."

James considered taking his part-time job at a retail store specializing in electronics and music more seriously: "I had a job that I really loved and all the people that I was working with were awesome to hang out with." Yet, the part-time job was not feasible in the long term—it offered little opportunity for promotion:

> Will I be happier just pushing on with [retail work]? And at that time a lot of my mates from [retail store] had tried to go for bigger positions and had lost

out and ended up quitting, and the ones that were still there, they ended up just sort of settling with the spots that they were in.

James decided to pursue a career with the NSW Police Force the day of his graduation. He said there was only one other policing student at his graduation: "All the people that were doing the cops, they were gone." They had "gone to Goulburn" (the NSW Police Force Academy) after finishing the first two years of their degree.[3] Most students, once they realized that university was not required (nor necessary), headed "straight to Goulburn," asserting some agency in the face of credentialism, where they worked toward an Associate Degree in Policing Practice, which involved twenty-eight weeks on campus, followed by on-the-job training, and distance education courses. Only students intent on joining the AFP completed the three-year program:

> And me and this girl were just left at the graduation ceremony like, "What are you going to do?". "Well I don't know, what are you going to do?". And she decided like a week beforehand to join New South Wales. So, the day of graduation I put my application to New South Wales because I just didn't have any other option.

A policing degree is not a prerequisite for entry into the academy, and although it made James's transition into the Police Force easier, James perceives his degree as "wasted time" producing a deaccelerated future: "Like I would've had a house sooner, I would've had a bigger house because it would've been cheaper back then, I don't know. Rather than buying a house last year I could've done it four years ago." If James had his time again, he would do things differently. He would bypass university altogether:

> If I could go back and sort of tell myself how to handle the next few years, I probably would've just said, you know, "Work in retail for maybe a year or two and just have fun and waste money on cars and whatever else. And then when you're done with that, straight down to the Academy and just get it done and finish it and be done with it."

James's narrative, then, is one of regret, missed opportunities, and wasted time. Wasted time is, indeed, a measurement of class. Movement in the social space, Bourdieu (1985, 725–6) explains, is "paid for in work, in efforts and above all in time (moving up means raising oneself, climbing, and acquiring the mark, the stigmata, of this effort). Distances within it are also measured in time (time taken to rise or to convert capital, for example)." James's narrative, like those of others, demonstrates how working-class students are often reliant on universities for knowledge about labor markets, and this dependency—when combined with limited social capital—can work to limit social mobilities.

Adrijana's (first degree awarded over five years ago) story is a little different: after completing degrees in art history, she found casual work at an auction house. She said, "And you work essentially as a consultant [...]. Like you know making the catalogue, you're processing like anything that people wanted to sell. Like checking whether or not an artwork or whatever is genuine." The work was insecure, and Adrijana described it as a niche where only the wealthy can survive. Like Morgan and Nelligan's (2018) "creative aspirants" who were forced to recalibrate their aspirations in the face of economic insecurity, Adrijana's story is one of optimism followed by disillusionment, and, in Adrijana's case, swift disillusionment. So, she moved on. Adrijana decided to retrain as a secondary school teacher in Western Sydney. She said, "I felt like I was making the decision to go back into the real world"—a world for her that was "homely" (Hage 1997) and offered security (as discussed in Chapter 3). Since graduating, Adrijana has worked as a casual teacher, but she does not see her position as precarious. She compares the teaching profession to the art world, and sees the former as more meritocratic, more hopeful. She also compares her work situation to her father's and acknowledges her comparatively advantageous position. The comparison is not about job insecurity, but rather about the physicality of labor and incomes. Adrijana said, "I definitely don't feel like I need to work as hard as my parents' do. [...] Like I might be on a lower step at the moment cause I'm four years in but I'm still earning very good money compared to . . . like, I'm earning what my dad is after decades."

School teaching is, however, a relatively low-paid form of professional employment (DET 2018). Historically, teaching (primary school teaching, at least) has been female dominated, and the low pay is very much about its historical designation as women's work. Teaching has more recently experienced "devaluation," and the profession, in Australia, now has difficulty attracting high-achieving school-leavers (McGowan 2019). It is also important to recognize that until the 1970s, teaching was about as far as working-class women could progress socially. Bright young women from working-class backgrounds were awarded teaching scholarships and very few studied degrees like law (Anderson and Vervoorn 1983). This describes a long-standing process of homely mobility, perhaps in which teaching (and teacher's college) was the conventional pathway for talented young women. Working-class communities always needed teachers, and, for many, this was the practical limit of aspiration. Aspirations, as Bourdieu (2000, 217) has argued, are adjusted to what is possible: "Thus power (that is, capital, social energy) governs the potentialities objectively offered to each player, her possibilities and impossibilities, her degrees of empowerment, of power-to-be and at the same time her desire for power, which, being fundamentally realistic, is roughly adjusted to the agent's actual empowerment" (Bourdieu 2000, 217).

Cruel Attachments

Other participants were waiting to secure permanent work in their field: they were blipping in a "stuck" phase and experienced this "gap" as overly protracted. They remained attached to the promise of university, yet they were not like Bourdieu and Passeron's (1979 [1964]) participants who remained hopeful, still invested in the promise of their qualification. Bernadette and Courtney were not suspended in relations of "cruel optimism" (Berlant 2011). Cruel optimism, as mentioned previously, is, "the affective structure of an optimistic attachment [that] involves a sustaining inclination to return to the scene of fantasy that enables you to expect that this time, nearness to this thing will help you or a world become different in just the right way" (Berlant 2011, 2). It is a relation of "negotiated sustenance" that makes life viable (Berlant 2011, 14). Bernadette and Courtney's relation to the promise of university is instead what I call a "cruel *attachment*." What makes it cruel is that there is very little optimism or sustenance in their attachments. Bernadette and Courtney remain attached to the promise of university not because they feel particularly hopeful, but because they feel they have no other choice. Unlike Nick and James who perceive waiting around as wasted time, Bernadette and Courtney see moving on as potentially wasted time.

Bernadette and Courtney both trained as primary school teachers, and despite teaching being perceived as a secure career choice, they are still waiting to secure permanent work. While there are teaching shortages in regional and rural areas, the STEM disciplines, and special and inclusive education, Western Sydney has an oversupply of teachers (Deehan 2014; Rorris 2021). Bernadette (first degree awarded over five years ago), for example, was a high-achieving student who attended Penrith High (an academically selective school)[4] for Years 7 to 10 and Xavier College for Years 11 to 12, and completed a bachelor of arts and master of teaching (primary) at Western Sydney University. Bernadette has secured a short-term casual teaching contract, but she is unable to secure a permanent position. At the time of our interview, Bernadette described herself as "technically unemployed." She has a newborn baby and no job to go back to. Bernadette and her husband have had to move into her parents' home to save money, and her mother is disappointed. She also described being the "big joke" of the family: her brothers, who are both tradesmen, think it's funny that Bernadette has two degrees, no permanent job, and is worse off economically than any other member of their family. She said, "I sometimes cop a lot of flak about it." Like Sheree and Jessica, Bernadette's self-assessment involves a glance to proximate social relations, her brothers.

This self-assessment is one of "affective alienation" (Ahmed 2010, 41) from the promise of university and her family who find her situation both disappointing and amusing. Feeling affectively alienated produced feelings of shame-rage. Bernadette blamed Western Sydney University. She said she would never study at Western Sydney University again, despite enjoying her undergraduate degree. Bernadette questioned why she did not complete her degree at the University of Sydney or the Australian Catholic University (the latter is a preferred pathway into the Catholic schooling system). QILT (www.qilt.edu.au, accessed July 21, 2019) data shows that graduates of teaching from the University of Sydney (86.5 percent) and the Australian Catholic University (91.3 percent) do have better full-time employment rates compared to Western Sydney University graduates (73.4 percent)—though, as mentioned previously, "full-time employment" is not indicative of "graduate employment." Teaching graduates from Western Sydney University also earn far below the national average: $65,600 per year, compared to $75,000 per year (www.qilt.edu.au, accessed July 21, 2019). Bernadette said she chose to attend Western Sydney University because she had "lowered my expectations of myself. [. . .] Oh, you idiot." She described her postgraduate teaching degree as "crap." "Crap" because she only had six weeks' worth of practicums. "Crap" because it lacked prestige. "Crap" because it did not teach her how to program curriculum. "Crap" because it did not teach her classroom management skills. The list goes on.

Bernadette said that Western Sydney University means very little to her:

> I have a degree. Doesn't matter where I got it from, I just have it. You know, I don't feel any connection to the university. I get letters about UWS alumni stuff and I don't give a rats. I don't feel UWS gave me enough for me to give back. I don't think UWS connects enough with its students. I think it's too impersonal. So, you know, when they come looking for alumni donations, I'm like, "Get stuffed." And then they want people to come and talk to prospective students. You think, "Well no, I haven't got a whole lot of positive things to say about UWS." I had a good time at university because I made friends with people and I connected with some of the lecturers, but as an institution, hell no.

The university asks Bernadette to give, but Bernadette feels no mutual obligation to give back. She has very little to give in monetary terms, and because of this, she feels the university has not fulfilled its side of the promise—to provide quality teacher training and pathways into permanent work. The promise, here, is a contract. Bernadette paid for her course in both time and money, and she expects economic returns. The breakdown of the promise of university signifies a breakdown in the postwar social democratic contract of working-class embourgeoisement. Bernadette is ambivalent though and oscillates between positive and negative experiences: Western Sydney University as personal and impersonal, and her undergraduate degree as good and her postgraduate degree as bad.

Courtney (first degree awarded under five years ago) also completed a bachelor of arts and a master of teaching (primary) at Western Sydney University, and two years after graduation is still waiting to secure a permanent position as a teacher. Unlike Bernadette, who was a high-achieving student, Courtney described school and university as a "struggle." She did not have the required ATAR (university admissions score) to enroll in a teaching program at Western Sydney University, but with "bonus points"[5] was able to secure an offer. She said she was not "gifted with the smarts." I asked Courtney what she needed to do to get a permanent job: "I think it's just being in the right place at the right time." She explained that casual work may lead to permanent work, but that casual work was very difficult to secure. Most of her peers work casually, one friend no longer teaches at all (she is helping her partner run his business), and two friends were "lucky" to secure blocks of teaching: "Um one girl she got a 12-month contract straight out of uni [. . .]. Yeah but that was at her prac school as well. There's another girl [. . .]. She's got a part-time relief job in a school and then she still just works casual."

Courtney has only had one three-week teaching block and is only asked to work one to two days a fortnight. There is, however, a more formalized waiting list for permanent teaching positions in NSW government schools. Courtney said, "Looking at that I wouldn't get a job for like 34 years." She is waiting, anxiously. Waiting, here, is experienced as "unduly prolonged" (Pardy 2009, 195). Pardy (2009, 200) calls this "chronic waiting." Chronic waiting, she writes, "is that where considerable or prolonged time has elapsed between the original desire for something and its failed attainment" (Pardy 2009, 199). It produces feelings of hopelessness where the possible now feels too impossible: "I have waited so long; the object of my desire continues to elude me; the wait and desire are hopeless" (Pardy 2009, 200). Many teaching graduates do, of course, secure work and do not have to wait "34 years." Courtney, however, has average marks, no social contacts within schools, and has difficulty establishing contacts once she does secure casual teaching work.

Courtney said that her grandmother warned her about the difficulties new teaching graduates face: "Like my Nan used to say to me, when I was at, in my final year. She goes, 'Like I keep hearing stuff on the news about the lack of jobs.'" Courtney would tell her Nan that the staff at university said, "There's plenty of jobs coming," particularly as "baby-boomers" retired. She said, "I was always like, 'No, no, like I'll get a job straight out of uni.'" Her lecturers and tutors constructed Western Sydney as a region of great challenges but also one of great opportunity: "So, I'm like, 'The uni's told me I'm, you know, you're gonna get a job if you're willing to work in this area'. Which I am! We come from here! I would want to live here! Like I've got no problem with me working here." For Courtney, the promise of university is tied to the promise of the region as a place of opportunity—the site of a good life where there is room to grow, socially and existentially. Yet, Western Sydney, here, is also pathologized, *if you're willing to work in the area,* and Courtney is pathologized through her inability to secure permanent employment in a region where there is supposedly plenty of work *if you're willing to work in the area.*

Courtney is desperate to secure permanent full-time work and would like to leave her other place of employment, a supermarket, where she works casually:

> Alex: So, did you work at the supermarket through uni?–
> Courtney: Yeah, yep [laughs]. I'm still there! [laughs]–
> Alex: Yeah that's good–
> Courtney: No, it's horrible. I hate it. I want to go. I've been there 8 years now–
> Alex: Oh yeah–
> Courtney: So, I started in Year 10 and then . . . it's good, it's gotten me through uni and when . . . also, now when I don't have casual work, like I've still got the supermarket [. . .]. I'm like "Oh, I'm done." I need a full-time teaching job. Get me out of here! [laughs].

Courtney feels like she is a burden to her partner and parents. Courtney and her partner (who is an automotive electrician) would like to buy their own home, and Courtney feels that she is slowing them down. Courtney also worries that her $30,000 university debt will "hinder" them when they apply for a home loan: "I'm more worried about it now." Courtney's parents also built them a "granny flat" to live in while they save for a home:

> So, it's basically like a little house. Um, so my boyfriend and I moved in there at the start of the year. And then basically they've done that for us so we can save money for a house. Me not working, not saving as much . . . so I kinda feel like, like I'm not, like they've done all this, like they've put all this money into doing this, and I'm not really using it for what they want, like they want me to . . . they used them as like . . . instead of us having to go out and rent a place and spend ridiculous amount on rent, we can pay like $150 a week on board. And we can stay there and save as much money as possible. So yeah, I just feel like if I had a job [laughs] we'd be out of there quicker and then I feel like what they have done, like I'd actually . . . yeah. Like it's annoying in that way that I don't have a job.

Courtney's parents and partner do not understand why she cannot secure more work in schools. She said, "Yeah, like I've tried to explain to them [pause] that [pause] there's no jobs kind of thing [laughs]."

Courtney also fends off queries from friends and acquaintances who ask why she is "still at the supermarket." For example, an acquaintance in her partner's soccer team: "And one of the boys on his team . . . Oh, cause they asked if they were gonna go out that night but I had to go work at the supermarket. And one of his friends goes, 'Oh, are you still at the supermarket? Why aren't you like teaching?'" Courtney said she was teaching but that there just wasn't enough work: "And I was embarrassed then cause I was kinda like well I can't get a job like . . . I was kinda like . . . So, when people say it to me I'm kinda like, 'Aww' [laughs]." Although Courtney recognizes that the issue is structural, it is still personal, and as she says, it makes her "embarrassed." This relation between waiting and *feeling embarrassed* is what Pardy (2009, 196) calls "waiting-shame": "Shame is like waiting, in the sense that it is about the feeling of not being in the right place or right relation to time and others. It is linked to and experienced in terms of an ideal other (someone whom I am not)." Reay (2002) argues that a shame of overreaching and failing haunts working-class students' relation to higher education. For Courtney, a fear of shame is no longer a haunting experience but is, indeed, a reality. Shame, here, acts as a metonym for social domination.

Courtney regrets attending university: "Cause I feel like I was 17, I was like, 'Yeah, I've got this big dream! Yeah, I want to be a teacher!' And now I'm like, 'Oh'. And it's not exactly what I expected to be." The job itself is difficult, "It's a lot more paperwork to teaching." Gallop, Kavanagh, and Lee (2021), indeed, found that there has been a sharp intensification of teacher workloads related to policy changes, student need, technology, curriculum, data collection, compliance, and higher community expectations. Courtney was also "upset and angry" about her career prospects, although her pay rate as a casual teacher provides some consolation:

> I have like . . . not like a breakdown . . . I have . . . I was really like upset and angry and that a few weeks ago. And I was like, "why did I do this?!". And I said . . . I actually said to my mum, I kind of wish I didn't get that acceptance into uni because then I would have done something else and I'd have a job and you know. Even though I wouldn't have the opportunity an' like the money an' stuff coming in that I have now . . . I'd have a job. And you need a job to survive so yeah, I'm kinda in two minds about it . . . about whether or not it's kinda been a good idea or not.

Courtney, here, oscillates between having an opportunity and having a job. Her university degree, following Hage's (in Zournazi and Hage 2002) metaphor, works like an imaginary bank account that Courtney has but cannot access, though it does offer some consolation, particularly as she assesses whether or not going to university was a good idea. This opportunity, or hope, is both one of fantasy and surrender, and Courtney is ambivalent about what to do next: to hold on or let go. Economic realities and university debt, however, prevent Courtney from retraining for another career:

In a way, I'm kinda like, do I just do something else? But then I'm like, well I've already got this HECS debt. Do I go back to uni and increase that HECS debt to do something else that at the end of that I could be in the same position anyway or do I go to TAFE? And again, TAFE is also really expensive as well. So, I'm like do I do the same thing and still end up in the same position after that with no job?

Courtney remains attached to teaching not because she feels particularly hopeful, but because she feels she has no other choice: "I'm just kind of floating." To float is to drift. It is a relation of suspension. Like Morgan and Nelligan's (2018) "creative aspirants" who were forced to eventually recalibrate their aspirations in the face of economic insecurity, Courtney's story is one of optimism followed by disillusionment. But unlike Morgan and Nelligan's (2018) "creative aspirants" who opted for more "secure" careers like teaching (and, indeed, like Adrijana), Courtney has no room to move or at least feels like she doesn't. Bourdieu (2000, 221-2) explains that a sense of powerless waiting, "by destroying potentialities, prevents investments in [the] social stakes [that] engender illusions. The link between the present and the future seems to be broken." Cruel attachments, then, involve a relation to both the past and future as wasted time or potentially wasted time. There is very little agency here—increased consciousness and economic realities, for both Bernadette and Courtney, produce a radical disenchanting.

Reconfiguring Class Identities and Social Mobility

The research participants' discussions about jobs and careers are shaped by their positionings in their microcosms, their localized horizons of aspirations, and their family's trajectories, *where I have come from and where my family have come from*—their habitus. Class distinctions and classed self-assessments, then, are relational and proximal—and in the absence of a hoped-for career and job, a sense of social mobility may be reconfigured in ways that involve an assessment of the relational and proximal. Courtney, for example, talked about "feeling" middle class because she had traveled overseas, despite working at a supermarket and struggling to secure casual teaching work. Courtney's discussion about travel and "feeling middle class" emerged out of a comment she made about her grandparents being "working class." I then prompted Courtney to define what she meant by "working class":

> Um well, my Nan worked in a factory and my Pop worked for the water board back when it was in St Marys. There was like a big thing there. Yeah so, they worked every day and they struggled to pay the bills. So that's what I define as working class. People who work really hard but still cause they don't have good jobs. Like they're good jobs. They don't have well-paying jobs. That they struggle a bit more to pay for things and stuff.

Courtney said that her grandparents worked double shifts: they worked all day, came home briefly for dinner and to tend to their garden, and then headed back to work in the evening. She said, "They still struggled to pay the mortgage and like to pay for food and stuff. [. . .] So yeah, I feel that working class is people who are struggling even though they work really hard." I then asked Courtney how she would define her parents in terms of class. She said that her parents were "better off" than her grandparents, but with some hesitation described them as working class too:

> Like we've always had what we wanted. We've never really gone without, but we don't really have anything else. Like . . . like my mum sees all her friends and stuff . . . they go out on holidays like overseas and stuff. My mum's been to like Bali when she was like a teenager and that was it. Like but yeah, I feel like she's always wanted to go on a cruise, but they've never been able to afford it. Like stuff like that. We've never gone without, but we've never had those luxuries. Like extra. She's still trying to pay off the mortgage.

Overseas travel, for Courtney, constitutes an important marker of class distinction: of economic comfort and the accumulation of cultural capital. Courtney, like Jacklyn (Chapter 2), does not distinguish between differently classed forms of travel—travel to Bali and cruises in the Pacific Ocean are often ridiculed as "bogan holidays" (see, e.g., the "Things Bogans Like" blog: https://thingsboganslike.com/?s=cruise).

I then asked Courtney how she would describe herself in terms of class: "I think if I were to have a job and I was working like I would then be . . . I feel like I would then be a different class then. So, at the moment I'm working-class [laughs]." Travel, however, makes Courtney *feel* middle class:

Courtney: I do feel middle class maybe because I just travelled for two months–
Alex: Oh, good on you–
Courtney: So yeah, I have that luxury that my parents never had. So yeah, all the casual teaching that I did last year, I saved the money–
Alex: Yeah–
Courtney: My parents never had that opportunity–
Alex: Yeah–
Courtney: Neither of my grandparents. So yeah, maybe for that reason I maybe feel middle class.

Courtney's partner was not interested in overseas travel and decided to save his money toward purchasing their first home, so Courtney traveled alone to London, and from London she traveled around Europe "on Contiki," following the hippie trails of the 1960s and 1970s, and the grand tours of the Victorian era. This form of pre- or post-university travel, though increasingly mainstream, is still a form of class distinction, and Heath (2007, 100) argues that it "nonetheless remains strongly associated with more privileged groups of students in pursuit of horizon-broadening experiences." It is also becoming a means for graduates to gain a competitive edge in the labor market and "contributes to the creation of an attractive 'personality package' within the overall economy of experience" (Heath 2007, 100).

Overseas travel, something Courtney's grandparents and parents have not experienced, fits with a narrative of progress that Courtney has constructed—of each generation "bettering themselves." She said, "Like they were always wanting us to do better." Travel then, provides Courtney with a sense of upward social mobility in comparison to her grandparents and parents. Yet, Courtney said, "Like I've gone to uni and now I'm in a worse off position." Courtney thinks she is better off than her parents and grandparents, but she also questions whether she is better off or worse off having gone to university. This complex self-assessment demonstrates the messiness of class identity and self-perceptions of social mobility, and the ways that it is variously experienced and defined in relation to those near, jobs, careers, and leisurely pursuits. It also points to the ways different forms of mobility materialize and comingle: Courtney feels at once both socially and existentially immobile in relation to her teaching career (she is stuck waiting), and socially and existentially mobile in relation to the physical mobility of leisurely travel. Courtney is not one or the other, and in both instances her assessment involves a glance at her family. Class distinctions are, after all, relational, and this relationality, as I argued in Chapter 2, makes possible micro-mobilities within place, but it also makes possible feelings of both social and existential mobility and social and existential immobility in relation to others.

Conclusions

In this chapter, I have examined how the research participants differentially negotiated the graduate labor market in the initial period after graduation, particularly how they remained invested in, or divested from, the promise of university. The transition from university into graduate employment can be extended, and many graduates move into an insecure buffer zone while waiting to secure graduate jobs related to their qualifications. This insecure buffer zone is what I called the "graduate waiting room." I examined three different ways that the research participants experienced the "graduate waiting room"—that is, how they configured or reconfigured their mobilities in the face of "diploma inflation" (Bourdieu and Passeron 1979 [1964], 90). Some "persevered" and eventually found work (though not necessarily in graduate roles), others "moved on" to other jobs and careers, and some remained blipping in a "stuck" phase. The latter is what I called a "cruel attachment" to denote an ambivalent and critical relation to the promise of university. I also examined how, in the absence of a permanent job in a desired career, social mobility may be reconfigured in new ways. Courtney, for example, talked about feeling middle class because she had traveled overseas. She did, however, feel at once both socially and existentially mobile *and* immobile, pointing to the ways that these mobilities comingle and materialize in relation to different socialities and places.

I argued that what we chase is determined by our habitus:

> The things to do, things to be done (*pragmata*) which are the correlate of practical knowledge, are defined in the relationship between the structure of the hopes or expectations constitutive of a habitus and the structure of probabilities which is constitutive of a social space. (Bourdieu 2000, 211)

Aspirations are unevenly distributed, and investments are not subject to chance, but involve regularity. The social world, Bourdieu (2000, 215) argues, resembles a "handicap race that has lasted for generations." Working-class students are often reliant on universities for knowledge about labor markets, and this dependency—combined with the pull of home, limited and localized stocks of social capital, and spatial inequalities—can work to reproduce classed inequalities. "Moving on" and "persevering" can involve moving very little. The "gap" between hopes and reality was not without challenge, tension, and frustration, and unlike Bourdieu and Passeron's (1979 [1964]) participants who experienced it as a personal crisis, the research participants, for the most part, were critical of their degree programs and universities. Diploma inflation was questioned and challenged. However, while some of the research participants may have questioned these structural difficulties, it is interesting that none of the research participants (bar one) questioned and challenged the localized and proximate nature of their aspirations. This dimension of symbolic violence remained hidden. These proximal and localized aspirations are "no doubt one of the most powerful factors of conservation of the established order" (Bourdieu 2000, 231).

5

On the Social Gravity of People and Place

Introduction

In 2016, I attended my sister's graduation ceremony for environmental science at Western Sydney University. The keynote speaker was Mark Bouris, a self-made multimillionaire best known as the founder of "Wizard Home Loans," a company that sells the dream of homeownership to ordinary Australians. He is also known as the chiseled and charming host of two television series: "The Mentor," where Bouris helps struggling small businesses get back on their feet, and "The Apprentice," an elimination-style business competition made popular in the United States by Donald Trump. Bouris spoke about how Western Sydney University increases the standard of living in the region and how an increase in the standard of living increases happiness. He also spoke about the "knowledge economy" and the "ideas boom." He said, "There are exciting careers waiting for you. Science is the way of the future." The atmosphere was feverish with anticipation. The future seemed ripe for the picking. Bouris spoke about his own rags-to-riches story: his father was a migrant from Greece and his mother was of Irish-Catholic stock. His parents taught him the meaning of a hard day's work. His father worked day and night, and his mother, too, worked in the evenings, including a stint behind the bar at Bankstown's historic "Three Swallows Hotel." Bouris grew up in Punchbowl and attended school in Lakemba and Bankstown (suburbs of Western Sydney). He graduated from the University of New South Wales, and was later mentored by billionaire media moguls Kerry and James Packer (graduates of Cranbrook, not Cranebrook), who invested in Bouris's business, Wizard Home Loans.

Bouris sold Wizard Home Loans for AU$500 million only eight years after its establishment and now has an honorary doctorate—from Western Sydney

University—and his success story, the self-made westie, or the westie made good, functions as an allegory for Western Sydney University itself. Bouris, too, represents the older capitalist fantasy of the hardworking entrepreneur from humble beginnings. Bouris was beaming. Others were beaming too. His background was familiar, similar, tangible. He was, it seemed, one of us who became one of them. The chancellor then reiterated Bouris's words, "I really liked what you said about university increasing the standard of living and happiness in Western Sydney." Together, their words fed into the capitalist fantasy that equates upward social mobility with happiness. Bouris's words, however, do not quite fit into normative narratives of social mobility, which often entail leaving places like Punchbowl behind. I was struck by Bouris's insistence on staying in Western Sydney—after all, he didn't. He left Punchbowl and now lives in Watsons Bay, one of Sydney's most exclusive harborside suburbs, a stone's throw from the Packers in Bellevue Hill.[1] But Bouris's emphasis on staying in Western Sydney, like Deng Adut, was interesting, nonetheless. In this chapter, I attend to the notion of "staying" through an examination of the post-university experiences of the research participants. Bouris's claim that social mobility increases happiness is, however, only part of the story—there are both gains and costs.

As discussed in Chapter 1, scholars have written about the emotional costs of social mobility from worlds marked as working class into worlds marked as middle class (Bourdieu 2008 [2004]; Hoggart 2009 [1957]; Lawler 1999; Munt 2000). Most of this work is autobiographical, or at least informed by personal histories, and has documented the emotional difficulties associated with upward social mobility. Friedman (2015, 2016) and Friedman and Savage's (2017) recent research on social mobility, as I have also discussed, is particularly significant. They examine various types of social mobility—the painful and not so painful. Friedman (2016) found that social mobility is painful for those who experience *sudden bursts* of upward mobility. This is because they don't have time to adjust to their new circumstances. On the other hand, the experience of *slow-speed* long-range mobility is relatively smooth (mobility from routine work to professional and managerial occupations), as is slow-speed short-range mobility. Friedman (2016, 137–8) argues that those who experienced slow-speed short-range mobility "rebuff[ed] change," which at times meant "actively stunting one's own upward trajectory." Stunting and rebuffing involved staying put in one's place of origin, holding onto one's working-class identity, and maintaining relationships with people from similar backgrounds. Finn (2017a, 428), too, has examined this idea of stunting—what she instead calls "proximate relationalities"—and the ways "changing course," or letting go of career ambitions is "embedded and [becomes] meaningful within the context of personal life." Finn (2017a), however, examines how staying put may involve ambivalence—it is not necessarily psychologically smooth.

I move away from associated ideas of "stunting" and "loss" to think seriously about "staying put" within the microcosm of Cranebrook and its surrounding suburbs, the wider Penrith, and the wider Western Sydney. "Stunting" implies a failed transition and an emphasis on "rebuffing change" ignores the changes already experienced by these participants—they are upwardly mobile, after all. Rebuffing change and stunting, then, ignore the weight of micromovements and degrees of social mobility *within* microcosms. Short-range mobility, I also argue, is not always psychologically smooth, and following Finn (2017a) I explain that it can involve ambivalence. This ambivalence, however, is not only related to the experience of letting go and changing course—as it is in Finn's (2017a) work. Social and existential mobility *within* a microcosm can also produce a deep sense of ambivalence. I argue for the importance of attending to Bourdieu's (in Bourdieu et al. 1999a, 3–5) work on "positional suffering," which describes the effects of hierarchy and degrees of social mobility *within* microcosms. As mentioned in Chapter 2, out of the twenty-six research participants I interviewed, twenty live in Penrith, and only six now live beyond the LGA's borders. Three live close by in neighboring regions: the Blue Mountains, the Hawkesbury, and Liverpool. Three live further afield in the Hunter Valley of NSW, Brisbane, and London.

I begin by attending to the notion of "staying put" and demonstrate that Cranebrook and its surrounding suburbs can be a place of desire and the site of a good life. Staying put, for most of the research participants, involves degrees of mobility in place. This movement may be about "getting out and getting away" in place. It may also be about staying put from a distance. I then examine how social obligations and commitments—to both people and place—shape mobilities in place. The pull of home, I argue, involves both good feeling and bad feeling, goodness and violence, care and domination. I explore how parental critique shapes mobilities, particularly how relations of "faithfulness" (Simmel 1950) can pull one back to place and curb the experience of social mobility, but also simultaneously work to make these mobilities meaningful.

I then examine "vertical" (Hage 2000) relations of "gratitude"—of care and reciprocity for people and place, of "giving back" to Cranebrook and the Penrith region. I examine how gratitude can pull one back to place, but also have a "flow-on effect" and involve acts of exchange to others beyond Cranebrook. Gratitude, however, can have a taste of bondage: it may work to bind one to people and place, even when the good life is a site of disappointment. This chapter, then, calls for a rethinking of class mobility through an attention to the pull of place and degrees of mobility in place, mobilities that may be both social and existential, and involve ambivalence.

Staying Put?

As discussed in Chapter 2, the research participants' location in Cranebrook, and their relations to the different pockets of Cranebrook, within a "plurality of visions and divisions" (Bourdieu 1987, 11), affected their self-perceptions of mobility and visions of a good life. Class is, after all, produced and reproduced through processes of distinction that are relational and positional. Typically, class relationality and positionality are understood in larger spatial terms: doing well means deciding to live in a nicer suburb. Jacklyn's story, however, is one of escape *within place*. Jacklyn (recent graduate), whom I introduced in Chapter 2, sought material comfort and a form of recognition based on invisibility—of not being seen, in her words, as "Housing Commission scum." Home was a recurring motif throughout our conversation: having an unhomely home, her mother's desires for homeownership, and the experience of being homeless. And although Jacklyn's story is one of escape from Housing Commission, it's not explicitly about escape from Cranebrook. It's about movement within her social milieu. Jacklyn is now working as a nurse at a local hospital and has moved out of Housing Commission (in Cranebrook) into a private rental property located on "the other side" of Cranebrook. Jacklyn said, "So we say there's a good half of Cranebrook and a bad half of Cranebrook and now we live on the good half that's very settled." She describes the "other side" of Cranebrook as being a place where the residents "like they've got jobs there. Like proper people that respect themselves and take care of themselves and go to work and all that. [. . .] More working-class area."

Moving into a different pocket of Cranebrook constitutes a dramatic form of social mobility. Jacklyn said, "I feel proud [. . .] cause I've achieved so much." Yet, Jacklyn still has moments where she feels like "scum." She says her neighbor "Doesn't say hello to me. She just looks at me. Very snobby, very competitive." On one occasion, Jacklyn's neighbor accused her of attempting to steal her post. Jacklyn explained that the postman asked her to collect her neighbor's package, "Like I was only trying to be nice you know." I'm not sure why Jacklyn's neighbor is less than neighborly, but in Australia where homeownership has traditionally signaled respectability, those who rent can still be subject to stigma. Jacklyn also talked about how she still negotiates negative comments about "housos" (residents of Housing Commission) from acquaintances, and though these comments are not directed at her, they're still wounding. She said, "A lot of people put down Housing Commission, and I got quite a few of my friends come from Housing Commission areas, and we've grew up and got out of it and we've got jobs." Jacklyn's comment does not break the Housing Commission/jobless line, but it does attempt to break another line: the idea that "housos" will always be "housos."

For other participants, Cranebrook and its surrounding suburbs are also sites of desire where there is room to grow. Lucy (degree awarded over five years ago), who grew up in Werrington Downs and attended Cranebrook High School, described herself as a being a real "Penrithian"—a term used to describe someone who was born at Nepean Hospital. She "loved" growing up in Werrington Downs. Her family had a "huge backyard," and she spoke fondly about "playing on the street" as a child. Lucy studied nursing and midwifery at Western Sydney University, and after graduating found work at Katoomba Hospital, which is located an hour or so from her family home in Werrington Downs. She joked that Katoomba was too far from a McDonald's (the nearest one was in Blaxland in the Lower Blue Mountains, just fifteen minutes from Penrith). Katoomba was, in fact, too distant from her friends who lived in Penrith:

> Lucy: Whereas Katoomba like the socialness, like the reason why I had to get away from it, there just wasn't as much to do up there–
> Alex: Yeah and I guess because all your friends are down here?–
> Lucy: Yeah. And like some of them would come up every now and then but it was a lot harder, so like I sort of had to plan it. I'm like "Geez, you guys, like it's not that far away! I do this all the time."

Lucy came back to Penrith, "Yeah I moved away for a little bit, but I came back happily." She said, "I can't imagine living anywhere else." The accumulation of being, as discussed in Chapter 1, is about accumulating a sense of "being at home" in our environments (Bourdieu 2000, 147). It is a relation of conatus, "of a tendency to perpetuate themselves in their being, to reproduce themselves in that which constitutes their existence and their identity" (Bourdieu 1993, 274). Lucy said, "And like I would, you know, raise my children here kind of thing and it's just great." The notion of *conatus* allows us to think about the pull of home, not just the trope of flight.

Conatus does not, however, involve a passive inertia: it involves an active striving to persevere in one's being, and this may involve an active striving to enhance one's being. The "pull" of home is fundamentally related to the "push" of going forth into the world. Lucy talked about Penrith as being ideally positioned: it's a safe distance from the "fast and loud" city, but proximate enough too. It's a desirable base for the intrepid Sydneysider: "It's far away from the CBD but you know it's not like the Mountains; we're in between and so it's not that far to travel to go somewhere new, beautiful, exciting." Penrith isn't just well positioned for adventure but, for Lucy, always has something new to offer:

> Lucy: . . . the other week, like probably a month ago–
> Alex: Mm-hmm–
> Lucy: I hadn't been to Penrith Gallery–
> Alex: Like the Lewers?–
> Lucy: Like I knew it was in Penrith, but I didn't even know where it was. And then we were going out for like Sunday brunch and that's where we went. I'm like "Oh, my God! That's, that's this place?" And it's just on the other side of the river–
> Alex: Yeah–
> Lucy: So, I'm still finding out stuff about Penrith when I've lived here my whole life–
> Alex: Yeah. How nice is the Lewers Gallery?–
> Lucy: Yeah–
> [. . .]
> Lucy: And it's like "How can I have not been here before just to like chill and hang out," you know–
> Alex: Yeah–
> Lucy: The water is just across the road.

Penrith, here, embodies the twin-logic of the "city-as-centre and suburbia-as-home" (Symonds 1997, 69). It does not, in contrast to Symonds (1997, 69), exist outside these "spaces of modernity." For Lucy, Western Sydney, specifically Penrith, is an embodiment of "suburbia-as-home."

Lucy was proud to be a nurse, proud to have a degree, and happy to be back living in Penrith. Yet, toward the end of our interview, she explained that she works at a clothing shop—the same shop where she worked while studying. I was thrown, and I didn't ask her to explain why she no longer works in a hospital. She continues to identify as a nurse and spoke about her experience with pride:

> And like still now something will come up and I'll talk about something health-related and like it's like, "Oh, like I didn't know you knew that; I didn't know you were that smart." I'm like, "Yeah, I've got all this secret knowledge hidden away. I'm a nurse, like we're just as smart as doctors."

Though she was not particularly socially mobile, she was moving well, existentially.

For Hannah (first degree awarded over five years ago), Penrith is also a site of desire where there is room to grow, but for her, "getting out and getting away" within place involves "staying put" from a distance. Like Lucy, Hannah was deeply connected to the local area: she was raised in Cranebrook and later Cambridge Gardens,[2] attended Cranebrook High School, married her high school boyfriend, and purchased her first home in Cambridge Gardens. Hannah studied at Western Sydney University, from where she earned a degree of bachelor of arts with honors and a PhD. After completing her PhD, she moved to London for a postdoctoral research position. She said, "We just, um, pretty much sold the house, um, and just packed up and moved. So, we've gone from a big three-bedroom house, so we live in a one-bedroom flat in London." Postdoctoral positions are difficult to find, and staying put in Penrith, at that stage, was not an option: "Um, I think that's kind of . . . I don't know, I never really thought about it, but I just assumed that just because I'd done this PhD in Psychology that I had to do a research position, you know it's what I had to do." I asked Hannah about her plans for the future. Her plans loosely involve coming back to Penrith:

> Hannah: But it's . . . yeah, so I mean immediate future? Here, London, working, research. I've got some teaching coming up. Um, so, 10 years down the

> track I'll be back. I'll probably be back in Penrith (laughs). My husband is always, always, always, always looking up on . . . what is it called? Like, um, realestate.com.au–
>
> Alex: Yeah?–
>
> Hannah: Yeah, he's always on there looking for houses and stuff. So, I almost guarantee if you ask me again in 10 years I'll be in Penrith–
>
> Alex: Penrith? Yeah–
>
> Hannah: Um, and you know we'll probably have a house and we'll just be hopefully just travelling and working. I don't want to just keep doing stuff because I have to do it; I'd rather just, you know, make enough money to just travel and enjoy life–
>
> Alex: Yeah–
>
> Hannah: That's my goal.

Hannah's laughter after saying, "I'll probably be back in Penrith," is both playful and self-deprecating, and filled with affection for place. She is aware that mobility from Penrith to London and London back to Penrith is a jarring trajectory—a geographical and social movement, or rather a return, not conventionally associated with "making it," fulfillment, and a good life. As discussed previously, Western Sydney, unlike other suburban regions, is perceived to be a place where "modern subjectivity is denied." Symonds (1997, 84) explains, "the modern subject, in search of itself, must leave such places." This last point helps to explain the contempt hurled at the so-called aspirational, a term of derision used to describe residents of the west who have accumulated economic capital but have decided to "stay put" rather than move to the east. The aspirational is socially and existentially mobile in Western Sydney.

Like Friedman's (2016) participants, who experienced long-range mobility but remained proud of their origins, Hannah also talked about a sense of pride for place and people:

> Hannah: Um, I guess so. I mean it's where I was raised and it's part of who I am. I think–
>
> Alex: Mm-hmm–
>
> Hannah: Identifying as . . . I always tell everyone, you know, "I'm from Western Sydney, I'm a westie." I have this . . . I think I do have that westie pride through and through–
>
> Alex: Yeah–
>
> Hannah: Like not feeling like someone who grew up, you know, getting everything handed to me on a silver platter; like I worked for my stuff. You know?–

Alex: Mm-hmm–
Hannah: If I have a car and a house it's because I've worked my arse off for it–
Alex: Yeah–
Hannah: And I think that's kind of . . . I think we kind of have that collective sense of like "Yeah, we did this," you know? Um, so, yeah, I would definitely say it's . . . I'm proud of it. I would never hide the fact that I'm from Penrith–
Alex: Mm-hmm–
Hannah: I think, yeah, definitely a part of us.

Westie, as discussed in the Introduction, is "both a self-identifying and externally imposed category; it has both positive and negative connotations" (Simic 2008, 226). It may be a source of pride and pleasure or scorn and derision. It reflects a geographical and class identity, and is embedded in national mythologies of battlers, convicts, and outcasts (Simic 2008). Hannah's insistence that she's worked for her success, and her "collective" understanding of Western Sydney battling against the odds work to increase her pride in place, people, and self. Being a graduate of Western Sydney University also provides a sense of continuity and coherence, it anchors her in the region. She said, "But there was something inherent in going to the University of Western Sydney that you still kind of felt like a westie. [. . .] Going to UWS it's kind of . . . I don't know . . . a good way." This may not have been the case if she attended another university: "I think if I went to Macquarie or to Sydney University, I might feel slightly different. Or if I went to New South Wales or something." Western Sydney University, here, extends into Hannah's life and identity even after she has moved on. As discussed in Chapter 3, Western Sydney University folds into Penrith, but it also folds into what it means to be a "westie." For Hannah, it's kept her rooted in place, grounded, down-to-earth—and all *in a good way*.

Intergenerational Criticisms

The research participants' imaginings of a good life are not only shaped by classed visions and divisions that operate in Cranebrook and the wider Penrith but also by their social obligations and commitments—particularly to family. Elise (recent graduate) earned a bachelor of communications degree from Western Sydney University, and now works for a marketing agency in

Sydney's CBD. Elise is socially mobile but doesn't feel like she is moving well, existentially. Elise is proud of her degree and profession, but is ambivalent about her current job. The commute is long (over two hours a day), overtime is expected, and her colleagues often make wounding jokes about Penrith. Like Hannah, Elise is "staying put" from a distance. She is on the lookout for work in Penrith, "even like admin," work that does not necessarily use her qualifications:

> Elise: To this day, not that my employer's going to listen to this, but to this day, we are totally trying to get me a job back here. [. . .] And if I ever have a bad day, which to be honest is most of them lately, get stressed out, Dad will say, "Oh, you know, 'F' the city. You don't need to be with them. Come back." You know?–
>
> Alex: Yeah–
>
> Elise: Like he really wants me to work out here and we'll often get into like little arguments. And I'll say like, "No. Everything I've worked so hard for is out there. There's nothing here for me. I can't use my skill out here"–
>
> Alex: Mmm–
>
> Elise: Which I can in other ways. And so, he hates it. He really hates it and he calls them "pen pushers," "city slickers," "silver spoons." He hates it. And whenever I tell him that, "Oh, they bagged out Penrith today," he goes off! He just hates it.

Elise's father, as the aforementioned extract reveals, wants her to "come back" to Penrith. The city, for him, is undesirable and unsafe, and he believes Elise can have a better quality of life in Penrith. Her father, who works in metal fabrication, boasts about earning more money than "pencil pushers" in the city, but she is a "pencil pusher," and media and marketing work is located in the city. Elise wants to "come back" too, but is ambivalent and oscillates between "we are trying to get me a job back here" and "we'll get into little arguments." Elise is torn between the pull of home, the pull of her career, and their perceived incompatibility: coming back home involves letting go of her career in marketing. This experience is similar to Finn's (2015) participants. Finn (2015, 134) writes, "there was often a reluctance to move away from family and home in order to see a return on investments in HE, even though home was experienced uneasily and with a heavy dose of ambivalence."

Later in our interview, Elise talked about reorientating her visions of a good life. As Ahmed (2010, 31) argues, happy objects can become sites of "personal and social tension," and in these instances disappointment can lead to reorientation. Elise said, "I've realised that it's not all about like [pause] career. Like [pause] I always want to work hard and use my profession and things like that [pause], but it's about family as well and making sure you have a life." This act of reorientation, as Elise's pauses reveal, does not foreclose feelings of uncertainty but it does lead to a prioritization of certain happy objects (home and family) over others (career). This is the inertia of "faithfulness" (Simmel 1950). Faithfulness, as discussed in Chapter 2, describes the forces that ensure the continuation of social relationships. Faithfulness, or the "inertia of the soul," is what gives continuity to life (Simmel 1950, 380). It also gives continuity to the social world: "Without this inertia of existing sociations, society as a whole would constantly collapse, or change in an unimaginable fashion" (Simmel 1950, 381). The homing disposition of the habitus, here, reorients Elise's movements in the world (Bourdieu and Wacquant 1992). Conatus, then, is not just about striving to persevere in one's own (individual) being. It is also about the perseverance of social relationships—being is, after all, social and relational.

Parental criticisms also work to shape Rachael's (degree awarded over five years ago) mobility. She is a graduate of Cranebrook High School and Western Sydney University, works as a nurse at a local hospital, and lives in Cranebrook. Her husband left school in Year 10 and works as a storeman at a paper factory. She said, "My husband's got a good work ethic. Like, he'll go to work rain, hail, shine. And he's not earning a lot of money, but he doesn't, it doesn't bother." Her husband's pay check, she later reveals, is becoming problematic. Rachael would like to buy a larger house, particularly as their young family grows, but house prices in Cranebrook have increased. She might not be able to "stay put" for much longer. They're now considering moving to Goulburn (a large country town closer to Canberra than Sydney). She explained: "With Goulburn, I think you can work in Goulburn Hospital, go to Canberra, a few other . . . Queanbeyan I think someone said? There's another. [. . .] And they're screaming for nurses in the country."

Rachael's mother-in-law is not happy and thinks Rachael should be content with what they have: "So, they're like, 'Why do you want so much? Like we had such a simple life' [. . .]. 'You people nowadays, you want your holiday, you want your nice car, you want your nice house. Just be happy with what you've got.'" Her mother-in-law would prefer Rachael to stay home and look after her newborn baby. Working and motherhood, for Rachael's mother-in-law, are incompatible. I am reminded of Skeggs's (1997, 71) participants (white working-class women) who inverted class distinctions and claimed moral superiority over middle-class women who "farmed out" their children. Happiness for Rachael's mother-in-law is a contentedness, a valuing of what you already have, that involves a gendered investment in family, not an investment in career, nor a desire for more and more material comforts. This is a critique of aspiration, of wanting too much, but unlike the criticisms hurled at Western Sydney's "aspirationals" for wanting too much of the wrong things (a bigger house, a better education, etc., *in Western Sydney*), this critique involves questioning those who do not want what Western Sydney already offers, no matter how humble the home.

Rachael planned to work full-time after having her baby, but later decided to work part-time, meeting her mother-in-law halfway. She said:

> When before I had my son, I said to them, "I'm going to come back to work full-time. Like I love nursing that much." But after having my son I'm like, "I think part-time work would be good." It's good to have time with him and like to be a nurse too. Like, I went to university, I don't want to let that go. That sort of part of me, yeah, I'm a mum but I'm also a nurse. [. . .] Yeah, whereas my in-laws are like, "That's not . . . you're the mum. You stay at home with the kids. You have the babies." I'm like, "No, no." I will have a few kids and then once they're grown up, I want to go back to work and then maybe I'll go into management or education or something like that. But at the moment, just part-time work, have a few babies and then see where it takes us.

Like Hannah, who holds onto the promise of Western Sydney University long after graduation, Rachael also holds onto its promise, *I don't want to let that go*. A degree, here, works to validate shifts in gendered expectations. She can be both a mother and a professional. Neoliberal discourses of aspiration are, as Allen (2013, 762) has argued, deeply gendered: "The figure of the young woman has played a symbolic role in the reproduction of neoliberal ideologies, where young women have been subject to an intensified gaze, constructed as reflexive, entrepreneurial, mobile and 'successful' subjects of the twenty-first century." This is, of course, complicated by the role of the mother: maternal involvement is central to these discourses of aspiration. Mothers have the role of "releasing the 'potential' of their child" (Allen 2013, 762). These competing gendered expectations—of being a mother and a professional—are in tension, particularly for young mothers. Guilt and judgment loom large.

Gratitude to Place

Like faithfulness, gratitude can pull one back to place, and in Chapter 2 I examined how gratitude can produce a pressure to follow parental desires. Gratitude, as I have explained, emerges from the act of receiving a gift (Simmel 1950). The very act of receiving a gift is the recognition of one's humanity, and "this act in its consequences, subjective meanings, and psychic echoes, sinks into the soul through gratitude" (Simmel 1950, 388). Gratitude is productive: it moves the receiver to reciprocate the exchange. It is, however, more than the act of reciprocation: "gratitude actually consists, not in the return of a gift, but in the consciousness that it cannot be returned" (Simmel 1950, 392). Simmel (1950, 388) writes, "It is an ideal bridge which the soul comes across again and again, so to speak, and which, upon provocations too slight to throw a *new* bridge to the other person, it uses to come closer to him." Acts of gratitude are not limited to "horizontal" relations between individuals but may also be "vertical" relations between individuals and society—or, between people and place, the research participants and Cranebrook. Vertical relations, Hage (2000, 32–3) writes, are not "only obligations to towards other people [. . .] but obligations towards our own sociality and our desire to live communally" (Hage 2000, 32). They, "exist when people are committed not so much to each other as to the relation they have to each other" (Hage 2000, 32). Vertical reciprocity, then, is the "idea of a relation to the relation" (Hage 2000, 33).

Adrijana (first degree awarded over five years ago) talked about "giving back" to Cranebrook: the place and the people. As discussed in Chapter 2, Adrijana spoke about Miss Harris, who was proud of the area, had an ethic of care for her students—which included encouraging Adrijana to go to university—and importantly nurtured a sense of belonging to place. At the "horizontal" level, Miss Harris offered, Adrijana received, but Miss Harris, through her gift of care, also exchanged recognition *for* Cranebrook, an act of exchange that Adrijana then reciprocated to her own students. Adrijana's first job teaching was at Cranebrook High School, where she worked alongside Miss Harris: "Well I went to Cranebrook first cause I dropped off my resume, and that was the first one I dropped off, cause it was comfortable and familiar." Adrijana described her teachers as being, "very happy to take me—they were excited!." She spoke about having the students "trust" because she was one of them: "They straight away sort of like dropped their guard. Like yeah, I was one of them." In a series of role reversals, she saw herself in the students and also saw herself in Miss Harris:

> Adrijana: Like something just didn't–
> Alex: Yeah–
> Adrijana: Wouldn't let them add those two together [going to university]. [. . .] I think that's why Miss Harris was such a big influence–
> Alex: Yeah–
> Adrijana: Cause I think I was them. Not really knowing anybody else in the local area–
> Alex: Mmm–
> Adrijana: And so her always talking about it–
> Alex: Yeah–
> Adrijana: So much–
> Alex: Yeah really important–
> Adrijana: Mmm.

Like "Miss Harris," Adrijana would tell her students that she went to university and that they could too. This is an act of gratitude: of throwing a "new bridge" to students at Cranebrook High School and reciprocating the gift of care that was initially offered by Miss Harris (Simmel 1950, 388). Adrijana has since worked at two other schools in Western Sydney: one in Casula and one in Penrith. She also sees herself in those students. Speaking about Casula High School, where there were "heaps of Serbs like me," she said:

> I felt like I could relate to a lot of the kids because so many were like migrants. So, I was like, "You know who went to summer school at Cambridge?". Giving them like the booklet like, "Look through it. [. . .] You'll travel when you get to uni, you know?". "What are you going to do at uni?". So, I think it really like impacted in the way that I sort of interact with kids as a teacher.

Gratitude, then, can be a generous affective relation, one that involves *throwing a new bridge* not only to Cranebrook but to others *outside* Cranebrook—not necessarily to the person or place that initiated the act of giving. "Exchange," Sennett (in Wise 2009, 37) argues, "turns people outwards."

Jenny (first degree awarded over ten years ago) also encourages students at Cranebrook High School to go to university. She said, "I'm always a great believer in, you know, you can make something of yourself *and* you can make something of where you live." She talked about making something of *herself* in Cranebrook and the wider Penrith region. Jenny holds a bachelor of economics/bachelor of law degree from Western Sydney University and a master's in corporate and commercial law from the University of New South Wales. After graduating, she worked as a paralegal in Parramatta and later at an "ivory tower law firm" in Sydney's CBD. The "ivory tower law firm" was an "old boys' club," and Jenny described being ridiculed for her postcode and being told to buy a nicer suit. She talked about "giving it back" to her city-based colleagues: "I give it back to them and say to them, I'd rather live on my 700 square metre block out in Western Sydney than in your shoebox [. . .]. Sorry, but I've got a barbeque and a blade of grass [laughs]." She left the "ivory tower law firm" not long after she married: "I knew it wasn't going to be conducive that if I had children [. . .] being on the train three hours every day." Rather than move closer to the city, she decided to "stay put" in Penrith and find a job locally. She wanted to raise a family where there was room to "throw a soccer ball around." This represents a gendered form of homely mobility: the desire to start a family also pulls her back to place. Jenny is now "the only female [specialization] lawyer in Penrith." She said, "I'm actually quite proud of where I've come from and where I've gone."

Jenny talked about *making something of where you live*. This is more than the self-betterment discussed earlier but involves a collective sense of betterment for Cranebrook and its surrounds. Jenny's sense of belonging to Cranebrook (the place, the people, the school), the care she received from her teachers, but also the discouragement she received from one teacher in particular (discussed in Chapter 2), created feelings of faithfulness and gratitude toward Cranebrook High School, to students like herself at Cranebrook High School, and to students at other schools like Cranebrook. Like Jenny's Year Coordinator, who told her to ignore others discouragement and disparagement (see Chapter 2), Jenny also tells students, students like herself, not to listen to teachers who say their dreams are unrealistic. Jenny, to paraphrase Simmel (1950), "throws" a "bridge" to others through her work with a university program that aims to encourage participation in higher education:

Um, and, and I do go back to the University [Western Sydney University] now and I speak to a lot of the kids from around this area because the University has that Fast Forward program. Um, and they've got the program where all the kids come in from Years 10, 11, and 12 and they hear about a career in law or a career in policing, and then you get some of these people together. That's one of the first things I say to the kids, especially the ones that come from, you know, Chifley College, Cranebrook High, Cambridge Park High, Kingswood High, or any of those. And I say to them, don't let anyone ever tell you that you can't do anything. [. . .] I actually, when I first started doing the Fast Forward program, Cranebrook High was actually in the audience and, um, I told the story about the teacher that told me that I'd never make anything of myself. I love talking to the students because, and I swear at them, too, and they love it because I'm real, I'm normal, I'm down-to-earth, I'm not their teacher. And, you know, I said, you know, I'd love, I'd love to go to the teacher and roll my practising certificate and shove it right up, right up her arse [laughs]. Um, the kids, the kids actually then take, take note, and they actually listen, I think, a little bit more.

Jenny prides herself on being like her audience: she may now be a lawyer, but she is still *real, normal, and down-to-earth*. Recognition, here, is not just one way. The audience's recognition of Jenny as one of them, evinced by their laughter and engagement, provides her with a sense of continuity and coherence. Jenny's gratitude to Western Sydney University is, however, at odds with Bernadette's resentment toward the university (as discussed in the previous chapter). Bernadette struggles to reproduce her version of a good life (homeownership and full-time employment) in Penrith, and so has no desire to reproduce the promise of Western Sydney University and reciprocate its offering, like Jenny does.

Gratitude to people and place is not, however, just about good feeling. It can involve ambivalence. Pat (first degree awarded over ten years ago), who works in Human Resources (HR) for a large multinational company, attended Cranebrook High School and lived in the Housing Commission pocket of Cranebrook with his mother and sister for "a good 27 years." Pat now lives in Leonay (a more affluent suburb in Penrith). Pat's partner, who grew up in South Penrith and is also a first-generation university student, thinks Pat is too fixated on "being from Cranebrook" but for Pat, "that's where I am from [. . .]. My mum's still there, you know. [. . .] It may be different, you know, if I only lived there for five years and mum, yeah, wow, mum's still in the same house

I grew up, you know." Pat talked about life in Cranebrook's pocket of Housing Commission as being "a" version of "normal":

Alex: What was it like for you growing up there?–
Pat: Normal–
Alex: Normal? Yeah–
Pat: Uh, it's now that I look back that I go, "Oh, it wasn't normal"–
Alex: Yeah, oh, that's interesting–
Pat: Uh, when you don't know any different–
Alex: Yeah–
Pat: It's normal–
Alex: Yeah, yeah–
Pat: It was my normal–
Alex: Yeah, yeah–
Pat: Uh, where growing up, out of my friends the odd friend was the one who had a mum and dad. All of my other friends were from sole parent families, you know? So, what was it like? It was normal for me, um, but you know it's now, uh, well, especially now having a professional job, having [a daughter] when I was 23. Out of all of my friends I was the last one to have a kid uh, but so, I thought I was quite normal and maybe even a little bit older to be having kids–
Alex: Yeah–
Pat: Yeah, so now working professionally everyone goes, "Wow! You're such a young father." You know, "You're 35 and you've got a teenager. Wow!"–
Alex: Yeah–
Pat: My colleagues at 35 are now just having kids.

As Pat recounted his experiences at school, at university, and in the workplace, he listed all the people who have helped him along the way—people who have offered bits of advice here and there, emotional support, academic support, and professional support. For example, his modern history teacher "went in to bat" for him when he was trying to convince the school council to let him repeat Year 11. There was the "older guy" he worked with at a supermarket, who said, "If you're ever midway through something, hang in." There was another person who said, "Like the hardest thing is starting. You've got your habits, you've got your behaviours, and when you start studying or you start anything new, adjusting or fitting in until you find your new norm is difficult." There was his former partner, who cared for their daughter while he was working and studying: "My ex did a lot more than I gave her credit for at the time."

There was his "professional mentor," who suggested he have elocution lessons: "I'd say 'free' for 'three' [...]. He's like, 'You're a smart young man but people switch off when they hear, you know, the lack of elocution. So, it doesn't matter what you're saying people will judge by how it sounds.'" There was his mother who typed his handwritten assignments on her 1970s typewriter. There was the time he met celebrity lawyer, Chris Murphy, who said, "If you get into law you've got a job as a clerk in my office." And there were his university lecturers, who were "very helpful."

Remembering their acts of care, Pat experienced feelings of gratitude—a gratitude that led to mutual obligation. Pat insisted on paying for our coffee. This was not unusual. It happened after a few other interviews. In all the other cases, I convinced the research participants that I would pay the bill, and so I did. They had given and it was my turn to give back, to show my gratitude in a very small way. This time, however, Pat paid the bill—a coffee each. He said, "I'm paying it back." We departed. Later that evening, Pat sent me a text. He wrote: "Thank you. Really appreciate you listening and taking an interest. Feeling very grateful for all of the people who have helped me over the years." Gratitude, however, can produce ambivalent feelings. Toward the end of our interview, moments before it ended, Pat questioned if the journey was worthwhile:

> Alex: What's it like looking back on that all, hey?–
> Pat: Yeah, it's an odd thing to do looking back. It's almost, just, I've done it, I've just–
> Alex: Yeah–
> Pat: There's been times, you know, where honestly, I think some days, I would be happier still living in Cranebrook on the dole, you know?–
> Alex: Yeah–
> Pat: Living that lifestyle. Like there's a lot of days where I think I would be happier doing that.

Given Pat's career success and gratitude to those who helped him along the way, this may seem like a surprising statement. Social mobility, as I outlined earlier, can be an emotionally costly process and one that is particularly fraught. Indeed, as Pat recounted all the help he has received, he was also reminded of all the times he had to learn the normalities of different settings—his "new normal." Learning the normalities of different settings was a reminder of some challenging experiences. There was the time he wore a tracksuit to his first day of university, and no one else was wearing a tracksuit. There was the time he wore jeans to his university graduation, and no one else was wearing jeans. There were some awkward dining experiences:

> Pat: Uh, I remember I had been there three months and had my first, well, it was just dinner, but it was dinner in North Sydney and having to use cutlery at a restaurant where it's like $80 (AUD) a head versus $10–
> Alex: Mm-hmm–
> Pat: I freaked and I'm there spilling and knocking–
> Alex: This is like out of the Titanic when–
> Pat: Everything–
> Alex: They have all the cutlery–
> Pat: And literally. And getting uptight and nervous and knocking over glasses and just not feeling comfortable. And then going out for, again, Cranebrook boy going out and, "Oh, we'll go out for lunch; we'll go to Chinese," and all of my colleagues are using chopsticks and–
> Alex: Oh, my gosh! I know–
> Pat: I've never used chopsticks before and going, like just feeling like socially awkward–
> Alex: Yeah, yeah, totally–
> Pat: Yeah, and in saying that, now I fast-forward 10 years ago, 10 years later, I'm great with chopsticks.

Developing new ways of being in the world and losing embodied aspects of the self to "move up" has meant that Pat has lost those embodied aspects of the self that connected him to his friends, particularly his speech. Like Hoggart (2009 [1957]), he finds himself chafing and oscillating between different social worlds:

> Pat: I get the judgement back the other way–
> Alex: Yes–
> Pat: Uh, and even people I grew up with, and you talk about language, you do become a product of your environment. If you start using different words you know, like I've had mates actually give it to me over my choice of language back the other way and it's–
> Alex: Oh, yes–
> Pat: Yeah, that's life, you know.

Pat's gratitude and his disappointment are turned into relations of sacrifice and deferral: "But I've got this opportunity and people would kill for it and so it would be kind of a little bit wrong if I just threw it away [laughs]. Am I right?." This involves a glance to those less fortunate than himself, to people he knows suffering material poverty, what Bourdieu (1999a, 4) calls "*la grande misere*." This is the conditionality of gratitude, and it simultaneously works to bind Pat to Cranebrook and his career. Simmel (1950, 393) writes, "A service, a sacrifice, a benefit, once accepted, may engender an inner relation which can never be eliminated completely, because gratitude is perhaps the only feeling which, under all circumstances, can be morally demanded and rendered." Disappointment, then, does not necessarily lead to reorientation. Gratitude can have a "taste of bondage" (Simmel 1950, 393). Pat then explained that it is also his job to give his daughter a better life than he has had. For Pat, then, there's no turning back. Like Elise, Pat is socially mobile but his sense of "moving well," of existential mobility, is ambivalent and tinged with "*la petite misere*," or ordinary suffering—the feeling of inferiority or alienation within, and, in Pat's case, between, microcosms (Bourdieu 1999a, 4).

Conclusions

In this chapter, I have examined relations of "staying put," or being oriented back, to place—to Cranebrook and the Penrith region more generally. "Staying put," I argued, is not necessarily psychologically smooth. Nor is upward social mobility in Western Sydney a straightforwardly "happy" journey—as Bouris's graduation speech would suggest. I argued that working-class places, places like Cranebrook, can be sites of a good life, not just places to be left behind, but places of agency and self-expansion. I attended to micro-mobilities *in* place, not just mobilities between differently classed worlds. Mobilities within microcosms, or "getting out and getting away" *within place,* can be significant emotionally and relationally and may constitute forms of existential or social mobility. This is what I call "homely mobility"—a term used to describe degrees of mobility in place and the social gravity of place. I examined how affective relations shape mobilities, particularly how one's positioning in Cranebrook, within webs of class distinctions, structure visions of a good life, and how one's social commitments and obligations to family and to Cranebrook—both vertical and horizontal exchanges—also shape mobilities. Relations of faithfulness and gratitude, I argued, have gravity: they can pull one back into place, give continuity and coherence to social life, and work to reorient social mobilities, or, in Pat's case, bond one to a "good life" that is a site of social tension.

Homely mobility within the microcosm of Cranebrook is a relation of domination—not just care (as I have argued previously). It is a form of symbolic violence—albeit a "gentle" and "disguised" (Bourdieu 1990 [1980], 133) form of domination. Homely mobility works to reproduce ways of being while providing room to grow but within limits. It, "makes absolute 'all or nothing' differences out of infinitesimal differences," and makes life worth living because, "the adjustment of expectations to real chances tends to limit subjective pretensions to the immediate neighbourhood" (Bourdieu 1990 [1980], 137). Jenny's movements, for example, away from the "ivory tower" law firm in the city and back to Penrith—to the site of her good life—offered a sufficient horizon for her aspiration, but her return home has the indirect effect of reinforcing the insulated privilege of the people and workplace she left behind (and in Australian society more generally). And as Pat's experiences have demonstrated, the effects of symbolic violence cannot easily be surmounted, but they can linger and persist through our social bonds, like the duty of gratitude. Bourdieu (2000, 180) explains:

> It is quite illusionary to think that symbolic violence can be overcome solely with the weapons of consciousness and will. The conditions of its efficacy are durably inscribed in bodies in the form of dispositions which, especially in the case of kinship relations and social relations conceived on this model, are expressed and experienced in the logic of feeling or duty, often merged in the experience of respect, affective devotion or love, and which can survive long after the disappearance of their social conditions of production.

Cranebrook, indeed, hangs heavily on Pat's shoulders and his experience of upward social mobility has left him existentially unsettled.

Conclusions

Libido Academica, Libido Homeliness

Education, as discussed, is a leitmotif of our times—it is a dominant way that hope for a good life is produced and distributed (Boltanski and Chiapello 2005 [1999]). This book examined these themes of hope, social mobility, and higher education, specifically in relation to the experiences of working-class students and graduates from Cranebrook and its surrounds in outer Western Sydney—a place, itself, that contests and embodies various elements of the Australian Dream. I chose to focus on Cranebrook for several reasons. First, Cranebrook is the most economically diverse suburb in Penrith and few residents have tertiary qualifications (as discussed in Chapter 2). Second, Penrith is perceived, from the outside, to be a marginal place on the peripheries of suburban Sydney, but within Penrith itself Cranebrook is seen to be the least desirable suburb (as discussed in Chapter 2). As Pat explains (Chapter 2), the Housing Commission estate becomes a metonym for Cranebrook and, by extension, for the wider Penrith. These webs of class distinction that operate in Cranebrook and the wider Penrith provided fertile ground to explore the micro-politics of class and social mobility. Penrith is also my hometown and its familiarity, as well as my own social networks within it, I assumed—naively—would ease the burden of fieldwork.

Recruiting twenty-six participants was a relatively straightforward exercise but my relation to the research field itself, over time, became too "thick and sticky" (Hage 2005, 465). The familiar was both productive and destructive. Hage (2005, 465) writes that ethnography immerses you in certain social relations, and the more you become involved in the social field, the more you are subject to its gravitational forces, forces that "make it very hard for you to remove yourself from it" (Hage 2005, 465). My life, for several years, has been consumed by this book. I have found myself—strangely—at funerals thinking about "homely mobility" in relation to the eulogized lives of loved ones. I have found myself analyzing the trajectories of family and friends as they move through university and beyond. I was just twenty-three when I began this research: my partner was still studying and working part-time at McDonald's, and both my sisters were also studying and working casually at our local Chinese Restaurant, the same restaurant where I also worked while completing part of this research. Unlike Hage (2005), I am of the research field. I am already subject to its gravitational forces and analyzing the lives of the research participants—people like myself, my partner, friends, and family— produced a deep sense of ambivalence.

Researching a topic "close to home," spatially and socially, can be suffocating. Writing about class and processes of social reproduction can be particularly unsettling (Bourdieu 1988 [1984]; Hoggart 1990; Skeggs 1997). Skeggs (1997, 15), in her book, *Formations of Class and Gender*, has documented the difficulties she faced writing about the experiences of working-class women:

> What I did not anticipate was how emotional the research process would be. The chapter on class was excruciating to write as I realized how I, too, had strongly invested in respectability when intimidated at university. I was forced to remember how I had lied about my mother's and father's occupations because I was scared to be recognized as inferior. I naively (over) "did" femininity, in a way I had never done before, in an attempt to generate distance from sexuality. My capacity to accrue educational and cultural capitals, however, has only increased my sense of marginalization. I am more aware of the "right" standards and knowledge and also of the judgements made of those who do not fit.

Bourdieu (in Wacquant and Bourdieu 1989), as I explained in the Introduction, argues that a smaller social distance between the researcher and the researched can reduce some of the symbolic violence inherent in the research encounter, but it also produces greater discomfort for the researcher. This is because objectifying the other involves objectifying oneself. This process, for me, was especially difficult because it involved objectifying not only my investments in home—what I call my *libido homeliness*—but my investments, or *illusio*, in higher education, resulting in a wearing down of what Bourdieu calls a "*libido academica*" (Bourdieu in Wacquant and Bourdieu 1989, 19). Demystifying the *illusio* of one's world can be paralyzing. You need *illusio* to move through the social world like "fish in water." A life without it becomes a state of violent predictability, a kind of sleepwalking, a life less hopeful.

This is, I argue, another one of the defining tensions of Bourdieu's sociology. Sociology, for Bourdieu (in Wacquant and Bourdieu 1989), is about denaturalizing and defatalizing the social world—that is, uncovering processes of symbolic domination for both the researcher and the researched. On the one hand, this relation can be one of goodness. It is an "extremely powerful instrument of self-analysis which allows one better to understand what he or she is by giving one an understanding of one's own conditions of production and of the position one occupies in the social world" (Bourdieu in Wacquant and Bourdieu 1989, 3). This process can produce possibilities for transformation, revolution even. But this relation can also be one of violence. It can produce a "radical disenchanting that makes this social world in which we must continue to struggle almost unliveable" (Wacquant in Wacquant and Bourdieu 1989, 22). One always haunts the other, and I found the latter—at times—demobilizing. A colleague, in an attempt to 'help me out of my stuckedness, once asked, "How close are you to being 'scum'?" "Scum" was a word Jacklyn used to describe herself and others (Chapter 2). His words, asked out of care, were an attempt—I think—to transition me from what Wacquant (in Wacquant and Akcaoglu 2017, 60) calls a "confused understanding of the heart" to "a rational grasp of the argument." But, as I learned from Pat (Chapter 5) and Bourdieu (1999c [1993], 629): "Producing awareness of these mechanisms that make life painful, even unliveable, does not neutralize them; bringing contradictions to light does not resolve them."

Researching a topic close to home also produced another anxiety: I worried about representation and doing violence to the research participants and their stories, a worry that stemmed from my own relation to processes of objectification. Bourdieu (1999d [1993], 1) in *The Weight of the World*, asks: "How can we not feel anxious about making *private* words *public*, revealing confidential statements made in the context of a relationship based on a trust that can only be established between two individuals?" I was haunted by a scene from one of my favorite novels, *Cloudstreet*, set in Perth (Western Australia) in the period during and after the Second World War (Winton 1991). Rose Pickles, a young working-class woman, dates a middle-class university student, Toby, who is also an aspiring author. Toby invites Rose to accompany him to a dinner party with book publishers, who—at the party—mistake him for another upcoming author, "Raven," and inquire about his upcoming work. Rose's family and neighbors become fodder for Toby's fiction:

> You should let us have some comic work, Raven, said George Headley. Toby's giggle mounted another sentence: well, well, well, actually I've been thinking of some very comic, funny, funny, material inspired only today. Rose tell them about where you live. Tell them about the lady in the backyard who lives in a tent. Tell them about the slow boy you used to love. Rose shook in surprise. (Winton 1991, 302)

Bourdieu (2000, 189–90), too, explains that those who are caught up in a game have little interest in seeing it objectified. Explaining Bourdieu's model of capital to friends and family—alone—has produced its fair share of frustration, shame, and anger. A family member once stormed out of a room when I attempted to explain our family's social class. Objectifying our accumulations of symbolic capital (or lack of), particularly social and cultural, produced denial, discomfiture, shock even. I came across as ungrateful, pretentious, and "bitchy." I avoid using what Winton (2013–14, 24) calls the "c-word" at the family dinner table now. When friends and family ask, "How's the research is going?" I hesitate; I change the subject. Class hurts. Skeggs (1995, 201), indeed, has described how her participants thought the original title for her research, *An Ethnography of Working-Class Women*, was deeply "offensive." She then renamed the manuscript *Formations of Class and Gender*.

It is, however, difficult to reduce the violence of objectification, yet I developed the concept of "homely mobility"—partly—in an attempt to do so. It is an attempt to understand the lives of the research participants, their hopes and mobilities, from within their microcosms. The tension in this project has, indeed, been between the goodness and violence of homely mobility. As discussed in Chapter 1, "home" comes from the root word *doma*: "to do violence; to tame" (Benveniste 1973 [1969], 248). Homeliness is not just a relation of goodness. It is entangled with "symbolic domination," a domination that is often disguised, concealed, and rarely revealed—what Bourdieu (in Bourdieu and Wacquant 1992, 167) calls "symbolic violence." This book has examined the micro-political, the goodness and violence of homely mobility, to better understand broader macro-political processes and the reproduction of social power—that is, how people make meaningful a world that makes them. I developed the concept of "homely mobility" to make sense of peoples' mobilities beyond a focus on structural inequalities, capital accumulation, and social mobility. I argued that while it is important to understand how education systems do or do not create the conditions for social mobility, mobility means more than social mobility. Moving beyond the existing work in the field, I examined how the research participants understood their own mobilities: their visions of a good life and what they perceived as "moving well," what Hage (2009) calls "existential mobility." So, rather than focus on university as a means to becoming middle class, I instead examined how university may become a means to a class-differentiated good life.

Nevertheless, the development of "homely mobility" wasn't just a response to my methodological preoccupations. I developed the concept of "homely mobility" out of my engagement with my research material and the existing scholarship. The project was initially guided by the following primary research question and four secondary research questions, but these questions shifted during the data production phase:

- Primary research question: What does an investigation into the experiences of young people who are first-generation university students from a geographically stigmatized suburb in Western Sydney reveal about place, identity formation, aspiration, and social mobility?
- Secondary research question one: How do the young people perceive themselves (learner identities and/or class identities) and the places they inhabit (the university and their geographical positioning in Sydney), and how does this impact on their attitudes to their peers (in the university community and their residential community) and studies (motivations and engagement)?
- Secondary research question two: How do the young people talk about their decisions to attend university, course selection, and the university choice process, and what do these conversations reveal about discourses of aspiration (personal, parental, governmental)?
- Secondary research question three: How do the differences between universities (elite and new university, location, etc.) impact on young people's experiences at university and constructions and reconstructions of their identities?
- Secondary research question four: How do the young people discuss their aspirations (fulfilled or unfulfilled) and talk about the value of their university qualification one to five years after graduation? Do institutional differences between universities and locational differences impact on the graduate experience and social (im)mobility?

As I began speaking to the participants, my analytical focus moved from class identity and social mobility to the accumulation of being and questions of a good life, and from mobility between working-class and middle-class worlds, to degrees of mobility within and between worlds. This marked a move away from a preoccupation with the sociological dimensions of Bourdieu's work, to a dual engagement with the sociological and philosophical dimensions of his work. I then developed the term "homely mobility" to refer to *micromobilities in microcosms—mobilities that may be social and existential, involve goodness and violence, and various degrees of integration in place*. I use this term to conceptualize how place and class shape aspirations and experiences of social mobility.

Bringing It Back Home

In Chapter 1, I reviewed the scholarship that informs the concept of "homely mobility." I demonstrated the uses and limits of the existing work and then previewed the book's argument. I began by demonstrating the significance and continuing relevance of Bourdieu and Passeron's (1979 [1964] and 1990 [1970]) scholarship on the reproduction of symbolic power in education, culture, and society. Contemporary Bourdieusian scholarship focuses on the struggle to accumulate symbolic capital, class disidentifications, and the emotional costs of social mobility. It does little, however, to think outside the binaries of social mobility and immobility, working-class and middle-class "fields," and transformations of, or investments in, working-class or middle-class identities. This work is a-placial and a-mobile. I then reviewed a small and emerging body of work associated with the "mobilities turn" in higher education that moves beyond the bounds of Bourdieu's field and a preoccupation with social mobility, to examine alternative mobilities and the significance of place (Donnelly and Evans 2016; Finn 2017a, 2017b; Finn and Holton 2019). This work, however, backgrounds structural inequalities—the pull back home, I argue, involves relations of domination.

To examine relations of symbolic power *and* the culturally specific ways people accumulate being, I turned toward and developed the philosophical dimensions of Bourdieu's work to understand how university becomes a means to a class-differentiated good life. I used the philosophical dimensions of Bourdieu's scholarship to inform a sociology of reproduction—something Bourdieu, himself, did not do. Indeed, the philosophical dimensions of Bourdieu's work are neglected in his own work on higher education. In Bourdieu's later philosophical work on home, he theorizes the pull of home—particularly in relation to habitus, *illusio*, and conatus—but he does not *empirically* examine the pull of home, and the accumulation of being, as an embodiment of structural inequalities embedded in the practical dimensions of everyday life and, importantly, place. And in his much earlier empirical work on home, specifically the Kabyle home, home is simply a place of socialization. On the other hand, in Bourdieu's empirical research on reproduction, specifically his scholarship on the French education system, cultural capital and habitus are used to examine processes of reproduction within the field of higher education itself. Bourdieu, in his work on home or education, then, does not examine the ways education becomes a means to a class-differentiated good life, and how visions of a good life are shaped by the push and pull of home (people and place).

The philosophical dimensions of Bourdieu's work are, too, absent in contemporary sociological scholarship on higher education—both in Bourdieusian-inspired scholarship and the emerging mobilities scholarship. Using Bourdieu's scholarship on the accumulation of being, I argued that we need to move beyond the field of higher education to explore what is meaningful within the research participants' microcosms. I developed the term "microcosm" to describe geographical places, specifically Cranebrook and its surrounding suburbs. Social spaces and fields are, after all, embedded in physical places. Microcosms, I explained, have elastic geographical boundaries and various scales of existence. I then demonstrated that we need to attend to degrees of existential and social mobility within microcosms. Both fields of study—the Bourdieusian and mobilities scholarship—conceptualize placial and social mobility in binary terms: moving up involves moving away from working-class places. This book, then, departs from these studies to consider micro-mobilities in microcosms.

In Chapter 2, I examined aspirations for university: how university became a means to a good life and how Cranebrook and the wider Penrith are sites of that good life. Contemporary Bourdieusian scholarship has examined how "the ultimate goal of [. . .] working-class students [. . .] is to actually enter the ranks of the middle class" (Lehmann 2009b, 643). But, as Lehmann (2013) points out, a focus on class escape can unwittingly pathologize working-class lives. Indeed, the trope of class escape doesn't leave much space for the possibilities of attachment to working-class lives and places. I instead argued that "working-class places" may be more than sites of stagnation and may indeed be sites of a good life—sites of possibility for social mobility. I began by profiling Cranebrook: its location, population, various pockets, and the research participants' perceptions of place. I demonstrated that class is produced and reproduced in "webs of material *and* symbolic ties" (Wacquant 2013, 275, emphasis my own) that operate in microcosms, as well as the wider social space, which make possible micro-mobilities within place. Class is diversely emplaced, or rather place is diversely classed. The research participants' self-perceptions of place, thus, affected their visions of a good life. Processes of class distinction can be experienced as more profound within microcosms and that this works to make possible degrees of mobility in Cranebrook and the wider Penrith.

The research participants' visions of a good life were shaped not just by their positioning in Cranebrook, Penrith, and Western Sydney but also by (a) embodied class realities and desires for greater economic comfort, and (b) the push and pull of family and teachers—an entanglement of social obligations and commitments, such as faithfulness and gratitude, shame and recognition. The accumulation of being is, indeed, a relational accomplishment. I showed how teachers can play a crucial role in shaping (or limiting) aspirations, particularly how they can nurture a sense of belonging to place and emplace a sense of hope in Cranebrook, but also how they can produce a defiant sense of belonging to place. Hope, I demonstrated, is not just relational, but emplaced too. I argued that the research participants' families not only pushed them toward particular futures, but they also functioned as representations of other possible futures—representations that worked to fuel ambivalence toward university as a means to a good life. Some participants, for example, ruminated on "the road not taken," such as becoming a manager at McDonald's or becoming an electrician. University, then, does not straightforwardly involve desires for class escape and escape from place. University is a means to a class-differentiated good life.

In Chapter 3, I examined how the research participants came to feel "at home" and "recognised" at university. I demonstrated that the notions of "class habitus," "institutional habitus," and "middle-class field" do not adequately capture the varied experiences of socialization and varied capacities to act in particular settings. I argued for the importance of attending to "degrees of integration" (Bourdieu 2000, 160). Habitus, Bourdieu (2000, 160) explains, "is not necessarily adapted to its situation nor necessarily coherent. It has degrees of integration." I began by making a case for the importance of attending to placial degrees of integration: how a sense of feeling "at home" in Penrith produced a sense of fit at Western Sydney University's (WSU's) Penrith Campuses. "Home" can, indeed, become a resource for homemaking at one's local university. Placial degrees of fit involve architectural and environmental fit but are also dependent on recognizing the people who populate a place as "one's own." The placial is, indeed, classed, raced, and gendered, and so on. Recognition, I demonstrated, involves processes of misrecognition, inclusion, and exclusion: it is about struggling for, and turning toward, what is homely, and effacing difference (what we are not, where we do not belong, the unhomely). Fit is, however, a precarious accomplishment. It is temporal and involves processes of recognition and misrecognition at various scales of existence—at the level of the setting, microcosm, subfield, and field. I argued that it is crucial to attend to Goffman's (1990 [1959], 32) notion of a "sense of one's place" in a setting to understand the situatedness of recognition, but it is also crucial to attend to Bourdieu's (2000, 241) notion of a "sense of one's place" to understand broader processes of symbolic violence and the uneven distribution of symbolic power. WSU, I argued, is always dangerously close to being misrecognized.

Furthermore, in contrast to existing scholarship (Reay et al. 2010), I demonstrated that the experience of feeling at home at one's local university is not necessarily a passive withdrawal from the world. Attending one's local university may involve the accumulation of being, such as scholarly accumulations, as well as the experience of "cultural enrichment" (Hage 1997, 136). I also examined how a sense of "at homeness" provided some of the research participants with the confidence to move out of their comfort zones. Feeling at home, as Noble (2015, 36) has explained, is "central to both a sense of self and to the possibility for future action." Though what constitutes getting out of one's comfort zone is unevenly distributed: for Adrijana that meant attending the University of Sydney and the University of Cambridge, but for Emma it meant attending the Parramatta Campus of WSU, not Penrith. Comfort was also experienced ambivalently and ambiguously and was both sought after and railed against. The gap between expectations and experiences may produce a sense of satisfaction, and a continuum of comfort-discomfort-comfort can become a *project* or a conscious aiming at the future. Yet, there are limits to the elasticity of horizons. A sense of social discomfort can ultimately pull one back to place. Hage (1997) explains that a homely space is one that is open for opportunities, whereas an unhomely space is like the lap of a possessive mother (or father), claustrophobic. I argued that the "mother's embrace" is both possessive and provides opportunities for transcendence. Like a spring, it can launch one forward, and pull one back—forcefully.

In Chapter 4, I examined how the graduate labor market was differentially negotiated by the research participants. The graduate labor market is increasingly competitive, and many graduates are left waiting to find full-time employment in the period after graduation. I called this period "the graduate waiting room." Waiting is a classed relation: movement in the social space and distances within it are measured in time. This chapter, thus, examined "waiting" as a period of forced suspension between graduation and securing desired forms of graduate employment. Bourdieu and Passeron (1979 [1964]), many decades ago, argued that victims of diploma inflation—those graduates who are left waiting—either remain invested in the promise of university, or that they disinvest from its promise and experience personal criticism and crisis. The former mode of attachment—remaining invested in an object whose realization is impossible but is considered to be a possibility—is similar to Berlant's (2011) notion of "cruel optimism," and scholars have likened the contemporary education system to one of cruel optimism (Reay 2017; Sellar 2013). Following Bourdieu and Passeron, I examined strategies of compensation, but I argued that not all attachments to the promise of university are relations of cruel optimism, nor do all disinvestments lead to personal criticism and crisis.

I began by examining three different ways the graduate waiting room was negotiated. In the first instance, participants "persevered" in the face of setback and eventually found employment, though not necessarily in graduate roles. "Moving on," on the other hand, involved making meaning from an alternative career path. These participants did not wait around, nor did they know how to (they did not know how to "play the game"). Others maintained what I called a "cruel attachment" to the promise of university. A cruel attachment is a relation toward the future that involves very little hope and very little sustenance. This relation is one of radical disenchantment: it involves a demystification of the social magic that disguises the symbolic violence of the education system. This exposure does not produce change and transformation but affords feelings of hopelessness. I then examined the experiences of one participant, Courtney, who reconfigured a sense of social mobility in the face of immobility through touristic travel and through an assessment of her proximal relations. Not all graduates, however, were left waiting, and some participants were able to move swiftly into graduate roles related to their qualifications. These participants used their localized accumulations of social capital to secure work, and their horizons of aspirations were, for the most part, local too.

In Chapter 5, I examined relations of "staying put," or being oriented back, to place—to Cranebrook and the Penrith region more generally. In contrast to contemporary scholarship on the experience of social mobility, I argued that "staying put" is not necessarily psychologically smooth. Nor is upward social mobility in Western Sydney a straightforwardly "happy" journey. Following Bourdieu's work on "positional suffering," I explained that we need to stay attuned to hierarchies and mobilities within microcosms. Small-scale changes within one's microcosm may be significant—emotionally and relationally. Most of the research participants "stayed put" in Cranebrook but "staying put" involved degrees of mobility in place, "getting out and getting away" in place. I returned to the arguments developed in Chapter 2 and demonstrated that the research participants' mobilities and visions of a good life are shaped by their positioning within their microcosms and by their social obligations and commitments to family and place. Drawing on Simmel's (1950) work, I examined how relations of "faithfulness" and "gratitude"—both vertical and horizontal—can reorient one's movements in the world and, in this instance, back to Cranebrook and its surrounds. This is the homing disposition of the habitus and involves relations of conatus. This is not a passive inertia, but an active striving to enhance one's being. The "pull" of home is fundamentally related to the "push" of going forth into the world. Homely mobility, then, works to reproduce ways of being while providing room to grow, but within limits. These relations have gravity and can bind one to a "good life," a life that can become a site of social tension, of good feeling and bad feeling, care and domination. Gratitude can, as I demonstrated, have a taste of bondage.

Cranebrook, Penrith, and Beyond

Penrith, the broader site of this study, has transformed considerably since I conducted my fieldwork. The world is, indeed, the result of endless construction and homely places can become unhomely over time. Penrith's environmental and architectural transformations are often obscured and diminished by those of nearby towns, such as Parramatta, where waves of migration, combined with intensive demolition and redevelopment, have rendered the landscape kaleidoscopic and unfamiliar (Castagna 2016). Recently, I was reminded of how much Penrith has changed while re-reading an older article on Western Sydney (Mee 2002). Mee (2002, 342), as discussed in the Introduction, argued that Western Sydney was valued as a "suburban home" because of its housing affordability, community spirit, spaciousness, and environment (and because it was much quieter than the city). Residents indicated that "higher population density" would be one of the most important issues over the next decade. Mee (2002, 342) explained that this was beginning to cause concern among residents, particularly those in Penrith who were fighting against the development of an airport at Badgerys Creek (on Penrith's peri-urban periphery) and a housing development on the old ADI site in Cranebrook. Residents were concerned about the destruction of bushland, pollution (noise, air, and water), and believed it would "negatively impact on children" (Mee 2002, 342).

In the years since Mee (2002) wrote her article, the ADI site has been controversially cleared and developed to make way for two housing developments, one of which is Jordan Springs (as discussed in Chapter 2). Jordan Springs is sometimes referred to as "Little India." Just over 30 percent of its residents were born overseas, and 7.4 percent were born in India (atlas.id.com, 2019). Though this percentage is relatively small, in Penrith it represents a significant shift—particularly in a region that is both whiter and blacker than the Sydney average. Badgerys Creek has also been cleared, and a 24/7 airport and aerotropolis are currently under construction. Penrith's landscape is being remade as it prepares for first take-off. Many older homes in its city centre have been bulldozed and replaced by apartment blocks, and its main arterial roads—as I write this book—are being widened to accommodate increased traffic congestion. The Northern Road, the road I use to get to Kingswood Library (WSU), is currently closed (a bridge is being dismantled). Before commuting to the library today, I checked a local citizens' page on Facebook to monitor the road closure, and many users wrote comments that bemoaned the recent changes to the area: Penrith was no longer "Penrith," and they expressed nostalgic desires for the "old" Penrith, as well as desires to move elsewhere—to areas like the "old" Penrith. I am interested to know how the research participants feel about these transformations. Is Penrith still a homely place and site of a good life?

I have followed some of the research participants from afar—as they make waves in the local press. Jenny, for example, has now opened her own law firm in Penrith and has attracted attention for "doing things her way." Her business model is different from the traditional "ivory tower" law firm she left behind. This book has primarily focused on the pull of home to examine the ways social worlds are reproduced, but future research could examine the duality of reproduction and transformation differently—that is, how working-class graduates, particularly those with deviant trajectories, "change the game" in local circuits of business, commerce, government, and schooling, and how their strategies open potential space for transformation (however small). I would also like to reinterview those participants who maintained "cruel attachments" to the promise of university: Where are they now? I write this question with a heavy heart. I, too, am near to the graduate labor market and have a keen awareness of hope's dark side. My father—a fitter-welder who spends his days in the steamy belly of garbage compactors and tugboats, or on workshop floors, in the breakdown lanes of motorways, or on construction sites, repairing trains, trucks, and cranes—is getting older, and years of hard labor have not been kind to his body. He is working as hard as ever—something his friends, who are winding down, do not understand: "I told them it's because I want you guys to have something one day." I understand the parental debt felt by Courtney.

I have, however, learned a lot more from the research participants than the purely sociological: throughout this journey, their words of practical advice have kept me keeping on. As Pat said in Chapter 5, "If you're ever midway through something, hang in." I am grateful for his wisdom—wisdom passed to Pat from a friend, and from Pat to me. Gratitude, as discussed, is a generous affective relation. Simmel (1950, 388) writes, "It is the ideal bridge which the soul comes across again and again, so to speak, and which, upon provocations too slights to throw a *new* bridge to the other person, it uses to come closer to him." But, here, like Pat demonstrated, and indeed Adrijana too (Chapter 5), *throwing a new bridge* can involve acts of reciprocation that involve others *outside* the initial relation. Gratitude can turn people outward (Sennett in Wise 2009, 37). When I almost gave up on this project, one of my colleagues reminded me of my ethical obligation to those like Pat. I needed to "do justice to and affirm the lives of those participants who entrusted me with their stories." Pat and my colleague's words of advice, which I am grateful for, become something of a mantra. They also reminded me of the social power of gratitude and faithfulness: even if we lose *illusio* in a game, our affective investments toward others can pull us back and pull us in. Faithfulness and gratitude are, indeed, the invisible threads that tie society together (Simmel 1950). They allow the coexistence of a heaviness of being (*illusio*) and lightness of being (*apathy*). *Illusio*, as I have demonstrated, involves ambivalence, degrees of gravity that ebb and flow, and pull and web in competing directions.

Policy Recommendations

The policy recommendations I offer are modest in scope and politicians, policymakers, and scholars have variously made similar recommendations for decades—regionally, nationally, and internationally. For example, Whitlam's "quality of life" agenda, which I discussed in the Introduction, continues to be relevant for Western Sydney. Against outsider and critical understandings of the region, Whitlam recognized that Western Sydney, for its residents, could be the site of "a good life." Decades on, "a good life," for the research participants, also involves "staying put" in the region, but Western Sydney continues to be spatially disadvantaged and its residents continue to experience a poorer "quality of life" than their neighbors in Sydney's east. This means, as I have shown, that not everyone can reproduce their version of a good life. For Whitlam, all Australians, no matter where they lived, should have access to the same social, cultural, and economic opportunities: "Equality and quality of opportunity, equality of life and more quality in life, go together" (Whitlam 1969, 2). And quality of life, Whitlam (1985, 3) wrote, "depends less and less on things which individuals obtain for themselves and can purchase for themselves from their personal incomes and depends more and more on the things which the community provides for all its members from the combined resources of the community." If we want real and lasting reform, we cannot focus on widening participation alone, but we need to take a regional and structural approach to the redistribution of opportunity—as Whitlam once did.

Since Whitlam's time, of course, the policy landscape has radically transformed from social democratic forms of governance to neoliberal forms of governance. The Dawkins Reforms in the 1980s, as discussed, abandoned Whitlam's visions for higher education and transformed the operating conditions of the sector from one of semi-equality into one of wild competition for funding and students (Marginson 2007). The Dawkins Reforms also transformed some Colleges of Advanced Education (CAEs) into universities, such as WSU, and these newer universities have struggled to accumulate the prestige and recognition attached to Australia's much older universities, such as the Group of Eight (Watkins 2020). And according to Whitlam (2004, 1–2), the "plan to turn CAEs into universities achieved the reverse of turning too many universities into CAEs." Equalizing opportunity must now involve redistributing recognition between universities so that a degree from one university isn't worth more than a degree from another. This means safeguarding the most disadvantaged institutions against processes of educational segregation that result from wild competition. This "big policy" recommendation could be described as utopian—yet, as the past shows, a return to a more equal system where universities are fairly and sufficiently resourced is possible.

There are, as also discussed, difficulties finding graduate opportunities in Western Sydney, and as Elise's experiences show, relations of faithfulness and gratitude to people and place can pull one back to place, give continuity and coherence to social life, but simultaneously work to reorient or curb social mobilities. We need to ensure that all Sydneysiders have equal access to professional employment opportunities. This may become easier for residents of Western Sydney in the wake of the Covid-19 pandemic: lower levels of migration may result in less competition for regional jobs and working from home may remove some geographical barriers to employment (O'Neill 2020). All levels of government have, as also discussed, recently prioritized jobs growth for Western Sydney—for blue-, white-, and pink-collar workers—through the development of an airport, an aerotropolis, and various other initiatives to create a thirty-minute city. But, as O'Neill (2020, 15) argues, "detail is lacking" and "each of these ventures carries risk." It is also sometime—

decades perhaps—until these job opportunities become available. Creating more jobs closer to home is no easy feat, and O'Neill (2020) also questions whether the aspiration for creating a cluster of professional jobs in Western Sydney is a realistic one—particularly when firms are reluctant to relocate from Sydney's CBD and inner city, and when they do, they will likely bring staff with them. He suggests that investing in public transport from Western Sydney into Sydney's CBD and inner city may instead be the solution:

> If there is genuine economic reason why large concentrations of professional services jobs are unlikely to be formed away from the CBD, then this impediment needs confronting and resolving. Perhaps government intervention can create the circumstances for growth away from Sydney's centre—as is the aspiration for Parramatta and the aerotropolis. However, if professional services firms can't be suburbanised, or seeded or grafted into specialist zones away from Sydney's centre, then investment in expensive public transit infrastructure is essential so that Western Sydney's emerging class of professional workers have access to jobs. The worst outcome would be to uphold the promise of a jobs-rich Western Sydney economy, with the assembly of an expectant labour force in greenfields residential suburbs, only to arrive at some future year, say 2036, and find that the jobs promise was an illusion. (O'Neill 2020, 17)

We also need to demystify the implicit strategies that operate in higher education and the graduate employment market, such as how to navigate the first year of university at an elite institution, or how to find a permanent teaching position in a primary school. We need to make those strategies explicit for all students and graduates—and where appropriate to career advisors, schoolteachers, and academics too. We also need to promote a plurality of post-school pathways—not just trades (as Jenny's experience reminds us), and not just university (as Nick's experience also shows). All post-school pathways should be seen as equal, legitimate, and important. While we should legitimize all post-school pathways, it does need to be acknowledged that the rewards associated with different pathways are unevenly distributed and "choice" is class differentiated and class differentiating. How many students at Cranbrook (in the east) will pursue an electrical apprenticeship? How many students at Cranebrook High School (in the west) will pursue law at Sydney University? Australia, like most nations around the world, is now seeing dramatic increases in wealth amongst high-income households and stagnant levels of wealth amongst the poorest (Adkins et al. 2021; Piketty 2014; Savage 2014), and so legitimizing and equalizing all post-school pathways also needs to involve a greater democratization of wealth.

Final Comments

It seems fitting that I write the final lines of this book from the Kingswood Library at WSU. The library sits on high ground. Its western side overlooks suburban Kingswood, South Penrith, and the Blue Mountains. It's a familiar view. Perched on a nearby hill is my old primary school, Mary MacKillop. From where I sit, I can pinpoint its playground: the foliage of an old Moreton Bay Fig, the stuff of childhood fun and fantasy, sits in my purview. My own mobility in and around the Penrith region, thus far, has been homely too. Homely mobility has a queasy intimacy. While it does seem fitting to end this book at Kingswood, it seems odd to end on this note, on this site in particular. The library's eastern side produces a different kind of queasiness, a discomfort related to radical change not continuity. It overlooks the Werrington escarpment—the site of the Mulgoa's camp when "white fellas" first arrived, stole the land, and renamed Muru-Murak after a place in the Cumberland of their distant motherland. Thinking about homely mobility and the social gravity of people and place inevitably involves a relation to stolen land—a colonial violence not just a state violence related to the uneven distribution of symbolic capital, but a violence of erasure and exploitation, a relation of very little goodness.

Notes

Introduction

1 Whitlam has something of a cult following, and, to my knowledge, is the only Australian prime minister who is also the namesake of a band, *The Whitlams*.
2 The Australian Dream is the dream of suburban homeownership (Gleeson 2006).
3 The "30-minute city" is the idea that residents can reach their nearest metropolitan center/cluster, strategic or large local center using public transport and/or walking within thirty minutes.
4 McCarthy Catholic College is a systemic Catholic school in Emu Plains, not far from Cranebrook. Catholic–Protestant sectarianism was rife in Australia until at least the early 1970s, and the Catholic community established their own church-run schools, while Protestants attended government schools. Historically, systemic Catholic schools were seen to be inferior to government schools but today—at least in Penrith—are seen, by some, to be "private schools." Visually, Catholic-school uniforms are "smarter" (blazers, ties, winter uniforms, summer uniforms, leather shoes, etc.) than those of the government schools in the region (polo shirts, tracksuit pants, sports shoes, etc.). When I attended McCarthy, only a very small handful of students had parents who were university educated. After school, most of my peers completed trades or entered office work—few enrolled in a university course. Since graduating in 2007, McCarthy has now become a "Trade School"—that is, students can complete a trade alongside the Higher School Certificate (HSC).

Chapter 1

1 There is a wide and contested body of work on "community," but I draw primarily on Hage's definition.

2. Hage draws on these arguments to write about whiteness, national belonging, and the uneven distribution of hope in Australia.

Chapter 2

1. "Deng Thiak Adut," https://www.youtube.com/watch?v=buA3tsGnp2s.
2. "Australian" ancestry describes those with Anglo-Celtic ancestry whose ancestors have lived in Australia for generations.
3. All the subsequent statistical information, unless otherwise stated, comes from profile.id.
4. I only interviewed one participant who identified as Aboriginal (Shannon). My sample, then, is whiter than the Cranebrook average.
5. The Blue Mountains are just to the west of Penrith, South-East Queensland is a ten-hour drive north, and the Central Coast is a two-hour drive north.
6. Including most of my paternal family who left Toongabbie for Wyongah. My Nan and Pop named their new home on the Central Coast "Toongabbie," after the suburb in Western Sydney they left behind, complete with a large sign made out of timber and horseshoes. Another home in their neighborhood was called "Girraween," after another suburb in Western Sydney. They too had a large timber sign mounted to their home.
7. The Holden Commodore is an iconic Australian car associated with white working-class masculinity.
8. Big W is a discount department store, and Lowes is a discount clothing store.
9. The "bogan" has been compared to the British "chav" but, as Rossiter (2013) explains, they are not the same thing.
10. It is interesting to note that Cranbrook's alumni include the Packers and Fairfax's (Australia's wealthiest families), as well as the geographer, Yi-Fu Tuan, and public intellectual, Craig McGregor, who is known, amongst other things, for his commentary on class in Australia.
11. These anxieties of proximity and threats to property value have been documented by Gwyther (2006) as one of the major motivating factors for relocation to Master Planned Communities.
12. Cronulla is a beachside suburb in South Sydney.
13. Centrelink provides social security payments and services to Australians.
14. St. Marys Senior High is a state school in St. Marys, a suburb located on the eastern fringes of Penrith.

Chapter 3

1. Torres Strait Islander peoples come from the islands of the Torres Strait, between the tip of Cape York in Queensland and Papua New Guinea. Torres Strait Islanders are of Melanesian origin with their own distinct identity, history, and cultural traditions.
2. Bankstown in a suburb in south-west Sydney. In 2016, the largest religious group was Islam (20.8 percent), and, as discussed previously, the largest ancestry group was Lebanese (15.1 percent) (profile.id. 2018, https://profile.id.com.au).
3. Penrith Plaza, aka "The Plaza," is a large shopping mall.

Chapter 4

1. I take the term "waiting room" from Pardy's (2009) work on multiculturalism and national belonging in Australia. She argues that, for some, multiculturalism is a "waiting room."
2. The Hawkesbury Campus was previously known as "Hawkesbury Agricultural College" before being incorporated into the University of Western Sydney. It was the first agricultural college in NSW.
3. The university has now institutionalized this pathway: it encourages students to "go to Goulburn," and once they have completed their training, Western Sydney University gives them some credits toward completing their third year of the bachelor of policing.
4. Academic selective secondary schools are run by the NSW government for high-achieving students.
5. Students applying to study at Western Sydney University may be eligible for up to ten "bonus" ATAR points if they meet one of the following criteria: (1) live in Western Sydney, (2) achieve outstanding results in relevant HSC or IB subjects, (3) elite athlete or performer, (4) experienced disadvantage, and (5) school recommendations based on performance in Year 11.

Chapter 5

1. Watsons Bay and Bellevue Hill are both located in Sydney's exclusive Eastern Suburbs.
2. Cambridge Gardens is a suburb located next to Cranebrook.

References

Abrahams, Jesse. 2017. "Honourable Mobility or Shameless Entitlement? Habitus and Graduate Employment." *British Journal of Sociology of Education* 38(5): 625–40.

Abrahams, Jessica, and Nicola Ingram. 2013. "The Chameleon Habitus: Exploring Local Students' Negotiations of Multiple Fields." *Sociological Research Online* 18(4): 213–26.

Adey, Peter. 2006. "If Mobility is Everything Then It is Nothing: Towards a Relational Politics of (Im)Mobilities." *Mobilities* 1(1): 75–94.

Adkins, Lisa, Melinda Cooper, and Martijn Konings. 2021. "Class in the 21st Century: Asset Inflation and the New Logic of Inequality." *EPA: Economy and Space* 53(3): 548–72.

Agnew, John. 2011. "Space and Place." In *The SAGE Handbook of Geographical Knowledge*, edited by John Agnew and David Livingstone, 316–30. London: SAGE.

Ahmed, Sara. 2008. "Sociable Happiness." *Emotions, Space, Society* 1(1): 10–13.

Ahmed, Sara. 2010. *The Promise of Happiness*. Durham: Duke University Press.

Ali, Aftab. 2015. "Western Sydney University's Powerful Refugee Student Recruitment Advert Takes the Internet by Storm." *The Independent*, September 7, 2015.

Allen, Kim. 2014. "'Blair's Children': Young Women as 'Aspirational Subjects' in the Psychic Landscape of Class." *The Sociological Review* 62(4): 760–79.

Allen, Kim and Sumi Hollingsworth. 2013. "'Sticky Subjects' or 'Cosmopolitan Creatives'? Social Class, Place and Urban Young People's Aspirations for Work in the Knowledge Economy." *Urban Studies* 50(3): 499–517.

Anderson, Donald, and Aat Vervoorn. 1983. *Access to Privilege: Patterns of Participation in Australian Post-Secondary Education*. Canberra: Australian National University Press.

Atkinson, Will. 2011. "From Sociological Fictions to Social Fictions: Some Bourdieusian Reflections on the Concepts of 'Institutional Habitus' and 'Family Habitus'." *British Journal of Sociology of Education* 32(3): 331–47.

Baik, Chi, Ryan Naylor, and Sophie Arkoudis. 2015. *The First Year Experience in Australian Universities: Findings from Two Decades, 1994-2014*. Melbourne Centre for the Study of Higher Education, the University of Melbourne.

Bathmaker, Ann-Marie, Nicola Ingram, Jessie Abrahams, Anthony Hoare, Richard Waller, and Harriette Bradley. 2016. *Higher Education, Social Class and Social Mobility: The Degree Generation*. London: Palgrave Macmillan.

Bathmaker, Ann-Marie, Nicola Ingram, and Richard Waller. 2013. "Higher Education, Social Class and the Mobilisation of Capitals: Recognising and Playing the Game." *British Journal of Sociology of Education*, 34(5–6): 723–43.

Becker, Gary. 1964. *Human Capital*. New York: The National Bureau of Economic Research.

Benveniste, Emile. 1973 [1969]. *Indo-European Language and Society*. Translated by Elizabeth Palmer. Florida: University of Miami Press.

Berlant, Lauren. 2011. *Cruel Optimism*. Durham: Duke University Press

Bernstein, Basil. 1971. *Class, Codes and Control*. London: Routledge.

Birani, Aisha, and Wolfgang Lehmann. 2013. "Ethnicity as Social Capital: An Examination of First-Generation, Ethnic-Minority Students at a Canadian University." *International Studies in Sociology of Education* 23(4): 281–97.

Boltanski, Luc, and Eve Chiapello. 2005 [1999]. *The New Spirit of Capitalism*. Translated by Gregory Elliot. London: Verso.

Bourdieu, Pierre. 1970. "The Berber House or the World Reversed." *Social Science Information* 9(2): 151–70.

Bourdieu, Pierre. 1977 [1972]. *Outline of a Theory of Practice*. Translated by Richard Nice. London: Cambridge University Press.

Bourdieu, Pierre. 1984 [1979]. *Distinction: A Social Critique of the Judgment of Taste*. Translated by Richard Nice. London: Routledge.

Bourdieu, Pierre. 1985. "The Social Space and the Genesis of Groups." *Theory and Society* 14(6): 723–44.

Bourdieu, Pierre. 1986. "The Forms of Capital." Translated by Richard Nice. In *Handbook of Theory of Research for the Sociology of Education*, edited by John Richardson, 241–58. New York: Greenwood Press.

Bourdieu, Pierre. 1987. "What Makes a Social Class? On the Theoretical and Practical Existence of Groups." *Berkeley Journal of Sociology* 32(1): 1–17.

Bourdieu, Pierre. 1988 [1984]. *Homo Academicus*. Translated by Peter Collier. Stanford: Stanford University Press.

Bourdieu, Pierre. 1989. "Social Space and Symbolic Power." *Sociological Theory* 7(1): 14–25.

Bourdieu, Pierre. 1990 [1980]. *The Logic of Practice*. Translated by Richard Nice. Cambridge: Polity Press.

Bourdieu, Pierre. 1993. "Concluding Remarks: For a Sociogenetic Understanding of Intellectual Works." Translated by Nicole Kaplan, Craig Calhoun, and Leah Florence. In *Bourdieu: Critical Perspectives*, edited by Craig Calhoun, Edward LiPuma, and Moishe Postone, 263–75. Cambridge: Polity Press.

Bourdieu, Pierre. 1999a [1993]. "The Space of Points of View." Translated by Priscilla Parkhurst Ferguson, Susan Emanuel, Joe Johnson and Shoggy Waryn. In *The

Weight of the World: Social Suffering in Contemporary Society, edited by Pierre Bourdieu, 3–5. Cambridge: Polity Press.
Bourdieu, Pierre. 1999b [1993]. "Understanding." Translated by Priscilla Parkhurst Ferguson, Susan Emanuel, Joe Johnson and Shoggy Waryn. In *The Weight of the World: Social Suffering in Contemporary Society*, edited by Pierre Bourdieu, 607–26. Cambridge: Polity Press.
Bourdieu, Pierre. 1999c [1993]. "Postscript." Translated by Priscilla Parkhurst Ferguson, Susan Emanuel, Joe Johnson and Shoggy Waryn. In *The Weight of the World: Social Suffering in Contemporary Society*, edited by Pierre Bourdieu, 627–9. Cambridge: Polity Press.
Bourdieu, Pierre. 1999d [1993]. "To the Reader." Translated by Priscilla Parkhurst Ferguson, Susan Emanuel, Joe Johnson and Shoggy Waryn. In *The Weight of the World: Social Suffering in Contemporary Society*, edited by Pierre Bourdieu, 1–5. Cambridge: Polity Press.
Bourdieu, Pierre. 1999e [1993]. "Site Effects." Translated by Priscilla Parkhurst Ferguson, Susan Emanuel, Joe Johnson and Shoggy Waryn. In *The Weight of the World: Social Suffering in Contemporary Society*, edited by Pierre Bourdieu, 123–9. Cambridge: Polity Press.
Bourdieu, Pierre. 2000. *Pascalian Meditations*. Translated by Richard Nice. Cambridge: Polity Press.
Bourdieu, Pierre. 2002. "Habitus." In *Habitus: A Sense of Place*, edited by Jean Hillier and Emma Rooksby, 43–9. London: Routledge.
Bourdieu, Pierre. 2008 [2004]. *Sketch for a Self-Analysis*. Translated by Richard Nice. Chicago: University of Chicago Press.
Bourdieu, Pierre, and Patrick Champagne. 1999 [1993]. "Outcasts on the Inside." In *The Weight of the World: Social Suffering in Contemporary Society*, edited by Pierre Bourdieu, 421–6. Translated by Priscilla Parkhurst Ferguson, Susan Emanuel, Joe Johnson, and Shoggy Waryn. Cambridge: Polity Press.
Bourdieu, Pierre, and Jean-Claude Passeron. 1979 [1964]. *The Inheritors: French Students and their Relation to Culture*. Translated by Richard Nice. Chicago: University of Chicago Press.
Bourdieu, Pierre, and Jean-Claude Passeron. 1990 [1970]. *Reproduction in Education, Society and Culture*. Translated by Richard Nice. London: SAGE.
Bourdieu, Pierre, Jean-Claude Passeron, and Monique De Saint Martin. 1994. *Academic Discourse*. Oxford: Polity Press.
Bourdieu, Pierre, and Loic Wacquant. 1992. *An Invitation to Reflexive Sociology*. Cambridge: Polity Press.
Bowles, Samuel, and Herbert Gintis. 1976. *Schooling in Capitalist America*. New York: Basic Books.

Bunn, Matthew, Anna Bennett, and Penny Burke. 2019. "In the Anytime: Flexible Time Structures, Student Experience and Temporal Equity in Higher Education." *Time and Society* 28(4): 1409–28.

Burke, Ciaran. 2015. "Bourdieu's Theory of Practice: Maintaining the Role of Capital." In *Bourdieu: The Next Generation*, edited by Jenny Thatcher, Nicola Ingram, Ciaran Burke, and Jessie Abrahams, 8–24. London: Routledge.

Byrom, Tina, and Nic Lightfoot. 2013. "Interrupted Trajectories: The Impact of Academic Failure on the Social Mobility of Working-Class Students." *British Journal of Sociology of Education* 34(5–6): 812–28.

Casey, Edward. 2001. "Body, Self, and Landscape: A Geographical Inquiry into the Place-World." In *Textures of Place: Exploring Humanist Geographies*, edited by Paul Adams, Steven Hoelscher, and Karen Till, 403–25. Minneapolis: University of Minnesota Press.

Castagna, Felicity. 2016. "We Are Here and We Are Significant." *Sydney Review of Books*, https://sydneyreviewofbooks.com/we-are-here-and-we-are-significant/

Christie, Hazel. 2009. "Emotional Journeys: Young People and Transitions to University." *British Journal of Sociology of Education* 30(2): 123–36.

Clayton, John, Gill Crozier, and Diane Reay. 2009. "Home and Away: Risk, Familiarity and the Multiple Geographies of the Higher Education Experience." *International Studies in Sociology of Education* 19(3–4): 157–74.

Deehan, James. 2014. "Teachers galore? A brief analysis of the 'Oversupply of Teachers' in NSW." *On Line Opinion*, http://www.onlineopinion.com.au/ view.asp?article=16801.

Department of Education, Employment and Workplace Relations [DEEWR]. 2009. *Transforming Australia's Higher Education System*. Accessed August 15, 2019. http://hdl.voced.edu.au/10707/131634.

Department of Education and Training [DET]. 2018. *2018 Graduate Outcomes Survey: National Report*. Accessed May 1, 2019. https://www.qilt.edu.au/docs/default- source/gos-reports/2018-gos/2018-gos-national-report- 2018.pdf?sfvrsn=a729e33c_4

Donnelly, Michael, and Ceryn Evans. 2016. "Framing the Geographies of Higher Education Participation: Schools, Place and National Identity." *British Educational Research Journal* 42(1): 74–92.

Douglas, Mary. 2001 [1966]. *Purity and Danger: An Analysis of the Concepts of Pollution and Taboo*. New York: Routledge.

Dreyfus, Hubert, and Paul Rabinow. 1993. "Can there be a Science of Existential Structure and Social Meaning?." In *Bourdieu: Critical Perspectives*, edited by Craig Calhoun, Edward LiPuma, and Moishe Postone, 35–44. Cambridge: Polity Press.

Farrugia, David. 2016. "The Mobility Imperative for Rural Youth: The Structural, Symbolic and Non-Representational Dimensions of Rural Youth Mobilities." *Journal of Youth Studies* 19(6): 836–51.

Finn, Kirsty. 2015. *Personal Life, Young Women and Higher Education: A Relational Approach to Student and Graduate Experience*. London: Palgrave Macmillan.

Finn, Kirsty. 2017a. "Relational Transitions, Emotional Decisions: New Directions for Theorising Graduate Employment." *Journal of Education and Work* 30(4): 419–31.

Finn, Kirsty. 2017b. "Multiple, Relational and Emotional Mobilities: Understanding Student Mobilities in Higher Education as More Than 'Staying Local' and 'Going Away'." *British Educational Research Journal* 43(4): 743–58.

Finn, Kirsty, and Mark Holton. 2019. *Everyday Mobile Belonging*. London: Bloomsbury.

Friedman, Sam. 2015. "The Limits of Capital Gains: Using Bourdieu to Understand Social Mobility into Elite Occupations." In *Bourdieu: The Next Generation*, edited by Jenny Thatcher, Nicola Ingram, Ciaran Burke, and Jessie Abrahams, 107–22. London: Routledge.

Friedman, Sam. 2016. "Habitus Clivé and the Emotional Imprint of Social Mobility." *The Sociological Review* 64(1): 129–47.

Friedman, Sam, and Mike Savage. 2017. "Time, Accumulation and Trajectory: Bourdieu and Social Mobility." In *Social Mobility for the 21st Century: Everyone a Winner?*, edited by Steph Lawler and Geoff Payne, 67–79. Oxon: Routledge.

Furlong, Andy, and Fred Cartmel. 2005. *Graduates from Disadvantaged Backgrounds: Early Labour Market Experiences*. York: Joseph Rowntree Foundation.

Gallop, Geoff, Tricia Kavanagh, and Patrick Lee. 2021. *Valuing the Teaching Profession*. Accessed October 28, 2021. https://apo.org.au/node/311068.

Gemici, Sinan, Alice Bednarz, Tom Karmel, and Patrick Lim. 2014. "The Factors Affecting the Educational and Occupational Aspirations of Young Australians." Accessed May 1, 2019. https://www.ncver.edu.au/research-and-statistics/publications/all-publications/the-factors-affecting-the- educational-and-occupational-aspirations-of-young-australians

Gleeson, Brendan. 2006. *Australian Heartlands: Making Space for Hope in the Suburbs*. Crows Nest: Allen and Unwin.

Goffman, Erving. 1990 [1959]. *The Presentation of the Self in Everyday Life*. London: Penguin.

Gwyther, Gabrielle. 2008a. "From Cowpastures to Pigs' Heads: The Development and Character of Western Sydney." *Sydney Journal* 1(3): 51–74.

Gwyther, Gabrielle. 2008b. "Once Were Westies." *Griffith Review* 20(1): 81–90.

Hage, Ghassan. 1997. "At Home in the Entrails of the West: Multiculturalism, 'Ethnic Food' and Migrant Home-Building." In *Home/World: Space, Community and Marginality in Sydney's West*, edited by Helen Grace, Ghassan Hage, Lesley Johnson, Julie Langsworth, and Michael Symonds, 99–153. Annandale: Pluto Press.

Hage, Ghassan. 2000. "On the Ethics of Pedestrian Crossings: Or Why 'Mutual Obligation' Does Not Belong in the Language of Neo-Liberal Economics." *Meanjin* 59(4), 27–37.

Hage, Ghassan. 2005. "A Not So Multi-Sited Ethnography of a Not So Imagined Community." *Anthropological Theory* 5(4): 463–75.

Hage, Ghassan. 2009. "Waiting Out the Crisis: On Stuckedness and Governmentality." In *Waiting*, edited by Ghassan Hage, 97–106. Carlton: Melbourne University Press.

Hage, Ghassan. 2011. "Social Gravity: Pierre Bourdieu's Phenomenological Social Physics." In *Force, Movement, Intensity: The Newtonian Imagination in the Humanities and Social Sciences*, edited by Ghassan Hage and Emma Kowal, 80–92. Carlton: Melbourne University Press.

Hage, Ghassan. 2013. "Eavesdropping on Bourdieu's Philosophers." *Thesis Eleven* 114(1): 76–93.

Hage, Ghassan. 2017. *Is Racism an Environmental Threat?*. Cambridge: Polity Press.

Heath, Sue. 2007. "Widening the Gap: Pre-University Gap Years and the 'Economy of Experience.'" *British Journal of Sociology of Education*, 28(1): 89–103.

Henderson, Holly. 2020. *Non-University Higher Education: Geographies of Place, Possibility and Inequality*. London: Bloomsbury.

Hoggart, Richard. 1990. *A Sort of Clowning: Life and Times, 1940–1959*. London: Chatto and Windus.

Hoggart, Richard. 2009 [1957]. *The Uses of Literacy: Aspects of Working-Class Life*. London: Penguin.

Holton, Mark. 2015. "'I Already Know the City, I Don't Have to Explore It': Adjustments to 'Sense of Place' for 'Local' UK University Students." *Population, Space and Place* 21(8): 820–31.

Holton, Mark, and Kirsty Finn. 2018a. "Belonging, Pausing, Feeling: A Framework of 'Mobile Dwelling' for U.K. University Students that Live at Home." *Applied Mobilities*, Online First.

Holton, Mark, and Kirsty Finn. 2018b. "Being in Motion: The Everyday (Gendered and Classed) Embodied Mobilities for UK University Students Who Commute." *Mobilities* 13(3): 426–40.

Honneth, Axel. 1995. *The Struggle for Recognition: The Moral Grammar of Social Conflicts*. Translated by Joel Anderson. Cambridge: MIT Press.

Husserl, Edmund. 1983 [1913]. *Ideas Pertaining to a Pure Phenomenology and to a Phenomenological Philosophy, First Book; General Introduction to a Pure Phenomenology*. The Hague: Martinus Nijhoff.

Hutchinson, Mark. 2013. *University of the People: A History of the University of Western Sydney*. Crows Nest: Allen & Unwin.

Idriss, Sherene. 2014. "The Just-In-Time Self: Young Arab Men, Skills and Narratives of Aspiration in the New Economy." PhD diss., Western Sydney University.

Lamaison, Pierre. 1986. "From Rules to Strategies: An Interview with Pierre Bourdieu." *Cultural Anthropology* 1(1): 110–20.

Lawler, Steph. 1999. "'Getting out and Getting Away': Women's Narratives of Class Mobility." *Feminist Review* 63(Autumn): 3–24.

Lawler, Steph. 2005. "Disgusted Subjects: The Making of Middle-Class Identities." *The Sociological Review* 53(3): 429–46.

Lehmann, Wolfgang. 2009a. "University as Vocational Education: Working-Class Students' Expectations for University." *British Journal of the Sociology of Education* 30(2): 137–49.

Lehmann, Wolfgang. 2009b. "Becoming Middle Class: How Working-Class University Students Draw and Transgress Moral Class Boundaries." *Sociology* 43(4): 631–47.

Lehmann, Wolfgang. 2012. "Extra-Credential Experiences and Social Closure: Working-Class Students at University." *British Educational Research Journal* 38(2): 203–18.

Lehmann, Wolfgang. 2013. "Habitus Transformation and Hidden Injuries: Successful Working- Class University Students." *Sociology of Education*, 87(1): 1–15.

Lehmann, Wolfgang. 2015. "Influences on Working-Class Students' Decisions to Go to University." In *The Working Classes and Higher Education: Inequality of Access Opportunity, and Outcome*, edited by Amy Stich and Carrie Freie, 13–29. New York: Routledge.

Lehmann, Wolfgang. 2019. "Forms of Capital in Working-Class Students' Transition from University to Employment." *Journal of Education and Work* 32(4): 347–59.

Loveday, Vik. 2015. "Working-Class Participation, Middle-Class Aspiration? Value, Upward Mobility and Symbolic Indebtedness in Higher Education." *The Sociological Review* 63(3): 570–88.

Mallman, Mark. 2017. "The Perceived Inherent Vice of Working-Class University Students." *The Sociological Review* 65(2): 235–50.

Marginson, Simon. 2006. "Dynamics of National and Global Competition in Higher Education." *Higher Education* 52(1): 1–39.

Marginson, Simon. 2007. "National and Global Competition in Higher Education." In *RoutledgeFalmer Reader in Education Policy and Politics*, edited by Bob Lingard and Jenny Ozga, 131–53. London: Routledge.

Marginson, Simon. 2011. "Equity, Status and Freedom: A Note on Higher Education." *Cambridge Journal of Education* 41(1): 23–36.

McGowan, Michael. 2019. "Labor to Introduce Minimum ATARs for Teaching Degrees if Unis Don't Lift Standards." *The Guardian*, January 6, 2019. https://www.theguardian.com/australia-news/2019/jan/06/labor-to-introduce-minimum-atars-for-teaching-degrees-if-unis-dont-lift-standards..

Mee, Kathleen. 2002. "Prosperity and the Suburban Dream: Quality of Life and Affordability in Western Sydney." *Australian Geographer* 33(3): 337–51.

Mill, John Stuart. 1998 [1859]. *On Liberty*. London: Routledge.

Miller, William. 1997. *The Anatomy of Disgust*. Cambridge: Harvard University Press.

Morgan, George. 2006. "A City of Two Tales: Distinction, Dispersal and Dissociation in Western Sydney," Paper presented to *Proceedings from Post-Suburban Sydney: The City in Transformation*, Centre for Cultural Research, University of Western Sydney, November 22–23, 2005.

Morgan, George, and Pariece Nelligan. 2018. *The Creativity Hoax: Precarious Work and the Gig Economy*. London: Anthem Press.

Munt, Sally. 2000. "Introduction." In *Cultural Studies and the Working Class: Subject to Change*, edited by Sally Munt, 1–18. London: Cassell.

Nanson, Gerald, and Robert Young, and Eugene Stockton. 1987. "Chronology and Palaeoenvironment of the Cranebrook Terrace (Near Sydney) Containing Artefacts More than 40,000 Years Old." *Archaeology in Oceania* 22(2): 72–8.

Noble, Greg. 2005. "The Discomfort of Strangers: Racism, Incivility and Ontological Security in a Relaxed and Comfortable Nation." *Journal of Intercultural Studies* 26(1): 107–20.

Noble, Greg. 2009. "'Countless Acts of Recognition': Young Men, Ethnicity, and the Messiness of Identities in Everyday Life." *Social and Cultural Geography* 10(8): 875–91.

Noble, Greg. 2015. "Pedagogies of Civic Belonging: Finding One's Way Through Social Space." In *Cultural Pedagogies and Human Conduct*, edited by Megan Watkins, Greg Noble, and Catherine Driscoll, 32–44. London: Routledge.

Norton, Andrew and Beni Cakitaki. 2016. *Mapping Australian Higher Education, 2016*. Melbourne: Grattan Institute.

Norton, Andrew, and Ittima Cherastidtham. 2014. *Mapping Australian Higher Education, 2014–2015*. Melbourne: Grattan Institute.

Norton, Andrew, and Ittima Cherastidtham. 2018. *Mapping Australian Higher Education, 2018*. Melbourne: Grattan Institute.

O'Neill, Phillip. 2017. "Regional Realities: Where to for Western Sydney, Industrial Rust Belt or Surging New Economy?." Address to Forum: The Future of Work and Curriculum Disruption Western Sydney University, 8 November.

O'Neill, Phillip. 2020. *Where Are the Jobs? Part 3: Western Sydney Workers in 2036*. Centre for Western Sydney, Western Sydney University, Parramatta.

O'Shea, Sara, Josephine May, Cathy Stone, and Janine Delahunty. 2017. *First-In-Family Students, University Experience and Family Life*. London: Palgrave Macmillan.

Pardy, Maree. 2009. "The Shame of Waiting." In *Waiting*, edited by Ghassan Hage 195–209. Carlton: Melbourne University Press.

Pearce, Jane, Barry Down, and Elizabeth Moore. 2008. "Social Class, Identity and the 'Good' Student: Negotiating University Culture." *Australian Journal of Education* 52(3): 257–71.

Peel, Mark. 2003. *The Lowest Rung: Voices of Australian Poverty*. Cambridge: Cambridge University Press.

Piketty, Thomas. 2014. "Capital in the Twenty-First Century: A Multidimensional Approach to the History of Capital and Social Classes." *The British Journal of Sociology* 65(4): 736–47.

Pink, Sarah, Michelle Catanzaro, Katrina Sandbach, Alison Barnes, Joanne Mcneill, Mitra Gusheh, Enrico Scotece, and Ciro Cantanzaro. 2015. "Making and Sharing the Commons: Reimagining 'the West' as Riverlands, Sydney Through a Dialogue Between Design and Ethnography." *Global Media Journal* 9(2). https://www.hca.westernsydney.edu.au/gmjau/?p=1939.

Powell, Diane. 1993. *Out West: Perceptions of Sydney's Western Suburbs*. St Leonards: Allen & Unwin.

Probyn, Elspeth. 2005. *Blush: Faces of Shame*. Sydney: NSW Press.

Raco, Mike. 2009. "From Expectations to Aspirations: State Modernisation, Urban Policy, and the Existential Politics of Welfare in the UK." *Political Geography* 28(7): 436–44.

Randolph, Bill, and Darren Holloway. 2005. "The Suburbanisation of Disadvantage in Sydney: New Problems, New Policies." *Opolis* 1(1): 49–65.

Randolph, Bill, and Andrew Tice. 2014. "Suburbanizing Disadvantage in Australian Cities: Sociospatial Change in an Era of Neoliberalism." *Journal of Urban Affairs* 36(1): 384–99.

Reay, Diane. 2002. "Class, Authenticity and the Transition to Higher Education for Mature Students." *The Sociological Review* 50(3): 398–418.

Reay, Diane. 2017. "The Cruelty of Social Mobility: Individual Success at the Cost of Collective Failure." In *Social Mobility for the 21st Century: Everyone a Winner?*, edited by Steph Lawler and Geoff Payne, 146–57. Oxon: Routledge.

Reay, Diane, Gill Crozier, and John Clayton. 2009. "'Strangers in Paradise?: Working-class Students in Elite Universities." *Sociology* 43(6): 1103–21.

Reay, Diane, Gill Crozier, and John Clayton. 2010. "'Fitting In' or 'Standing Out': Working-Class Students in UK Higher Education." *British Educational Research Journal* 36(1): 107–24.

Rorris, Adam. 2021. *NSW Public Schools to 2031: Impact of Enrolment Growth on Demand for Teachers*. Accessed October 28, 2021. https://apo.org.au/node/31186.

Rose, Nikolas. 1999. *Powers of Freedom: Reframing Political Thought*. Cambridge: Cambridge University Press.

Rossiter, Penny. 2013. "Bogans: A Sticky Subject." *Continuum: Journal of Media and Cultural Studies* 27(1): 80–92.

Rowse, Tim. 1978. "Heaven and a Hills Hoist: Australian Critics on Suburbia." *Meanjin* 37(1): 3–13.

Savage, Mike. 2014. "Piketty's Challenge for Sociology." *The British Journal of Sociology* 65(4): 591–606.

Sellar, Sam. 2013. "Equity Markets and the Politics of Aspiration in Australian Higher Education." *Discourse: Studies in the Cultural Politics of Education* 34(2): 245–58.

Sheller, Mimi. 2014. "The New Mobilities Paradigm for a Live Sociology." *Current Sociology Review* 62(6): 789–811.

Sheller, Mimi, and John Urry. 2006. "The New Mobilities Paradigm." *Environment and Planning A: Economy and Space* 38(2): 207–25.

Simic, Zora. 2008. "'What Are Ya?': Negotiating Identities in the Western Suburbs of Sydney During the 1980s." *Journal of Australian Studies* 32(2): 223–36.

Simmel, Georg. 1950. "Faithfulness and Gratitude." In *The Sociology of Georg Simmel*, translated and edited by Kurt Wolff, 379–95. Glencoe: The Free Press.

Singhal, Pallavi. 2017. "'You End Up Behind A Bar': 22 Graduates Fighting for Every Job." *The Sydney Morning Herald*, October 10, 2017.

Skeggs, Beverley. 1995. "Theorising, Ethics and Representation in Feminist Ethnography." In *Feminist Cultural Theory: Process and Production*, edited by Beverley Skeggs, 190–206. Manchester: Manchester University Press.

Skeggs, Beverley. 1997. *Formations of Class and Gender: Becoming Respectable*. London: SAGE.

Skeggs, Beverley, and Vik Loveday. 2012. "Struggles for Value: Value Practices, Injustice, Judgment, Affect and the Ideas of Class." *The British Journal of Sociology* 63(3): 472–90.

Stretton, Hugh. 1975. *Ideas for Australian Cities*. Melbourne: Georgian House.

Symonds, Michael. 1997. "Outside the Spaces of Modernity: Western Sydney and the Logic of the European City." In *Home/World: Space, Community and Marginality in Sydney's West*, edited by Helen Grace, Ghassan Hage, Lesley Johnson, Julie Langsworth, and Michael Symonds, 99–153. Annandale: Pluto Press.

Threadgold, Steven. 2020. *Bourdieu and Affect: Towards a Theory of Affective Affinities*. Bristol: Bristol University Press.

Tuan, Yi-Fu. 1977. *Space and Place: The Perspective of Experience*. Minneapolis: University of Minnesota Press.

Tyler, Imogen. 2008. "'CHAV MUM/CHAV SCUM': Class Disgust in Contemporary Britain." *Feminist Media Studies* 8(1): 17–34.

Wacquant, Loic. 1993. "On the Tracks of Symbolic Power: Prefatory Notes on Bourdieu's 'State of Nobility'." *Theory, Culture and Society* 10(1): 1–17.

Wacquant, Loic. 2013. "Symbolic Power and Group-Making: On Pierre Bourdieu's Reframing of Class." *Journal of Classical Sociology* 13(2): 274–91.

Wacquant, Loic, and Aksu Akcaoglu. 2017. "Practice and Symbolic Power in Bourdieu: The View From Berkeley." *Journal of Classical Sociology* 17(1): 55–69.

Wacquant, Loic, and Pierre Bourdieu. 1989. "For a Socio-Analysis of Intellectuals: On 'Homo Academicus'." *Berkeley Journal of Sociology* 34(1): 1–29.

Watkins, Megan. 2020. "The Persistence of Inequality: Education, Class and Cultural Capital." In *Fields, Capital, Habitus: Australian Culture, Inequalities, and Social Divisions*, edited by Tony Bennett, David Carter, Modesto Gayo, Michelle Kelly and Greg Noble, 188–207. Abingdon: Routledge.

Watkins, Megan, and Greg Noble. 2013. *Disposed to Learn: Schooling, Ethnicity, and the Scholarly Habitus*. London: Bloomsbury Academic.

Western Sydney University. 2018. "WSU Pocket Profile." Accessed December 8, 2021. https://www.westernsydney.edu.au/__data/assets/pdf_file/0018/1243233/Pocket _Profile_2019.pdf.

Western Sydney University. 2018. "WSU Securing Success 2018-2020 Strategic Plan." Accessed December 8, 2021. https://www.westernsydney.edu.au/__data/assets/pdf_ file/0004/844672/STRA2627_Securing_Success_Strategic_Plan_2018-2020_Web.pdf.

Whitlam, Gough. 1969. "Into the Seventies with Labor," *Policy Speech, Sydney Town Hall*, October 1, 1969.

Whitlam, Gough. 1973. "The First Twelve Months," *Statement Made in the House of Representatives*, December 13, 1973.

Whitlam, Gough. 1985. *The Whitlam Government 1972–1975*. Ringwood: Penguin Books.

Whitlam, Gough. 2004. "Australian Postgraduate Association," *Speech, The Boulevard, Sydney*, May 29, 2004.

Winton, Tim. 1991. *Cloudstreet*. Oxford: Picador.

Winton, Tim. 2013–2014. "The C-Word: Some Thoughts About Class in Australia." *The Monthly*, December 2013–January 2014, 24–31.

Willis, Paul. 1977. *Learning to Labour: How Working Class Kids Get Working Class Jobs*. Farnborough: Saxon House.

Wise, Amanda. 2009. "Everyday Multiculturalism: Transversal Crossings and Working-Class Cosmopolitans." In *Everyday Multiculturalism*, edited by Amanda Wise and Selvaraj Velayutham, 21–45. Hampshire: Palgrave Macmillan.

Yeatman, Anna. 2016. "Gough Whitlam's Vison of the Australian *Res Publica*: Creating Civil Possibility in Rhetoric and Action." *The Whitlam Legacy: A Series of Occasional Papers Published by the Whitlam Institute* 6(1): 3–12.

Young, Michael. 1958. *The Rise of Meritocracy 1870–2011: An Essay on Education and Equality*. London: Thames and Hudson.

Zipin, Lew, Sam Sellar, Marie Brennan, and Trevor Gale. 2015. "Educating for Futures in Marginalized Regions: A Sociological Framework for Rethinking and Researching Aspirations." *Educational Philosophy and Theory* 47(3): 227–46.

Zournazi, Mary, and Ghassan Hage. 2002. "'On the Side of Life' – Joy and the Capacity of Being: A Conversation with Ghassan Hage." In *Hope: New Philosophies for Change*, edited by Mary Zournazi, 150–71. Annandale: Pluto Press.

Index

Aboriginal Australians 5, 50, 53, 77–8, 159
Abrahams, Jesse 30, 73
academic capacities 80–3
accumulation of being 33–5, 61, 126, 146
accumulation of homeliness 36–7, 61, 146
Adey, Peter 31
Adkins, Lisa 159
Adut, Deng 47–8, 122
affect alien 43, 63, 67, 110
agency 74, 88–96, 105, 107, 115, 140
Agnew, John 4
Ahmed, Sara
  affect alien 43, 63, 67, 110
  happiness and ambivalence 42, 45, 68
  happy objects 42–3, 130–1
  promise of happiness 42–3
  sacrifice of migration 40, 62–3
  sociable happiness 42
Allen, Kim 38, 49, 132–3
amor fati 34
Arab Australians 86–8
aspirational, the 8–9, 12, 57, 128, 132
aspirational citizenship 2, 48
aspiration and hope
  agency and comfort 88–96
  changing 68–72, 97–120, 129–33
  class differentiated 30–5, 47–72, 97–141
  emplaced 47–72
  unfulfilled 97–120
  university, for 47–72
Atkinson, Will 17, 74, 95
Australian Cultural Fields 29
Australian Defence Industries (ADI) site 51–2, 154
Australian Dream 3–4, 9, 52, 57, 65, 143
Australian Labor Party 10

Australian Tertiary Admissions Rank (ATAR) 111
Australian Youth Studies 3–4

Baik, Chi 73, 94
Bathmaker, Ann-Marie 21, 30, 36, 44, 73, 104–6
Becker, Howard 23–4
belonging at university 27, 73–96
Benveniste, Emile 43, 146
Berlant, Lauren 41, 98–9, 109, 152
bogan 10, 56–9, 116
Bourdieu, Pierre
  accumulation of being 34–5, 61, 126, 146
  amor fati 34
  aspiration and hope 33–5, 102, 109, 118–19
  class distinction 4, 55
  class reproduction 4, 23–30, 55
  compensatory strategies 41–2, 98–9
  conatus 34, 126
  cultural capital 25–6
  diploma inflation 28–30, 98–9
  economic capital 25
  field 26–30
  habitus 4, 25–44, 91–2
  human capital theory 23–4
  illusio 16, 34–5, 98
  la grande misere 140
  la petite misere 140
  libido academica 16, 144
  lusiones 98
  microcosm 37–8
  participant objectivation 14–16
  philosophical scholarship 33–5
  place 37–8, 76
  positional suffering 39–40, 123, 153
  project and pretention 91, 95
  recognition 75–6, 80, 85
  researching class 13, 16, 144–5

sense of one's place   4, 26, 40, 86
social capital   25
social phenomenology   34
social physics   34, 55
social space   24–8, 37
social symmetry   13–16
sociological scholarship   23–30, 145
subfield   26–7
symbolic capital   23–30
symbolic violence   27–30
time   107
waiting   41, 98, 115
Bouris, Mark   122–3, 140
Bunn, Matthew   41
Burke, Ciaran   16, 21, 30, 44
Byrom, Tina   49

Cambridge Park High School   13
Casey, Edward   74, 76, 79, 88
Castagna, Felicity   154
Charlton, Andrew   97
chase, the, *see illusio*
Christie, Hazel   3, 49
chronic waiting   112
class contempt   8–9, 58, 128
class disgust   55–6
class distinction
    emplaced   4, 40, 47–72, 121–41
    relational and proximal   40, 115–18, 121–41
    research interviews, in   14–16
    symbolic domination   42
    university   73–96
class escape   2–3, 34, 48–9, 72, 98, 124
class identity   12–13, 55–61, 115–18, 124–5, 146
class reproduction   4, 23–30, 47–72, 97–140
Clayton, John   80, 82–3
Cloudstreet (Winton)   145–6
colleges of advanced education (CAE)   10, 156
colonial violence   5, 50, 159
compensatory strategies   41–2, 98–115
conatus   34, 126, 131, 149, 153
cosmo-multiculturalism   8, 87
Cranbrook School   58–9, 121, 158
Cranebrook   12–16, 50–68
Cranebrook High School   13, 58–9, 66–8, 81–2, 133–7

cruel attachments   18, 42, 99, 109–15, 118, 152
cruel optimism   41, 98–9, 109, 152
Cumberland County Council   5–6
Cumberland Plain   5–6, 51–2, 159

Dawkins Reforms   10, 157
Dharug   5, 50, 159
diploma inflation   18, 21, 28–30, 98–119
Donnelly, Michael   3, 16, 22, 30–3, 36
Douglas, Mary   56
drifter   104, 106, 115

economic capital   25
economic security   47–72, 97–120
embourgeoisement   111
existential mobility   35, 38, 87, 102, 117–18
existential politics   48
extra-credential experience   101, 104, 117

faithfulness   40–3, 63, 131, 156
Farrugia, David   4
fibro housing   6, 47
field   26–30
Finn, Kirsty
    proximate relationalities   99, 123, 130
    relationality and place   30–3, 36
    waithood   98–9
Friedman, Sam   24, 38–9, 122, 128

Gandangara   5
gendered expectations   67–8, 131–3, 135–6
giving back, *see* faithfulness; gratitude
Goffman, Irving   4, 75, 85–6, 151
good life   1–5, 47–72, 121–41
Graduate Outcomes Survey   102–3
graduate premium   100
graduate waiting room   41, 97–119
gratitude   40–3, 63, 133–41, 155–6
Grattan Institute   29
Group of Eight   10–11, 26–9, 157, *see also* Sandstone
Gwyther, Gabrielle   5–9, 53, 57

habitus
    aspiration   118–19
    class reproduction   4, 42

cultural capital   25–6
disrupted   39
emplaced   37, 76
homing disposition   4, 34, 38,
    42, 76, 131
hysteresis effect   39
institutional habitus   73
relationality   32–3
shame   64–5
well-fitted habitus   25–6, 76
Hage, Ghassan
  accumulation of
    homeliness   36–7, 61
  agency   88–9, 105
  cosmo-multiculturalism   8, 87
  cultural enrichment   87
  ethnography   16, 143–4
  etymological roots of home   43
  existential mobility   35, 38
  home and domination   43
  hope   114
  horizontal relations of
    gratitude   12, 41
  intercultural interaction   87
  migration   3
  political economy of being   34
  social gravity   34
  social mobility   38
  stuckedness   92, 105
  vertical relations of
    gratitude   12, 41, 133
  well-fitted habitus   25–6
happy objects   42–3, 130–1
Heath, Sue   117
Henderson, Holly   31–2, 38
Hoggart, Richard   16, 38, 122, 139, 144
homelessness   64, 72, 124
homely mobility   4, 38, 43, 148
homeownership   65, 107, 113,
    124–5, 131–3
Honneth, Axel   88
Housing Commission, *see also* public
    housing; social housing
  Cranebrook   5, 52, 55–61
  experiences   124–5, 136–40
  government department (NSW)   6
  housos   124
human capital theory   23–4
Husserl, Edmund   22, 34, 91
Hutchinson, Mark   10, 85

Idriss, Sherene   88
illusio   16, 34–5, 40–2, 66, 98, 156
The Independent   47
interest, *see illusio*
internships   30, 104
invisibility   65, 124

Keynesian economics   48

labile labour   105
la grande misere   140
la petite misere   140
Lawler, Steph   38–40, 56, 122
learner identities   73
Lehmann, Wolfgang
  extra-credential experiences   30
  fit at university   73
  parental hope   3, 36, 61
  social mobility project   3, 16, 21, 36,
    44, 49, 149–50
  teachers and hope   66; vocational
    education   99
libido, *see illusio*
libido academica   16, 144
libido homeliness   144
Longitudinal Surveys of Australian
    Youth (LSAY)   61
Loveday, Vik   4, 36, 38
lusiones   41, 98

McDonald's Restaurant   14–15, 17, 50,
    68–70, 125, 144, 150
McMansions   6, 7
Mallman, Mark   73, 83
Marginson, Simon   10, 16, 21, 26–
    9, 44, 157
Master Planned Communities
    (MPC)   6–9, 57
Mee, Kathleen   9, 52, 154
meritocracy   24, 30, 48, 108
microcosm
  accumulation of being   34
  class distinctions   42, 55
  Cranebrook, as a   4–5, 60–1
  definition   4, 37
migration   3, 5–9, 40, 53, 62–3, 154, 157
Miller, William   56
Miss Harris   49, 66–7, 133–4
mobilities turn   16, 22, 30–3, 44, 148
Morgan, George   7, 104–5, 108, 115

motherhood 131–3, 135
Mount Pleasant 59
multicultural enrichment 86–8
Munt, Sally 38, 122

neoliberalism 2, 48, 65, 105, 132, 157
Noble, Greg
   agency 18, 88–9, 151
   Arab Other 86–8
   competence 81
   invisibility 65
   scholarly habitus 17, 74, 80, 95
   settings 74, 85
Norton, Andrew 11, 29, 100–3

O'Neill, Phillip 6, 11, 98, 157–8
O'Shea, Sara 36

Pardy, Maree 112, 114
parental debt 63, 113, 155
participant objectivation 14–16
Pascal, Blaise 35, 98
Peel, Mark 15
pencil pusher 130
Penrith 50–61
Penrithian 125
Piketty, Thomas 159
Pink, Sarah 8–9
placial bearing 74, 76, 79, 88
placial degrees of integration 17, 18, 73–96, 148, 151
policy recommendations 156–9
politics of expectation 2, 48
positional suffering 39–40, 123, 153
Powell, Diane 3, 7, 8, 52–3, 85
Probyn, Elspeth 64–5
project and protention 91, 95
promise of happiness 42–3
promise of university
   accumulation of being 61–71
   ambivalence 68–71
   desire for economic security 61–5
   emplaced hope 66–8
   golden ticket, as a 97–8
   holding onto 129, 132
   parental hope 61–5
   unevenly distributed 41
public housing, *see* Housing Commission

Quality Indicators for Teaching and Learning (QILT) 103

Raco, Mike 2, 48
Randolph, Bill 7
Reay, Diane 27, 41, 73–4, 86, 98, 114
research methods 12–16, 33, 143–8, 155–6
Rose, Nikolas 2, 48, 105
Rossiter, Penny 10, 56, 58
Rowse, Tim 3, 7

sacrifice 40–3, 62–3, 139–40
St Paul's Grammar School 13
Sandstone, *see* Group of Eight
Savage, Mike 24, 38–9, 122, 159
scholarly habitus 80
scholarship boy 38
Sellar, Sam 41, 98, 152
Sennett, Richard 12, 134, 156
sense of one's place 4, 26, 40, 75–6, 85–6
setting 73–4, 83–6
shame 30, 39, 56–65, 110–14, 150
Sheller, Mimi 30–1
Simic, Zora 9, 129
Simmel, Georg 40–3, 63, 131–41, 155–6
Skeggs, Beverley 4, 12, 16, 59, 132, 144
social capital 18, 25, 104, 108, 119, 153
social democracy 2
social gravity 34, 40, 121–41
social housing, *see* Housing Commission
social mobility
   ambivalence 78–81, 129–41
   degrees of 121–41
   emotional costs 136–40
   existential mobility, relationship to 38, 102, 117–18, 121–41
   intergenerational criticisms 129–33
   relational and proximal, as 57–72, 115–18
   social gravity 40, 121–41
social phenomenology 34, 55
social physics 34
social space 24–8, 37
social symmetry 13–16
Stretton, Hugh 3, 7, 52
stuckedness 92, 105, 145
subfield 26–7
symbolic capital 23–30

symbolic power   28–30, 83–6
symbolic violence   28–30, 44, 119, 141, 143–8
Symonds, Michael   4, 7, 38, 127, 128

Tharawal   5
thirty-minute city   11, 157
Threadgold, Steven   33, 35
Tomkins, Silvan   64
travel   69–70, 115–18, 134
Tuan, Yi-Fu   4
Tyler, Imogen   56

umwelt   22, 34
university debt   69, 113–15
University of Sydney   13, 73–96
Urry, John   30–1

Wacquant, Loic
   agency   96
   class reproduction   4, 60
   field   26
   microcosm   37–8
   recognition   75–6
   research   145
   social phenomenology   34
   social physics   34
   social space   27
   symbolic capital   24
waiting   41, 97–119
Waterside   7, 51–2

Watkins, Megan   10–11, 29, 74, 80, 98–100, 157
Western Sydney, the region   5–12, 157–8
Western Sydney Airport and Aerotropolis   11, 154, 157–8
Western Sydney University
   advertisement with Deng Adut   47–8
   belonging   74–95
   Fast Forward program   135–6
   history   10–12
   prestige and stigma   10, 84–6, 103, 110–11
   pride   129
westie   8–9, 12, 53, 128–9
Whitlam, Gough
   Dawkins Reforms   157
   higher education   2, 9–11
   quality of life   2, 156
   social democracy   2
   Werriwa   2
   Western Sydney   2, 9–11
   Western Sydney University   80, 85
Willis, Paul   42
Winnicott, Donald   88
Winton, Tim   12, 145–6
work ethic   70, 104–5, 131
Wran, Neville   10

Xavier College   13

Zipin, Lew   49

www.ingramcontent.com/pod-product-compliance
Lightning Source LLC
Chambersburg PA
CBHW061836300426
44115CB00013B/2402